TALES
FROM A
HUNGRY
LIFE

A MEMOIR WITH RECIPES

Published by Coqui Press
Like us on Facebook
Or, email us at coquipress@gmail.com

First Print Edition June 2014

ISBN 978-0-9912850-1-3

MARIA SCHULZ

TALES
FROM A
HUNGRY
LIFE

A MEMOIR WITH RECIPES

For Mom and Dad, who made life happy and full.

Table of Contents

Foreword
Meet the Family: Notes from an Insider

By Tom Ciotti

Our current age of sensationalism and voyeurism has given me the courage to broadcast my earliest fantasy as the foreword to this remarkable book. As it primarily occupied me from the age of three to about seven, it sadly lacks the raw sizzle of lust, power, or greed. Dominating the world with a gold scepter in hand while wearing nothing but leather chaps would not become an obsession until I was at least nine.

The fantasy involved family or, more specifically, siblings—lots of them. As an only child until my twenty-first birthday, born into a family that did not have the wealth to spoil me, I spent most of my time bored and kind of lonely.

The thought of being one of many—forced to share bathroom time, wear hand-me-downs from siblings who were twice my height and half my weight, and fight for a sliver of the last Twinkie—can still make me sigh rapturously even after all these years.

You may ask, as my wife did when she started reading this over my shoulder, why a talented but unknown author would choose a talented and equally unknown writer to pen a foreword. It's a fair question with a relatively logical answer; you see, I am a subject matter expert.

My cousins, the Lagalantes, were the singular objects of my desire throughout most of my early years.

Who are the Lagalantes, you ask? They are a family of seven children, two unique parents, and an extended bunch of neurotics and eccentrics whom you will happily learn all about as you read on.

The Lagalantes are also perfect, at least from the perspective of a shy only child who always looked forward to family visits. They were loud, disheveled, and each possessed a wit that was similarly sharp but completely unique in the same breath. I dreamed my bed was squeezed into a corner of the attic, right next to the spot where Joey sat on Paul's head and farted as I looked on, longingly.

As I write this, I somehow feel that perhaps this fantasy is actually more twisted than my infatuation with Agnes Moorehead, but I digress.

To call them a family, in truth, is somehow a slight. They would be more accurately described as a clan. Nothing I could share about them can equal what Maria has put in this book, so I won't try.

The stories that follow are so hilarious they really beg for more than can be contained in these pages. There should be a movie and animated series made as soon as humanly possible. I want to be able to buy a Joey action figure or an authentic nylon Jude beard that I can wear to Phish concerts. Read this book and you too will demand these things!

I dreamed about being one of them and am proud to have become an honorary sibling, the cousin Oliver to their deviant version of the Brady Bunch.

Oh—and the recipes in the book are really great too!

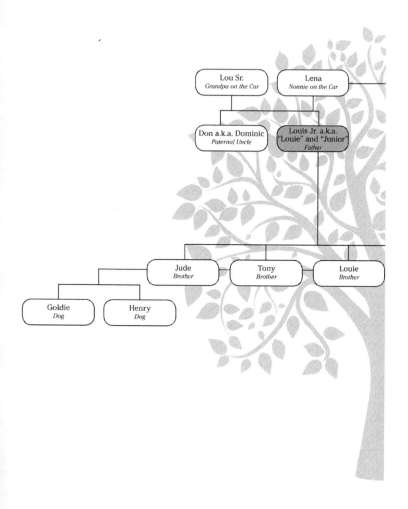

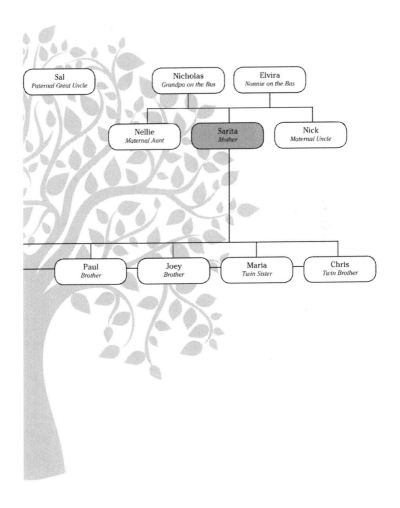

Chapter 1: We Didn't Start the Fire

They say that God answers all prayers. So why is my father's house burning to the ground?

Flames shot into the sky as I parked my car a block away and fought through the crowd around my childhood home in Bayside, New York.

Smoke choked me and made the already humid air even more dense. Or maybe I just couldn't breathe because I wasn't sure if my father was alive or trapped inside the burning house.

He should have been with my mother at her nursing home by now, but uncharacteristically, no one had seen him there yet.

Today might just be the day that he died.

I finally saw my brothers Jude, Chris, and Tony, and my sister-in-law Kathie, in front of the crowd, watching.

"Where's Dad?" I yelled above the din.

I scanned up and down the block until my eyes caught sight of what would have made me laugh any other day: my father, running up and down the block, wearing his Italian undershirt, old jeans, and black shoes with no socks.

I ran to my father and hugged him.

"I thought you were trapped inside! I thought you were dead!" I said.

"Ah," my father yelled, pushing me away. "I'm not dead. Don't cry yet."

Oh well…so much for the touching father/daughter moment.

My eyes stung from the smoke billowing out of our house, and I wondered if everything inside would be destroyed. The flames shooting up into the air were burning down the house my parents, six brothers, one rock-'n'-roll band, hordes of friends, countless dogs, cats, birds, and an albino rat, and I once called home.

The temperature hovered around 97 degrees and there was nowhere to go for relief. So we all just stood there, roasting in the summer sun, watching the flames dance like an apple flambé.

The house had become too much for my father. The boiler kept breaking down; the windows let cold air in during the winter and hot air during the summer; the carpets were frayed and torn; and every room was cluttered with junk left behind by my brothers and me.

While it was never exactly the cleanest place on earth before, now it was a disaster. Dad had begun praying in earnest to God: "Please, God, give me a sign. Show me what to do about the house."

Apparently, God's answer came in the form of a lightning strike.

"I saw the flames and heard the sirens while I was driving Uncle Don to the nursing home to see mom and Nonnie," Tony said. "I had no idea it was Dad's house."

At this point, my brother Joey pulled up. "Whew," he whistled. "Just another day in paradise."

We stood there for a while, and then I looked at my watch. "I'm going to call Uncle Don," I said to my brothers. "Maybe he can feed Mom after he takes care of Nonnie."

I called the nursing home and they put my uncle on the phone.

"Maria!" he boomed. I could tell he didn't know what was going on.

"Listen, Uncle Don," I said. "Dad's house got hit by lightning and burned down. We need you to make sure Mom gets fed today."

"Oh, Maria," Uncle Don said. "Stop kidding around."

"I'm not kidding," I said. "Now make sure Mom gets fed."

"What do you mean the house burned down?" he said, panic filling his fragile voice.

"Well, at 9:33 this morning, lightning struck and now Dad's house is rubble. That's what I mean."

"Oh, my gosh," he said, over and over again. "Tell me you're kidding."

"I wish I could," I replied. "Now make sure my mother and your mother eat."

We watched the flames get stamped out as the firefighters made one last sweep through the house. A big, burly fireman came out and motioned to my father.

"You can go in now," he said, "but you can't stay long. The building isn't safe. Go in and get what you want, and then come back out. The rest is probably water damaged or burned anyhow."

I ran through the living room, where our family photos hung sideways or had fallen to the floor, and darted through the soggy dining room where water was now gushing from the ceiling. I was bobbing and weaving to avoid falling ceiling chunks and taking each step gingerly in case the floorboards beneath me were about to collapse. I raced back to my parents' bedroom. Oh, how my mother would have cried if she knew what was going on.

I ran straight to my mother's closet and pulled the door open a few inches. The heat and the water made the door hard to move, and it was pitch-black inside. Water streamed into the closet from the ceiling above as I stuck my hand in and rooted around until I found my parents' wedding album. I yanked it from the closet, along with some X-rays my mother had kept that showed my twin brother, Chris, and me the day before we were born, some more photo albums, and a few grade-school drawings and love notes I'd made for her.

I ran outside and handed them to my sister-in-law, Kathie. "I have to go back," I said, as I darted inside.

I ran to my bedroom, my special refuge in all those years

growing up, now pretty much obliterated. The smell of charred wood and soggy carpets made the dense air suffocating. An oversized attorney's desk that I had gotten from my beloved English teacher many years before now lay in ruins; most of the furniture in the room was dripping and sagging. Water seeped from the ceiling where the firefighters had doused the flames that consumed the entire upstairs floor; everything we had up there was charred.

I had gotten married and moved away many years before, but I always thought there would be time to come back for the treasures I'd left behind. Just the year before, I'd been rifling through the attic, finding the first story I ever wrote—a third-grade saga about an Eskimo girl named Lola, her Alaskan malamute, and their quest for food.

I had also found a series of restaurant menus I'd written in the sixth grade for both good and bad restaurants, including an Italian restaurant I affectionately called *Mangia Tutti Cosi* because my mother always used to tell us to "eat everything," and another for a bad Chinese restaurant that I'd called *The Hong Kong Hit Man*. I had put everything in a pile on Chris's old bed.

I was going to come back for everything the next week, or the next time I was in visiting my mother, who ironically could no longer feed herself. But now everything that had been up in the attic was gone. Even my Charlie Brown cookbook, with the bread recipe my mother and I used to make every Thanksgiving, had disappeared in a blaze of glory.

My obsession with food began long before. In our house, a Sunday dinner meant a four-hour meal that began with antipasto and ended with a tray of pastries, cakes, and pies. My Italian grandmother taught my Puerto Rican mother everything she knew about cooking, and what my grandmother didn't teach her, my mother learned from the cookbook her Puerto Rican father gave her many years before.

I used to sit for hours, rifling through the recipes and laughing at the 1950s drawings of the mom, wearing a dress and pearls and a perfectly starched apron, setting down a feast before her husband (in a suit and tie), while their two perfectly washed and groomed children waited with patient, blissful smiles.

Dinners at our house went something more like this: seven screaming children raced for the kitchen table, where only six kids could fit comfortably, and if the seventh child was lucky, one of the other six would squeeze over so the latecomer didn't have to eat alone in the dark, empty dining room. My brothers and I would all scream over each other while my mother, who looked tired, bedraggled, and stressed beyond belief, would hand us steaming plates of food.

Sometimes, my brother Jude would invite all of his band-mates and his girlfriend to join us for dinner. My friends were always welcome (it never occurred to me, or my mother, that she could say no), and sometimes as many as a dozen children sat at the dining room table, screaming over each other, arguing, laughing, and, most of all, eating.

My mother, whose first language was Spanish, used to walk around the table saying "Mangia tutti cosi," which was Italian; what she was telling us was: "Eat everything!" Some nights, that was terrific. Spaghetti and Meatballs night, Pot Pie night, La Choy Makes Chinese Food That Swings American night—those were the good times. Then, there were the not-so-good nights. Tuna Casserole Tuesdays. Eggplant Parmesan Fridays. Go Back to the Five and Dime, Jimmy Dean, Jimmy Dean Sausage and Eggs night.

Sunday dinners usually meant an appearance by my grandmother (my father's mom), my Uncle Sal (my grandmother's "baby" brother), and my father's older brother, Don. Extended family would come by for desserts, and sometimes there would be twenty people sitting at tables that extended from the dining room to the living room. The air rang with loud voices and laughter, and everywhere there was the smell of something delicious that was about to be shared.

Now, the kitchen and dining room looked like a war zone, and not because all of us had just eaten there. The sagging ceilings dripped brown, murky water and the rooms reeked of fire. Dishes had fallen from the cabinets and smashed to bits, while chunks of falling plaster and weak floorboards made me anxious to get out of these rooms that I never would have dreamed of avoiding while I was growing up.

Where to start? How could I begin choosing what treasures to keep and what I would part with forever? I looked around my old bedroom and started to pull down the photos that lined my wall next to the window. There were pictures of Chris and me in the high school band, photos of all six of my brothers and me at Tony's and Kathie's wedding, graduation photos, and snapshots of my husband, kids, parents, grandparents, aunts, uncles, nieces, and nephews.

I looked outside and saw Chris rifling through some band equipment that had fallen from the second-story window. Everything was now twisted and burned beyond recognition. Tears streamed down my face as our eyes locked, and suddenly, we shrugged and laughed.

As sweat poured off our faces, my brothers, sister-in-law, and I loaded up our cars with as many photographs and albums as we could find. We grabbed all the sentimental things that we could lay our hands on: the portrait of Grandpa when he was a child trumpet player back in Italy, the picture of Uncle Sal in his vaudeville days, Mom and Dad's wedding photo, Mom's jewelry box, the pig in a chef's hat cookie jar, statues of the Blessed Virgin Mary and Jesus with his crown of thorns. My hair, skin, and hands reeked of ashes and water.

People I hadn't seen in decades stopped me on the street while I loaded up my car with ash-covered mementoes of life before the fire.

"You should have seen your Dad," one longtime neighbor said to me. "The rain was coming down pretty hard and there he was, running up and down the block, waving his arms and pointing at his house like a crazy man. Want to see the video?"

Another neighbor stopped me with a big smile on his

face. "Wow, I haven't seen you here in a while! I guess it would take a fire to get you here!"

Still an idiot, I thought to myself.

After an hour or two, when our car trunks were full and our heads swirling from the heat and the enormity of my father's loss, the firefighter who was in charge came back into the living room.

"Time to go, folks," he said. "I hope you have everything, because the place has to be boarded up before the next storm hits."

My brothers, sister-in-law, father, and I trudged out the door.

There were so many things to leave behind…a lifetime of treasures that no one but I would ever miss, but that could never be replaced. I forgot to take my Shirley Temple doll, and the Bionic Woman…even my Cher doll perished in the fire. Worst of all, I never found my mother's cookbook, the one her father had given her so many years before.

We walked out the door and to our cars. There was nothing more we could do here. We stood there, smelling like soot, drenched straight through our clothes, laden with soggy treasures. My Uncle Don pulled up and lurched from his car.

"So you weren't kidding!" he said.

My brothers, father, and I laughed while Uncle Don stared at the house and fought back tears. He rubbed his bald head and his now too-skinny body shook. I wrapped my arms around him and rubbed his back as I consoled him.

"What should we do now?" Kathie said, as we stood on the street looking at each other.

"Well," my father said, as we headed to our cars. "Let's eat."

Recipe: Blackened Chicken

This chicken is delicious if you marinate it before throwing it on the fire (much like we marinated in our own juices while the firefighters put out the flames).

1½ pounds skinless, boneless chicken breasts (thin sliced)

½ teaspoon salt

1 teaspoon black pepper, freshly ground

1 teaspoon Italian herbs

½ teaspoon dried thyme leaves

½ teaspoon dried oregano leaves

2 teaspoons paprika

1 teaspoon onion powder

1 teaspoon garlic powder

¼ teaspoon cayenne pepper

½ teaspoon white pepper

Butter

Combine spices. Coat each piece of chicken with spice mix. Adjust the spiciness level according to taste. Baste each piece of chicken with melted butter. Grill chicken, basting with butter after turning once. Grill about 10 minutes.

Serves 4.

Ten Things You Shouldn't Say When Someone's Childhood Home Gets Hit by Lightning:

10) It was time to redecorate anyway.

9) Your father looked hilarious running in the rain.

8) So your dad wears wife-beater Ts?

7) What do you think your mom would say?

6) What brings you here?

5) You know what the odds are of a lightning strike?

4) Ben Franklin invented this antenna that stops lightning strikes. Didn't you guys have one?

3) If your parents didn't have bad luck, they'd have no luck at all!

2) We should start calling your dad "Job."

1) So what's new?

Chapter 2: Going Home

We had been living with boxes for so long in our tiny attached house in Queens that it never actually occurred to me that we'd move someday. But that day was now.

The sun was high and bright by the time our mother drove us in the station wagon to the new house. It was only a few blocks away, but we might as well have moved to France.

My whole world was the alley behind our house. It was the place where all our friends rode bikes, played tag, and screamed over the fence to get us to come out and play.

There were the seven of us: Jude, Tony, Louie, Paul, Joey, Maria, and Chris. My five older brothers were born in five years; then, my mother had a three-year hiatus before she had twins: my brother Chris and me. Eight years was all that separated the seven of us. It made for a very noisy, raucous, fun, and chaotic household.

Besides our family, every house on that block had children: the Reichs had two, the Wongs had five, the Rosenbergs had three, the Romans had two, the Prestons had three, and the Primianos had three. There was a Polish family of four girls and one boy who lived around the block (and they all had first names that started with "W") and a Colombian family that had three children on the other side of the alley.

I ate bagels with lox for the first time at Muriel Reich's house. At Marty Rosenberg's, his grandmother gave me a steaming bowl of chicken noodle soup that she called "Jewish penicillin" when I was suffering from a nasty cold. In the Wongs' house, we scampered after live shellfish and threw them in a big pot of water so I could try crabs for the first time. Mrs. Roman made me potato pancakes and apple sauce one night, and the Prestons were happy to share some corned beef and cabbage.

The neighborhood around our Queens home was a veritable United Nations, and I was always eager to try something new and delicious with my neighbors. In turn, my friends would come over to sample my mother's meatballs or enjoy that staple of my early childhood, deviled ham. No matter what the season or reason, there was always something new and exciting to eat.

But the new house, just a mile away, didn't have an alley, or neighbors bearing food, or kids for that matter. What it did have was old people, and lots of them. Most of them were the original owners of the houses, and they were proud of the quiet, clean atmosphere.

It's not that our neighbors weren't nice people. They were. But they were about 300 years old, on average, and were horrified that a family with seven children was moving onto their quiet little block. When we got there, we didn't exactly prove their fears unjustified.

We were like monkeys let loose from a cage. We pulled up in our lime-green station wagon, threw down the back hatch, and came roaring out, fighting, screaming, and shattering the illusion that we were going to be good, quiet neighbors.

My grandmother came running out of the house in a panic before any of us could get inside. "Louie," she called. "Don't let them in there. Call Father McNulty right now, or I won't go back in there."

"Ma! What are you talking about?"

"I want this house blessed before you send the kids in there."

My father thought my grandmother was being ridiculous, but she was still his mother, so he ran around the block and brought back Father McNulty. We stayed outside while our parents, grandmother, and parish priest walked around, sprinkling holy water and exorcising the house.

The night before, my grandmother slept over to watch the place and get it ready for our arrival. But just before dawn, as she sat on the couch, a man dressed in a sea captain's suit came marching down the stairs, frowned at her, and disappeared. He apparently then proceeded to make lots of noise upstairs since he was not so happy about the new homeowners who would be coming his way.

Well, my grandmother wasn't looking to star in her own TV show called *The Ghost and Mrs. Lagalante.* No, as far as she was concerned, someone had to go—and it was going to be the captain.

So it wasn't until after Father McNulty left that we were allowed to enter. We piled inside, each lugging a box to our respective rooms, laughing and screaming and wondering if the captain needed his own room, or would he mind bunk beds?

We had big plans for that little house. The one that would go into effect almost immediately was that Jude, my oldest brother, would finally be able to have a band in the basement. This was something of a lifelong dream, and now, at the age of fourteen, he was going to see it come true.

"As long as you stop practicing by 10 pm, I don't see why it should be a problem," said my father, who liked to nurture my brother's musical ambitions. Nobody realized at that moment that Jude's greatest musical ambition was to rock the house from its foundation.

Our second goal was to have a dog. Not just any dog: this dog was one that we'd seen the day it was born to our next-door neighbor's dog, Ginger. Mom and Dad had promised us we could get a puppy once we moved to the new house. So imagine our delight when Ginger gave birth on my parent's fifteenth wedding anniversary, just six weeks before our move.

So all these dreams were bubbling up in my head that

day while we tore open cartons, reassembled furniture, and shouted "Mom! Where's my football?" "Mom! Which box did you put my school bag in?" and "Mom! Why do Maria and Chris get the room on the first floor but we have to live upstairs?"

My father was up and down the stairs, struggling to get beds in place. His hair, which he wore in a comb-over to hide his bald spot, was lying across the side of his head and he was sweating.

"What are you standing around for?" my father boomed. "Go do something useful."

I wandered into the kitchen, where my mother was trying to put away pots, pans, and groceries. I realized I was starving.

"Mom," I said. "I'm hungry."

"You're always hungry," my mother replied. "We won't be eating for awhile."

"Can't I have a snack?" I said.

"I haven't unpacked yet," my mother said. "Why don't you go outside and play for a while? It will make the day go by faster for you."

I realized that this was my mother's nice way of saying "Get lost," so I did just that. Since my brothers were busy helping my father unpack the upstairs room, I went outside to explore by myself.

Within ten minutes, I met Nancy, a little girl from down the block who wanted to introduce me to all the neighbors. One neighbor, in particular, was my favorite. Her name was Mrs. Ida Murray.

"Are you hungry?" Mrs. Murray said.

"No, thanks, I have to go home," Nancy replied.

"Too bad. What about you, Maria?"

"I can stay," I replied.

We waved goodbye to Nancy and, within moments, we were sitting around a sunny kitchen table, sipping lemonade and eating homemade ladyfingers. I told Mrs. Murray about the block I'd just left and how worried I'd been about moving. Mrs. Murray told me about her life growing up on an Iowa farm, where her mother mistakenly cooked her pet chicken, Georgiana.

I laughed over my lemonade. "Weren't you upset?"

"Oh, I was devastated. My brothers and sisters were too. We all loved Georgie. She had such a friendly way about her. But our Pa marched us right downstairs and told us to eat up. He said that's what you get when you name dinner."

I liked Mrs. Murray. She obviously could bake with the best of them, and she was fun company. She had beautiful white hair, clear blue eyes, and slender hands that were always busy with something. While we sat there, she shucked peas and her eyes twinkled while she told me about life on the farm.

Two doors down, I could hear the sound of a pounding hammer and my father's voice. "Maria!" he was booming. I lurched from my chair.

"Thanks for the cookies and lemonade, Mrs. Murray, but

I have to go. My dad's calling me."

"Okay, Maria. Come back again real soon."

I ran out the back door and sped across the lawn that separated our new house from Mrs. Murray's house. When I raced through the door, my father took a swat at me.

"Where have you been?" he yelled. "We're unpacking your room and you're out playing?"

"Mom told me to go outside," I replied. I didn't tell him about the afternoon snack, because he looked pretty thirsty and would probably get annoyed. I just grabbed an unopened box and tore it open before he could ask me anything else.

We laughed and worked while I dreamed of dinner, which felt about two years away. Moving was an awful lot of work, but my parents seemed happy. We were off on a new adventure. It didn't include my old friends or an alley, but it had some surprises in store, I was sure.

"The pizza's here!" Mom called, and we all dropped our boxes and ran for the dining room table. First, we made sure that Nonnie got to choose her seat, and then the rest of us scrambled for any seats we could get. My grandmother called us by nicknames: the boys were all Sugarplums, and I was Rosebud (no, not the sled). Sugarplum #1 (Jude) got to sit next to Nonnie because he was her self-proclaimed favorite. I sat next to my father, my mother sat directly across from him on the other side, and Tony, Louie, Paul, Joey, and Chris sat in different spots around the new dining room table.

"Dig in!" my mother said, as she handed cheesy slices to each of us.

"Sarita, do you have anything for me?" my grandmother said. My grandmother hated cheese with a passion. She claimed it smelled like feet.

"Yes, Mom," my mother replied. She went into the kitchen and came back out carrying a small, cheese-less pizza and a salad.

"How can you eat that with no cheese?" I asked her.

"Easy," she replied, taking a bite. "How can you eat it WITH cheese?"

"I wonder what the captain would eat," Jude said.

My grandmother swatted Sugarplum #1 and everybody laughed.

We ate our fill that night and then sat around the television in the new basement and watched *All in the Family* and *Mary Tyler Moore*. I wanted to stay up for *The Carol Burnett Show*, but I felt my eyes being dragged down like cement weights had been placed on top of them.

Finally, exhausted by the heat, the work, and the food, I staggered off to bed. Chris and I snuggled under the covers of my top bunk bed while Nonnie slept in the bunk below us.

The following morning, Chris and I sat around our new kitchen table while Nonnie served us breakfast.

"Do you think we'll get that new puppy now?" I said.

"Why not? Mom and Dad said we could."

"Oh, just forget about getting a puppy," my grandmother said. There were times when my grandmother was a bucket of ice water on the struggling fires of our hopes and dreams. "Your parents have a lot of work ahead of them, and the last thing they need is another creature to take care of…"

Her last words hung there as we heard a banging on the front door. We ran for the door just in time to see my dad let in our former next-door neighbor, Mario, holding a six-week-old puppy. She was a typical German shepherd, like her mother, Ginger, except that her coloring was golden instead of brown and black.

"Mario, what are you doing here?" my father said.

"Listen, Louie, I'm going to the pound. If you don't take this puppy, we're dropping her off there. Her brothers and sisters are in the car right now."

My father turned to look at my mother. She shrugged her shoulders. "Okay, hand her over."

My father held the puppy high. "Everybody, meet Goldie."

My brothers and I all ran up to kiss her and hold her. "What should we do first?"

"Well," said my father, "she should eat. And come to think of it, so should we."

Recipe: Nonnie's Eggs-In-a-Basket

This one is easy, but it tastes great and the kids always love it!

Cooking spray or butter

4 slices bread

4 eggs

12 strips of bacon (optional)

Spray pan with cooking spray (or use butter, whichever you prefer). Cut out a circle in the center of the bread with the rim of a juice glass. Put the bread into the hot pan and crack the eggs into the hole in the middle. Be sure not to break the yolks. Put the circles of bread in the pan to brown. Let harden, and then flip. When golden brown, serve. Serve 3 strips of bacon on the side.

Serves 2.

Chapter 3: The Dog Who Came to Dinner

It didn't take long before we were all settled in our new home. My brothers Tony, Louie, Joey, and Paul slept upstairs in bunk beds in a dormitory-style room; Jude slept downstairs in his own bedroom with Goldie as company. Chris and I shared the bedroom next to our parents' master bedroom on the first floor.

Since we had spent so much time in the finished basement of our last home, my parents initially set up the basement the same way in the new house. There was a television and a full bar in the larger room, with the laundry room perched behind it. Next to the television room was a long, large room with the boiler room on one end and a workroom tucked into the back on the other end. It seemed like a perfect playroom for us younger kids. Our mother encouraged Chris and me to play down there often, preferably all day, to stay out of her hair.

But one day, Jude came into our playroom with his friends.

"Get out," Jude said.

"But Mom said this is our playroom," I replied.

Jude and his friends started covering the walls with posters of Johnny Winter, Edgar Winter, The Rolling Stones, The Beatles, and Eric Clapton.

"Not anymore," Jude replied.

We grabbed our toys and ran upstairs to find our mother. By the time we returned, the room had been transformed into the band's personal space. There were lava lamps and band instruments everywhere.

"This isn't fair!" Chris and I whined. Our toys were thrown in a corner to make room for the band's things.

"Dad said we could use this room," Jude said. "So it looks like you're out of here."

Now, Chris and I could have complained to our father, but there was no winning in this situation. If we said nothing, we lost; if we went to our father and he took our side, we would infuriate Jude and live in fear for the day he would retaliate. We gathered up our toys and went back upstairs to our bedrooms to play.

Having the band in the house meant a lot of activity at all times. There was always a surplus of boys, the "Yoko Ono's" who dated the band members, and the friends and groupies who came with them. Everyone had long, straggly hair and wore concert jerseys and jeans.

On show nights, the band would sport hot pants and tops

that opened to their navels. In many ways, it was like having another three brothers. I really thought six was enough when it came to brothers, but I had no choice in the matter.

First, there was Gary, the drummer. Gary towered over all of us at 6' 3" tall, and he had big arms, huge feet, and wavy red hair. He was the kindest to us little ones, always with a smile and a joke. He used to wear a T-shirt of Wile E. Coyote holding the Road Runner by the neck and saying, "Beep, beep your ass." I was never afraid of Gary, because he was always kind and gentle with my brother Chris and me. I remembered him from when I was very little, walking his boxer down the street and stopping to let us pet the dog.

Gary started dating a girl named Karla. Karla had long brown hair that was perfectly feathered. She was always very vivacious and friendly. One night, while I struggled to make jewelry for my seventh-grade social studies project, Karla sat down beside me and helped me string beads and feathers to make feather earrings and bracelets.

"Do they look like something the Iroquois would wear?" I said, showing her the textbook pictures.

"Close enough!" she said.

The next band member, Gerry, was Gary's brother. Gerry looked a little bit like his older brother; he also had wavy red hair, fair skin, and a ready laugh. He wasn't as tall as Gary, but he still towered over me. Gerry played lead guitar and could often be found eating one of my brother's sandwiches. He liked teasing Paul and Chris, but unless I left food out unattended, he never bothered me.

Mike, the keyboardist, had dirty blond hair that he wore long. He looked a little bit like Rod Stewart in his Maggie May days. Mike was quiet and polite, and all the girls (and some of the guys) loved him.

My brother Jude was the bass guitarist. He wore his hair hanging down his back and often put red, blue, or blond streaks in it. When my brothers were little, my father used to march them all down the block to the barber, where they would get buzz cuts; they spent most of the summer almost bald. Once Jude got into high school, he drew a picture that resembled Jesus and told my father, "This is what I want to look like."

My father replied, "Fine, as long as you keep your hair clean."

So at any given time, you could find Jude in the bathroom, washing his hair.

This fabulous foursome created a band that went by many names, but the one that always stuck for me was "New York's Unemployed."

Almost every night the band descended into our basement and practiced for hours and hours, laboring over the same song. They played cover songs like "All the Young Dudes," "Gimme Three Steps," "It's Only Rock-'n'-Roll," "Purple Haze," and the theme song from *Barney Miller*. We would sit upstairs, doing homework, eating dinner, or watching TV while the walls shook. Since this went on every night until 10 pm, the neighbors understandably hated us.

My brother and his band eventually even wrote and produced their own songs and cut a 45 single featuring "Abusement Park" on Side A, an homage of sorts to the Rolling Stones' "Violence," and "This Route Before" on Side B, a remarkably mature love song for four guys I never considered romantic in the least.

All four guys in the band loved animals and would always play with our new puppy, Goldie. For her part, she enjoyed being the belle of the ball and followed those boys around like the love-struck puppy she was. Goldie was the kind of dog that every child should have: she was patient and playful and always up for a good time.

Like the rest of us, Goldie was obsessed with eating. She ate her share of toys: GI Joe lost a few legs, my Dawn doll became a cripple thanks to her, and Thumbelina died an untimely death with Goldie responsible for the homicide.

Unfortunately, toys weren't the only thing that Goldie ate. Jude had a turtle tank out in the backyard where he kept his two prize giant turtles, Oscar and Felix. Jude and Gary got the turtles from Oakland Lake and were thrilled to keep them in our yard. It was the ideal situation...until a curious puppy named Goldie came along. Poor Oscar never stood a chance. Goldie pulled him out of the tank and threw him down on the ground. She poked, prodded, and pulled until she managed to rip his shell apart and play with the now dead creature inside.

When Goldie came back into the house with blood all over her face and paws, it was clear that she'd been eating. We wondered what, exactly, she'd feasted on. It didn't take Jude long to discover Oscar's remains strewn all over the backyard. Jude, of course, did what anyone in that situation would do; he refused to talk to Goldie or have anything to do with her.

We all found this hilarious; we weren't sure if Goldie knew anything now except that turtle was delicious. But for at least a week, Jude shunned Goldie like the plague. Poor Goldie was confused. Before Oscar's untimely demise at her paws, she and Jude were always together. She slept in the basement with Jude and often tagged along with him and his friends wherever he went in the house.

Ever since that day that she'd enjoyed the turtle dinner, Jude started yelling. What, exactly, he was yelling about Goldie would never know, but for the rest of her life, whenever anyone said to her, "Did you eat that turtle?" Goldie looked heartily sorry…and maybe a little bit hungry.

Eventually, Jude realized that dogs will be dogs and that turtle pens needed to be more secure. Plus, one night as my father walked around with the now downcast Goldie, turning off lights and tucking in blankets, he watched while Goldie ran over to Jude and kissed him while he slept. Jude was a sucker for those kinds of stories, so he decided to forgive Goldie once and for all.

So, somehow, life began to take on some semblance of normalcy. It was normal to have twelve kids in the house at any time, because Jude's band-mates and their cronies were always over. It was normal to eat dinner with the TV blasting so we could hear over the amplifiers roaring "Suffragette City," "Fire," "Drivin' Sister," and other rock songs in the basement. It was even normal to do our homework while the band played so loud underneath us that the walls, shelves, and books in our hands shook.

At some point in all this, Jude decided that he needed a clubhouse. So he moved some furniture into the garage and that's where he and his friends would gather when they weren't having band practice. They built a loft in the top part of the garage and set up a radio and a little black-and-white TV. It was very homey. The only thing missing was a dog!

As luck would have it, a pack of stray dogs that was wandering the neighborhood started hanging out at Mike's house. One of them had beautiful caramel-colored fur and what looked like thick black mascara around his soulful eyes. His ears flopped over and his nose was jet-black. Except for the ears, he looked a little bit like Goldie.

As Mike looked at him, he realized the dog was missing one of his feet. Someone had taken a knife to his back paw and hacked it off, leaving a stub—what we called a hoof—in its place. His bad foot didn't slow him down at all, and now it made sense why the dog seemed friendly but a little bit scared. Mike started putting food out for him and told the rest of the band about him.

"We should bring him to my house," Jude said. "My father will let us keep him."

My father was usually a soft touch when it came to animals, but not this time.

"We already have a dog," Dad said. "If you want Goldie to hang around in your clubhouse, just take her out there."

"But this dog needs a home! He's so sweet."

"No," my father said. "I don't want another dog in this house."

That was the loophole Jude needed.

"Let's keep him in the garage," Jude said to Mike. "What's his name, anyway?"

"Henry," Mike said. "Or Hank."

"Why Henry?" Jude said, as he petted the wriggling dog.

"He looks like a Henry to me," Mike said.

So Henry started living in our garage. I thought Mike brought him over every day, because I knew that my father had said "no dog" and I couldn't imagine that Jude would break that law. Henry continued to live out there in his own private apartment until the morning of February 14, 1974, when my father, coming home from mass on a bone-chilling, snowy Valentine's Day, saw that the light was on in the garage.

"Dumb kids left the light on again," my father said, as he went to the yard to turn it off.

"What the…" my father said, as a dog that looked just like Goldie jumped up at him when he entered the garage. "What is Goldie doing out here?"

It took only a moment for my father to realize that this wasn't Goldie at all. "JUDE!" he yelled, running for the house.

Since Chris and I could no longer sleep with all the screaming going on, we sat at the kitchen table and started having breakfast. Our mother filled us in on the story as we ate our corn flakes.

"Where will the dog go?" I said, as we watched Jude and Henry trudge out into the snow.

"Dad said he'll have to take him to the shelter or get him into The Bide-a-Wee Home," Mom explained. "Your father was really angry with your brother."

Chris and I watched Jude and Henry disappear down the street. "I guess I'll never see him again," I said. I meant Henry, but if my father was mad enough, maybe I'd never see Jude again either.

I came home from school at lunchtime, starving and ready to eat a peanut butter and jelly sandwich with Chris while we watched *Bewitched* until it was time to head back to school. My mother greeted us at the door and waved us toward the basement. The sounds of two dogs playing and barking came up the stairs.

I ran down and saw Henry playing happily with Goldie. "What's he doing here?"

"Your Dad had a change of heart," Mom said.

Apparently, my father went off to work in midtown Manhattan and stopped at St. Patrick's Cathedral that morning to pray. He asked God to give him guidance and help him make the right decision where that dog was concerned. It dawned on him, at this point, that he was acting old and mean toward Jude and Henry.

"That's when he called Jude at Mike's house and said he could bring Henry back," Mom explained. "But just until we find him a home."

I saw Henry rolling on the ground with Goldie. "It looks like he's home to me."

"Don't get your hopes up, Maria," my mother said. "Your father was pretty adamant."

A month went by. Henry was happy to be indoors, but as a dog just exiting puppyhood, he got himself into trouble. He chewed carpets and toys and stole food from Goldie. One night as we slept, he chewed the cord to the TV set and got a shock that left him squealing as he ran away and hid. My father found the TV, still plugged in, with a bit of blackened wall next to the outlet. Funny, but Henry never did that again.

As the days went by, my father grew more and more attached to Henry and so did the rest of us. As my father petted him one day, he realized that Henry had stitches that went down his chest and across his stomach. There was also the missing paw and the way he cringed whenever someone raised a hand to him. Somebody had done a real job on that poor dog, and now we worked hard to get him to trust us.

Henry was a great lover of treats, and bones, and apples. He never met a meal he didn't like, and sometimes he would rip open the garbage bags and help himself to seconds. Life on the street had made Henry a food thief, but he quickly discovered that he didn't have to steal at our house. Within a few days of his arrival, he stopped wolfing down the food in his plate and trying to steal Goldie's. When it came to food, there was always plenty to go around from the nine of us to the two of them.

Henry was thin and bedraggled, but after one month with us, he was starting to fill out. His coat took on a lustrous sheen, and no one was happier than Henry when eggplant parmesan was on the menu. On Friday afternoons that month, Henry helped Goldie eat as much eggplant as they could while we made believe we were enjoying it. After every big, happy meal, he liked to lie on his back and get a tummy rub.

Since my mother took my father at his word, she started telling everyone she ever knew about our foster dog, Henry, and how much he needed a home. My father agreed with her, even though Henry turned out to be sweet, affectionate, and the perfect playmate for Goldie. He didn't even eat turtles!

"There's a family coming over on Saturday," my mother said.

"You found someone who wants Henry?" my father said, incredulous.

"Yes," my mother replied. "And they really seem interested."

My mother was not a dog person, but rather one forced into dog care by the eight of us. She had meals to cook, clothes to wash and mend, children to wash and mend, and a dog named Goldie to bring back and forth to the vet. Adding

Henry to her already staggering load was a chore she was trying to avoid. Mom welcomed that family like they came bearing gold, frankincense, and myrrh.

Henry ran right over to the newcomers and lay down near them. They gave him treats and rubbed his belly while we watched.

"You know," my father said, as the mother petted Henry and cooed at him, "he's missing one paw, and he has stitches up and down his stomach. He must have been really abused."

"Really?" the mother said, as she stepped back a little.

"Absolutely," my father said. "And you know the problem with abused dogs is that they can't always be trusted."

"He looks like a sweet dog," the woman said. "I think we can trust him."

My father hesitated. "No," he said. "Forget it. Henry stays here."

The family left, surprised and disappointed. Henry wagged his tail as my father scratched his head and my mother shook hers.

"Louie, you said he'd only be here two weeks."

"So he'll stay a little longer," Dad said, as Goldie and Henry chomped on Milk-Bones.

Henry, the dog who came to dinner and was supposed to stay for just a couple of weeks, ended up finding his forever home with us. With Goldie by his side, he lived for twelve more very happy, hunger-free years.

Recipe: Eggplant Parmesan

What made my mother's eggplant the bane of our existence but the joy of Goldie's and Henry's? I'm not sure, but I think it was because she never had the time to drain the eggplant, so it was like a big oily sponge. Goldie and Henry didn't mind—it made their coats shine. Here's a recipe that the rest of us can enjoy! Note the salting and draining trick—do it or your dogs will be the only ones enjoying themselves.

2 large eggplants

Salt

1 28-ounce can crushed tomatoes

1 12-ounce can stewed tomatoes (with basil and celery)

1 6-ounce can of tomato paste

1 cup water

¼ cup sugar (to make the sauce sweet)

1 clove garlic, peeled and minced

⅓ cup olive oil

2 bay leaves

1 teaspoon Italian seasoning

Freshly ground black pepper

1 cup bread crumbs

½ cup milled flax seed

4 large eggs, beaten

Olive oil (enough to coat the pan)

1½ pounds fresh mozzarella cheese, sliced into ¼-inch rounds

1 cup freshly grated parmesan cheese

1 cup fresh basil leaves or ½ cup dried

1. Cut eggplants lengthwise into ¼-inch slices. Arrange one layer on a large plate or platter and sprinkle evenly with salt. Put paper towels on top. Repeat with remaining eggplant, salting each layer, until all eggplant is on the platter. Weigh down the slices with a couple of plates and let drain for 2 hours. This process makes the eggplant release some of its moisture and makes it less likely to soak up excess oil while cooking.

2. While the eggplant is draining, prepare tomato sauce. Combine all tomato products, water, sugar, garlic, and ⅓ cup olive oil in a big pot. Season with salt and pepper, bay leaves (remember to remove them after cooking is done) and Italian seasonings to taste and let simmer.

3. When eggplant has drained, press down on it to remove excess water, wipe off the excess salt, and lay the slices on new paper towels to remove all the moisture. In a wide, shallow bowl, combine bread crumbs and milled flax seed. Mix well. Pour beaten eggs into another wide shallow bowl. Place a large, deep skillet over medium heat, and pour in half an inch of olive oil. When oil is hot, dredge the eggplant slices first in the bread crumb mixture, then in the beaten egg. Working in batches, slide coated eggplant into hot oil and fry until golden brown on both sides, turning once. Drain on new paper towels.

4. Preheat the oven to 350°F. In the bottom of a 10x15-inch glass baking dish, spread 1 cup of tomato sauce. Top with one-third of the eggplant slices. Top eggplant with half of the mozzarella slices. Sprinkle with one-third of the parmesan cheese and half of the basil leaves.

5. Make a second layer of eggplant slices, topped by 1 cup of sauce, remaining mozzarella, half the remaining parmesan, and all of the remaining basil. Add remaining eggplant, and top with the remaining tomato sauce and parmesan.

6. Bake until cheese has melted and top is slightly brown, about 30 minutes. Allow to cool at room temperature for about 10 minutes before cutting and serving.

Serves 8.

Chapter 4: Jude

Whenever people hear that I was the only girl in a family of seven children, they invariably say things like "Oh! You must've been so spoiled!" or "You must've lived like a princess!"

But let me tell you: I was no princess. I never lived in fear that my brothers would kill me with kindness. Kill me, maybe, but not with kindness.

I don't think my brothers meant me any harm, but they were rough-and-tumble boys. They never treated me like a dainty little girl. They treated me like one of them. So I suppose I should thank them for making me feel that girls had just as many rights as boys, including the right to be pummeled, punched, and pushed downstairs.

Jude was my oldest brother and, in my eyes, the ruler of our universe. My parents were like overlords, but Jude was definitely the leader on the ground.

It was Jude we looked to when it came time to settle squabbles; if Jude was with you, who could be against you? Eight years older and cooler than I could ever hope to be, Jude was a wise though sometimes merciless ruler. If he felt that he needed to right a wrong, he could be brutal.

When a neighborhood kid picked on our brother Louie, Jude's vengeance was swift. Jude waited for the boy to come riding by on his bicycle, and then he stuck a large stick into the spokes. The kid went flying, and we never had to worry about that particular bully messing with us again.

While the other girls in my neighborhood had to run screaming when gangs of boys tried to rub Nair into their hair one Halloween, I walked around with my waist-length tresses gleaming and my head held high. Only Cher tossed her hair more than I did. When one boy had the audacity to grab me, I uttered the fateful words "My brother is Jude Lagalante," and not a hair on my head was touched.

Life with Jude was fun, but sometimes dangerous. One day when I was about three years old, my brother was sick and stayed home from school.

"Jude," my mother said, as she clutched her keys. "You watch Maria and Chris while I go pick up my parents."

"Okay," Jude said.

Once my mother was gone, my brother turned to me and said, "Say, want to play a game called Superman?"

"What do you have to do?" I asked.

"I pick you up and throw you toward the couch. You

pretend you're flying. That makes you Superman. Come on, it's fun!"

"All right," I said, since I always wanted to fly and the couch looked pretty safe.

We were laughing and screaming for a good five minutes. I loved the feeling of flying through the air and landing on the couch with a great big WHOOSH!

"I'm Superman!" I yelled.

What I didn't bank on was the wall next to the couch, where I actually landed when Jude's arm began to tire and his calculations were off.

I realized within a second of impact that I was headed for the wall. I tried to break my fall with the plant beside the couch, but my elbow and knee scraped along the carpet as I smashed into the wall.

My mother came in as I lay bleeding and crying, wrapped around the potted plant.

"JUDE!" my mother screamed, as my grandmother gathered me into her arms and took me to the bathroom, kissing my tear-streaked face and searching for bandages and Mercurochrome.

Jude was always looking for adventure. This penchant for doing the wrong thing happened to be matched by a mischievous sense of timing. The time my parents went away for a Marriage Encounter weekend and left my Italian grandmother in charge seemed like the perfect time to throw a party.

Of course, there would be no parties as long as my grandmother was breathing, but this didn't stop Jude. Since he lived in the basement, he simply went downstairs with three of his band-mates after dinner and left my grandmother busy cleaning up and getting the little ones ready for bed. Several hours later, while my grandmother sat on the couch for some much-deserved rest, she heard girls' voices coming from downstairs.

"Who's down there?" my grandmother said, from the top of the staircase.

Stifled girlish giggles were the only response. My grandmother got a sinking feeling that Sugarplum #1, her beloved eldest grandson, was up to no good.

Whoever said that grandmothers were not able to move at lightning speed obviously never saw my grandmother. She descended those stairs like a chimpanzee on crack as she searched for the girls hiding there.

Using the basement windows as stand-in doors, Jude had smuggled in three girls, along with copious quantities of beer, and the whole gang was having a wild '70s party. As my grandmother burst through the basement door, the sounds of Edgar Winter and the laughter of at least ten teenagers greeted her.

"*Putana!*" my grandmother yelled, grabbing all three girls by the hair. "Get out of this house NOW!"

Faster and more powerful than a speeding locomotive and now able to leap tall teenagers in a single bound, my grandmother catapulted those kids out the side door of our house with a few swift kicks.

When my parents came home that Sunday, my grandmother resigned from weekend babysitting forever. And she never looked at Sugarplum #1 quite the same way again.

Recipe: Turtle Pie

Remember Jude and his beloved turtle, Oscar? Well, here's a recipe that represents him perfectly. I think Goldie would approve.

Vanilla ice cream

2 ready-made chocolate piecrusts

Caramel sauce

Nuts

Chocolate sauce (try to get the kind that hardens)

Put small amount of ice cream in bottom crust. Drizzle with caramel, nuts, and chocolate sauce. Then add more ice cream and more caramel, nuts, and chocolate sauce. Put top crust on. Store in the freezer until ready to serve.

Serves 4-6.

Chapter 5: Tony

My brother Tony should have been the oldest. He was always an old soul, capable of herding us all together and establishing order when Jude just wanted to invite every last kid in the neighborhood over to play in discarded refrigerator boxes.

While Jude and his friends were busy establishing their band, New York's Unemployed, my brother Tony was often our babysitter. He was the benevolent leader, as opposed to the vicious leader Jude could sometimes be when he was left in charge. However, when pushed, Tony could be as merciless as the next one.

One day, when left to mind us as my mother ironed clothes, Tony instigated a rousing game of hide-and-seek. I saw the dryer door open and I climbed in. Tony watched me go in there and thought it would be great to have a little fun at my expense. So he shut the door and turned the dryer on.

I didn't panic too much as the dryer started to tumble me in great big circles. But as the dryer started to heat up, I must admit, I began to sweat. Thankfully, it occurred to my mother that she wasn't doing any wash and she threw the door open.

"Tony! I expect better than this from you!" my mother screamed, as I cried in her arms.

But whether my parents liked it or not, Tony was their best hope for a babysitter within—or without—our family. Our cousin, Diane, had been our babysitter once, and she was possibly the only person who had taken the reins forcefully and without fear. She would gather all seven of us together and tell us that we were about to experience an amazing game.

"It's called Who Can Fall Asleep Fastest," Diane said. "Now, everybody get into bed!"

Morons that we were, we'd pile into our rooms and jump into our beds without ever asking her what the rules were. Sometimes, it was still sunny outside when Diane put down the challenge to us.

But it didn't matter; if someone put down a challenge to us—even one that required us to go to sleep—we would not show any weakness by refusing it. Only Louie had brains enough to ask about the terms of the contest.

"What do we get if we win?" he said.

"Oh, your prize is simply amazing," Diane said. "If you win, I will wake you up and let you stay up for the rest of the night with me. No bedtime at all! And," she said, with a pause for added dramatic effect, "you can have all the ice cream you can eat."

There were loud whoops and cries of joy from both bedrooms.

"But," Diane said, "whoever wins CAN'T TELL. It's our secret, or I won't play this game with any of you ever again."

So each of us was dispatched to la-la land, determined to be the first to fall asleep and gain the prize of a lifetime: no bedtime! Endless ice cream! That Diane was the greatest!

When the following morning came and I woke up in my bed, I realized that I had lost. I didn't get to stay up or eat ice cream. Although I was tempted to start asking around about who won, I realized that to do so would jeopardize the future prizes my cousin intended to give me, when it was my turn.

And so Diane continued to babysit for us, much to my parents' delight. The only time I saw them sadder than the day my grandfather died was when they realized that Diane now had a social life and couldn't come over anymore.

They had some marginal success finding girls from the neighborhood to watch us so they could go out to dinner every now and then. But my parents had to give up the hope of ever getting a babysitter again after Jude, Tony, and Louie locked one in the upstairs closet and left her there for three hours.

I came out of my bedroom and found Louie in the hallway.

"We should let Lisa out of the closet."

"Don't be silly," Louie said. "This is a game. She's having fun."

When my parents came home and liberated her several hours later, her own father's screams were only slightly louder when he returned with his sobbing daughter. I watched as my father apologized profusely to him and promised it would never happen again.

"Damn straight it won't," the father replied. "I'd never let my daughter anywhere near those animals again!"

Of course this was a blow to me, because Lisa had great long hair and I used to sit and brush it for hours while she sat there wringing her hands and wondering aloud how she was ever going to get my brothers to do anything she told them to do. That's how she ended up in the closet; she should've just stayed there and let me brush her hair while the boys behaved badly.

Having been a part of the mutiny that led to Lisa's demise—and knowing the enemy like he did—Tony was never going to end up locked in our closet. He ruled with an iron fist, and when he said we had to do something, he meant it. This resulted in my being sent to bed while it was still perfectly light out on more than one occasion because I dared to question his authority.

But Tony was a kind older brother. If I was ever in trouble, I knew I could go to Tony and he would bail me out, whether by talking to our parents to get my bike fixed or saving me a seat at the kitchen table so I wasn't forced to eat alone at the dining room table while everyone else had fun in the kitchen.

Tony was the one who taught me how to read a clock, the difference between dinosaurs, and the joy to be found in an episode of *Dallas* or *Dynasty*.

When Chris and I were in first grade and Tony was in the

eighth grade, we younger kids were paired up with the big kids in school to make sailboats out of Ivory Snow soap bars. Tony made a beeline for Chris and me and helped us carve the boats just enough so that they didn't sink. Then he patiently helped us make the sails that would wave triumphantly over our little soap boats. Tony's patience was endless and we felt proud. How many other kids there could boast that THEIR brother helped them carve their boats?

Well, quite a few (big families were the norm in our Catholic school), but the other older kids didn't run to help their little brothers and sisters like our brother did. If they got paired up with their little brother or sister, fine. But Tony made it his business to be there for us, a trait that has never faded.

When Tony went off to Queens College, he had to get a job in the student work program in order to afford the modest tuition. The "plum" job he landed was as a lab technician in the vivisectionist's lab. Tony, the animal lover, had to work in a lab where he regularly put electrodes in rats' heads, probed and prodded monkeys and cats, and tested rabbits. In an atmosphere that was by definition cruel, Tony injected calm and caring.

He started bringing me with him just before dawn on Saturday mornings to feed the animals and clean their cages. We would walk across the Queens College campus, which was then so wide open that you could see the Manhattan skyline in dawn's early light. The lights would still be twinkling in the Empire State Building; if you looked a bit to the left, you could see the Twin Towers sparkling in the sky.

We'd go into the lab and get hit by a wave of noxious smells, including animal feces, vomit, urine, and the sting of chemicals used to keep the roaches from multiplying beyond control. Not exactly glamorous, but the stink was the least of it.

Tony would let me clean the crates in the cats' room, where we tried to be kind to the poor animals kept there. I'd help Tony as he cleaned the cages in the rats' section, and I almost jumped out of my skin the time an albino rat leaped up and bit Tony on the thumb.

As he bled, Tony gently pushed the rat down into its crate and calmly said, "Now let's go get some Band-Aids."

I would've needed a sedative, but Tony walked to the office, bandaged his finger, and went about his business.

After an hour or two, we finished the job, and then we would go to the Bagel Nosh for breakfast. We'd meet our parents, Joey, Paul, and Chris, who were all going to volunteer at St. Kevin's Catholic Church at a program for the mentally retarded, and grab a table big enough for the seven of us. Tony would treat me to any bagel I wanted, plus hot chocolate with whipped cream and a banana. We'd sit around and trade stories until it was time to leave for St. Kevin's.

Tony was a good brother, but he was no saint. When illness struck him at sixteen and Joey was busy hiding his cane to torment him, Tony waited and watched. When he was feeling better, he hid the cane behind the couch, and when Joey got within striking distance, Tony whacked him repeatedly with it until Joey cried "Uncle!"

Tony may have been more merciful than Jude, but it was important to remember that you should never trifle with him.

Recipe: Monkey Bread

If the monkeys could have elected a king, they would have gladly elected Tony. Here's a recipe that reminds me of our days working with the monkeys at the laboratory.

1-pound frozen bread dough

1 stick butter

1½ teaspoons cinnamon

¾ cup sugar

½ cup chopped pecans

Thaw bread dough. Cut into 20 pieces (any shape). Melt butter. Mix cinnamon, sugar, and pecans in bowl. Dip pieces of dough into melted butter, then in cinnamon mixture. Stack in tube or Bundt pan. Cover and put in warm place; let rise until doubled in bulk, 1 to 3 hours. Bake at 350 degrees for 25 minutes. Immediately after baking, turn out on a plate while warm.

Serves 8-10.

Chapter 6: Louie

Then there was Louie, who was blessed with a charm and charisma far beyond his years. Life was always a party when Louie was around. Always laughing, always happy, always surrounded by friends, Louie was the brother that everyone agreed was destined to reign over the Favorite Brother of the Week Awards.

My father instituted this little popularity contest after there was some argument over who would get the one and only chocolate doughnut on Sunday mornings. For whatever reason, my father would always buy nine jelly doughnuts and one chocolate doughnut and then ask us to vote for the most popular brother of the week, whose prize would be that chocolate doughnut. Almost every week, Louie would come away with the most votes, the chocolate doughnut firmly in his hand.

After many years of objecting, I got the awards officially renamed Favorite Sister of the Week Awards and was finally able to compete. My brothers rewarded me by voting, by an overwhelming margin, for our dog, Goldie. She enjoyed the doughnut while Louie went back to campaigning for his rightful place as Favorite Brother of the Week Award winner.

Louie often felt compelled to fight Jude for supremacy. When we would get locked in a long-drawn-out battle over a game of Monopoly, Louie would stop at nothing to come out victorious. Once, he had Park Place and I had Boardwalk. He wanted to buy it from me; I wanted to sell it to him.

But…Jude stepped in and offered me pretty much every piece of property he owned and loads of cash. I could see the veins bulging out of Louie's head. Now I was in for it; if I did what Louie wanted, he would win and the game would mercifully be over. But if I didn't do what Jude wanted, I would live in fear of being the victim of a painful "hit" that would strike whenever Jude got around to it. Tony tried to help.

"Why don't you two leave her alone? She's just a little kid."

"Shut up," Jude replied, and then turned to me. "Come on now, Maria. Decide."

I looked around the table at my brothers and paused. Either way, I was doomed. I handed the deed to Jude.

"You can't do that!" Louie said, as he jumped to his feet. "You made a promise! We had a deal!"

"Tough luck, loser!" Jude yelled, and laughed.

Louie was so incensed that he grabbed the Monopoly

board, threw it up into the air, and smashed all the hotels, money, and playing pieces off the table. "I'm outtalk here!" he yelled, and he stomped out of the house. We never did play Monopoly together again, but it was just as well. Louie got over his blinding rage and forgave me for selling Broadway to Jude. Really, what choice did I have? He seemed to understand that.

Louie continued to hone his skills as a negotiator as we hurtled through life. When my twin, Chris, came home with a report card that featured one A, one B, one D, and five Fs, it was Louie's charm and reasoning that saved Chris's life.

"Dad, I know this seems really bad," Louie said. "But there is a silver lining!"

"And what's that?" my father replied.

"He got an A in religion and a B in speech. Maybe he'll be a priest!"

My father was so busy doubling over in laughter that he could barely speak. Louie had this magical effect on my father, and thank God, because Chris went on to get more Fs and Ds in the future.

But there was one time that Louie's sense of humor failed to hit the mark.

I was home one Friday night, panic-stricken because I had seen some bits of *The Exorcist* and I was convinced that the Devil had booked his flight and would be on my doorstep any minute now. My parents were out for their weekly Friday night with their best friends, Rita and Gary, when I called them at 11 pm.

"Mom," I said through tears, "I'm afraid. Please come home soon."

My mother clucked at me and tried to jolly me through it. "Come on, Maria. It's just a silly movie."

"No, it's not," I insisted. "Please don't leave me here alone."

"You're not alone," Mom said. "Chris and Paul are home!"

"They're asleep already," I said. "Besides, why would the Devil be afraid of Chris or Paul?"

My mother laughed. "Okay, we're on our way."

My parents came home an hour or two earlier that night than they would've normally come home. My father laughed at me and told me to pray and everything would be fine. That's when the phone rang.

"Who the hell would call now?" my father said.

I wondered if the Devil knew our phone number.

"We'll be right there," my father said, as he hung up the phone. "Seems Louie and his friend John were in a car accident. They're at North Shore University Hospital right now."

My parents ran back out the door, leaving me to deal with my own demons, with no one but Chris, Paul, Goldie, and Henry as protectors.

What seemed like an eternity later, the phone rang, and Paul answered.

Paul's face was a mask of fear. "Yeah. Yeah? Oh no! Okay, Dad," he said as he hung up the phone.

Chris stood nearby. "What's wrong?"

Paul shook his head and gulped. "Louie didn't make it."

Chris was gripped with panic. He grabbed Paul's arm and started shouting, "No! Paul, please, Paul! Tell me it's not true."

Paul stood there for a moment and then started to laugh. "No, he's fine," he said. Poor Chris didn't know whether to be overjoyed or to end up with one less brother by killing Paul.

My parents realized that this incident could have had a very different ending, and they were grateful to have Louie home, alive if not well. This time, Louie got off the hook. But the next time his teenage escapades had him coming home from a party way too late, my father was not quite as benevolent.

The next day, our father turned to him.

"So what do you think of this incident?" my father said to him.

"Well, Dad," Louie began, sporting his most philosophical voice and a warm hand on my Dad's shoulder, "these things happen."

Normally, this was the kind of remark that would have my dad barreled over laughing. After all, hadn't he been just like Louie when he was a teenager? Didn't he get in trouble for staying out all night, driving his car up onto the neighbor's lawn, and worrying his mother half to death?

But now a dark, angry look clouded his features.

"Let me tell you what's going to happen now," Dad replied through gritted teeth. "I'm going to gather up your siblings and they are going to impose your punishment."

Louie looked delighted. "Okay," he said, a little too brightly.

"But only on one condition," my father said, as he summoned

my other brothers and me into the living room. "This Star Chamber had better mete out a punishment that I feel is worthy of the crime, or I will throw out the punishment and impose one that's even stiffer. Got it?"

Jude, now in charge, nodded. "We'll come up with something," he said, and for the first time since the Monopoly incident, Louie looked alarmed.

After about an hour of back-and-forth talking, Jude, Tony, Paul, Joey, Chris, and I hashed out a punishment that we thought fit the crime. "For every five minutes that Louie was late, we'll deduct an hour off his curfew," Jude announced. "Louie came home forty-five minutes late. That means he has to come home 9 hours early, at 3 pm every day, for two solid weeks. Plus, he can't have any friends over during that time."

"That's not fair!" Louie exploded. "That covers Labor Day! I have parties to go to that weekend!"

My dad smiled. "I like it," he said. "And just remember, Louie: these things happen."

Somehow, babysitting skipped over Louie entirely, so while Tony was often stuck at home with us younger kids, Louie was out at parties all the time. So for him to be home with us, every day from 3 pm on, was probably the cruelest punishment we could have meted out.

He paced the floors like a tortured lion. Life was a party to Louie, and our house had become a party he didn't want to crash. When those two weeks were up, Louie raced out the door and out into the world. And boy, did he smile.

Recipe: Alabama Slammers

For years, Louie was the bartender at the local pub, Peter T's. I chose this drink for the end of his chapter because I can still remember when I was old enough to have one and he made it just for me. I loved it, and I hope you like it too.

4 ounces Southern Comfort liqueur

4 ounces amaretto liqueur

4 ounces grenadine syrup

16 ounces orange juice

In a glass of ice, combine Southern Comfort, amaretto, and grenadine. Fill with orange juice and stir.

Serves 4.

Chapter 7: Paul

My brother Paul could be both very kind and very sadistic. I don't think it was in Paul's nature to be rotten, but my brother Joey was right behind him in age, and he made Paul's life miserable when we were little kids. There were times that Paul could be sensitive and creative, and Joey could be completely insensitive and destructive.

That's not to say that Joey wasn't creative too. The ways that he came up with to torment us were hilarious and innovative, especially when he wasn't teasing me.

Noting Paul's love for the comic strip Peanuts, Joey created his own comic strip making fun of Paul. It was called Paul Is Nuts and featured a very Charlie Brown–like Paul character, sporting the same tortured look that Paul often wore after spending any amount of time with Joey. Everybody thought this comic strip was hilarious...everyone, except for

Paul. All Paul wanted to do was to get Joey to stop teasing him. But how could he do it?

Paul decided to tease me just to divert Joey's attention from him. Joey didn't care which sibling he was teasing, so Paul would start bothering someone else just so he wouldn't get the worst from Joey. When I was very young, Paul would make up songs about me, calling me fat, ugly, stupid, and useless. I was tormented for years, until I learned something: Paul was easier to hurt than I was.

One day, we watched a commercial for milk in which the outline of a man jumped from a glass of milk, danced around a bit, and then dove back into that big cold glass. For some reason, this made us all laugh uproariously, including Paul. That is, until Joey pointed to the TV and said, "Hey! That's Paul! Let's call him Milk from now on."

Never mind that Milk had no particular meaning and shouldn't have been insulting in the least; it unnerved Paul, and I got my first glimpse into information that might be useful some day.

That day came when I was about nine years old. Paul and I were sitting in the living room watching *The Gong Show* when he launched into one of those songs about me being fat and stupid. I responded by singing about my favorite dairy product, Milk, until Paul came running after me with a speed that would've made a cheetah look blindingly slow. I thought I would make it to my bedroom in time, but Paul was on top of me in a flash just as I reached the door.

Before I could lock the door with that plank of wood I kept for just these kinds of occasions, Paul grabbed me with both hands and lifted me high over his head. He bench pressed me and threw me twelve feet across the room. I crashed into the shelves, pulling down horse and dog statues; slammed my head and arms against the metal railings of my bed frame; and felt every last bit of air deflate out of my lungs as I rolled beneath the bed.

I could just see Paul's worried expression as he stood in the doorway from my vantage point beneath the mattress. He looked terrified that he had killed me; I thought for a moment that it was nice that he was actually concerned. Then I pulled myself up on the bed and launched back into my song about Milk.

Paul grabbed his head and wisely (for me, at least) ran from the house. Later that afternoon, my father called us all together to play a game of hearts. I came out of my room, sporting a bruise that stretched from my shoulder to my bicep and a scratch over my eye where some of the broken bric-a-brac had cut me.

"What happened to you?" my father said.

I looked at Paul, who immediately cracked like a watermelon on wet cement and told my father the whole tortured story.

My father looked confused. "So you beat her up because she called you Milk?"

My dad was laughing so hard that even Paul cracked a smile.

The following year, I got my first look at the Paul that the rest of the world saw. I was minding my own business in my fifth-grade math class when Mrs. Costello told me I was to go downstairs to the auditorium for a show. It was supposed to be for the sixth to the eighth grades, but for some reason, I was allowed to go. Since I never liked math class anyway, I joyfully ran down to the auditorium, where my mother was already seated. She waved me over and I sat down beside her.

A few minutes later, the lights went dark and the spotlight shone on the stage. The curtains opened, and there stood my brother Paul.

"What's this all about?" I whispered to my mother.

"Shush," my mother said. "He's starting."

I couldn't understand what I was going to see. "Maybe he's going to do a one-man show with our waxed fruit," I thought. We were forever teasing Paul for playing with knives, forks, or the fake fruit on the kitchen table.

Suddenly, Paul began to do a soliloquy from *Moby Dick*. He ranted and raved about the Great White Whale; the veins in his neck bulged and he looked as angry as he did that day I called him Milk. I couldn't understand a word of what he was talking about, but I noticed that he transfixed the usually boisterous crowd of eleven- to thirteen-year-olds. He was amazing.

"Hey," I said. "He's actually good."

I turned to look at my mother, and there she was with tears streaming down her face, delighted to see Paul shine at something he was born to do.

The crowd broke into a mighty roar when he finished and the curtains closed. I had an odd feeling; I wasn't quite sure what to make of it. It was the first time in my life that I was not looking at Paul like a tortured little sister. I was seeing him as someone worthy to be admired.

For all of Paul's teasing and baboon-like strength, he could be very kind and gentle. When high school began for me, I went off to a gigantic school where I didn't know anyone and couldn't find any of my classes. That first day at school, I had four minutes to get from the third-floor to the basement for a mechanical drawing class.

The bell had already rung when I realized I would never make it. There was only one staircase that was open and led down to the basement; you could come up the stairs but not down most of them (to keep kids from skipping classes). I spent the next half-hour frantically trying every door to the basement that I could find while upperclassmen laughed at me or ignored me.

I had given up hope of ever finding my class when, through tears, I saw Paul.

"What's wrong?" Paul said.

"I can't find the stairs to my class," I sobbed.

Paul took me by the hand and walked me to the correct staircase, then went down to the basement with me and took me directly to my class. Apparently, he was not worried about looking cool.

"When your class is over, go up this staircase here and you'll be back by the front doors," Paul instructed as he looked at my program card. "Then you can get to your sixth-period class on the second floor in a snap."

I hugged him to me like he was my lifeline and sobbed, "Thank you. I feel like such an idiot."

"Everyone gets lost the first day." Paul laughed and pushed me toward my class. "Get going already."

Being a freshman while Paul and Joey were seniors was always a revelation. I began to notice that, now that they were older, they didn't live to make me miserable. In fact, quite often, they were protective, loving, and kind. I found it funny when Paul would burst through the door of my classes and yell hello to me, or throw the door open to Mr. Reines's class and yell "It's Reines in the morning!" This was funny, since *Imus in the Morning* was a very popular radio program back then and "Reines," pronounced "Rine-us," sort of rhymed with "Imus." What can I say? We were easily amused.

Paul's and Joey's behavior was very different in high school than it was when Chris and I were around ten years old and we would join hands in prayer as we implored God to strike them both dead, or at least immobilized, so they would stop torturing us.

Recipe: Chocolate Malted Milk Cookies

I can't think of my brother Paul without the word "milk" coming to mind. This recipe makes me think of him: surprisingly sweet and hard to forget.

1 cup butter, softened

¾ cup granulated sugar

¾ cup brown sugar, packed

1 teaspoon baking soda

2 large eggs

2 (1-ounce) squares baking chocolate, melted and cooled

1 teaspoon vanilla extract

2 ¼ cups all-purpose flour

½ cup instant hot cocoa powder

1 cup chopped malted milk balls

1. Preheat oven to 375 degrees.

2. In a large mixing bowl, use an electric mixer set on medium to high speed to cream the butter for 30 seconds. Add the sugar, brown sugar, and baking soda, scraping the sides as necessary.

3. Beat in the eggs, melted chocolate, and vanilla until completely combined. Stir in the flour until just mixed. Next, fold in the cocoa powder and malted milk balls.

4. Using a teaspoon, drop spoonfuls of dough about 2 inches apart onto an ungreased cookie sheet.

5. Place in preheated oven and bake for 10 minutes, or until edges are firm.

Cool on cookie sheet for a minute or two, and then transfer to wire rack to cool completely.

Yield: About 3 dozen cookies

Chapter 8: Joey

When I was little, I firmly believed that my brother Joey was bent on my destruction. He told me early on that I ruined our family's softball team; they'd been thrilled to welcome Christopher home, but when they saw me, well…

"When Chris came home, everyone from the neighborhood ran to our house to see him," Joey said. "But when you came home, no one could be bothered."

I was always running away from Joey because:

1) He liked to tease me until I cried.

2) Then he'd laugh at me for crying.

3) Next, he'd punch me when I made fun of him in return.

4) So no matter what, I'd be bruised and crying.

Running away from Joey caused me any number of injuries, including skinned knees, black eyes, and sprained ankles. I can still hear my mother saying: "Joey, leave your sister alone! And Maria, stop crying." His penchant for teasing was unparalleled. So it was only a matter of time until my need to run away and his need to torment me would result in a spectacular injury.

One day when I was in the third grade, I was waiting for a play date with a friend. We planned to go roller-skating around the neighborhood.

My mother was in the basement airing out mattresses when she asked me to go upstairs and get her the dustpan. I raced up the cement stairs from our unfinished basement and immediately ran into Joey.

"Re-re," he said, "go get me a sandwich and a glass of milk."

"I can't," I replied. "I have to get Mom the dustpan."

"If you don't," he said, his voice grave, "I'll be forced to turn into the Wolfman."

My pulse quickened. My brother did a drop-dead impersonation of Lon Chaney Jr. turning into the Wolfman. With Joey's voluminous hair and ability to go from calm friendly brother to frenzied lunatic threatening to kill me, I was convinced he could actually turn into that beast. And then what would become of me? I had no silver bullets and Abbott & Costello were nowhere to be found.

But despite the imminent threat posed to me by my brother's possible transmutation, I didn't want to make him a sandwich. So instead of just slipping away quietly, I grabbed the dustpan and made a break for it.

So certain was I that my brother, aka Lon Chaney Jr., was hot on my heels and about to rip me limb from limb that I ran to the basement stairs like a cheetah on amphetamines. I almost made it to the safe harbor that was my mother when I tripped on my own feet and fell headfirst down the flight of cement steps.

I lay there in a heap, my little body twisted and my head at an odd angle. I began to sense that I was watching myself from the ceiling when my mother walked into that part of the basement. Since she'd spent most of my childhood convinced that my brothers would eventually kill me, she immediately went into panic mode.

"MARIA!!!!!" she screamed, grabbing me.

I immediately snapped to and looked into her panic-stricken face. I started screaming. While the two of us shrieked, my mother dragged my broken little body over to the nearest mattress and dumped me onto it. She started to slap my face, which hurt quite a bit.

"Maria! What's your name?" she screamed.

"You just said it. It's Maria," I muttered.

"Oh, my God, I thought you were dead. DEAD!!!" My mother screamed again, as she pulled me into her arms and kissed me frantically.

Now I liked affection and attention as much as the next person, but my neck, back, and head were killing me and I was afraid that my mother's love was going to snuff out what little life I had left in me.

"I'm alive, Ma," I said.

"What on earth were you running from?" my mother said. "Did you call Paul 'Milk' again?"

"No," I said, as I tried to clear the cobwebs from my eyes. "Joey was turning into the Wolfman."

My mother looked at me like I had just burst into Cantonese. "I don't understand you kids sometimes," she muttered.

Within an hour, the woozy feeling left me and I was overtaken with an adrenaline rush. When my friend, Mona, and her mother showed up at our door for our play date, Mrs. P. looked alarmed at the sight of me.

"Obviously, you want her to rest and not play this afternoon," she said.

My mother looked at me. "Well, she says she feels okay and wants to go play. So why not?"

With that, I put on my roller skates and Mona and I rode all over the neighborhood. For the next two days, I played as if my life depended on it.

But by Sunday night, I was feeling as if someone had beaten me repeatedly with a cane...and no, it wasn't Tony.

As my family sat around watching *Airport*, I started to feel sweaty. I couldn't blame it on Dean Martin, although I was pretty sure that my grandmother was right to adore him the way she did; boy, was he handsome. No, it was more than that.

I started to notice that the McDonald's commercials were making me sick. "Two all-beef patties, special sauce, lettuce, cheese, pickles, onions on a sesame seed bun" rang out in my head, and my stomach began to gurgle ominously.

I ran to the bathroom, only to find Jude inside for the duration. I banged on the door and begged him to come out. But apparently it was his night to wash his now silky, long brown hair, and I could not impress upon him the urgency of the situation.

I finally gave up and ran into the kitchen, desperate to find a place to throw up. I knew I would never make it to the upstairs bathroom. I looked into the sink; it was full of unwashed dishes. I tried to run to the garbage pail, but I didn't make it.

My parents came in to find me on the floor, caked in vomit, with puke everywhere. I explained that Jude wouldn't get out of the bathroom.

My father banged on the bathroom door. "Jude, get out here. And bring the mop with you. You've got some cleaning to do."

The next morning, my mother broke down and called our family doctor to make a house call. Dr. Smith arrived, bag in hand, ready to look not just at me, but at Jude and Louie as well. Since they were both home with fevers, my mother figured a doctor's visit was not only a necessity, but also an economic coup. One house call fee for three sick kids! She could hardly believe her good luck.

Normally, my parents called the doctor only if a fever

was out of control or they couldn't get the hemorrhaging to stop. Broken bones usually necessitated a trip to the hospital emergency room, but only after a day or two of your limb hanging at an odd angle and your constant whining convinced them that, in fact, you may actually need medical attention.

Dr. Smith came into my room, wearing that slightly disturbed expression he normally had on his face whenever he was looking at me. My penchant for bizarre accidents and multiple contusions always had him shaking his head at both my mother and me. He put his ice-cold stethoscope on my chest and put one finger up.

"Now follow my finger!" he said, which I thought was kind of funny. I could see at least a dozen fingers (although he insisted there was only one) and the question made me laugh uncontrollably. I thought his next question would be "Pull my finger." I laughed even harder.

"Jeez," he said, as he poked and prodded my purple face and tried to compress the swelling that made the left side of my face look like an eggplant. "What the heck happened to you?"

"I fell down the basement stairs," I said, in between the giggles.

"Did someone push you?" Dr. Smith said.

"No," I replied. "But Joey was threatening to become the Wolfman if I didn't make him a sandwich."

Dr. Smith shook his head and summoned my mother to my bedside. "She can't focus her eyes, plus she sees loads of fingers when I've only got one up. Her head is purple and swollen, and she's not making any sense when she talks. Plus,

I think her neck is sprained. She's got a concussion."

My mother nodded. "When can she go back to school?" This seemed to be my mother's first and always most pressing concern. The doctor shot her an angry look.

"Do you know what a concussion is? Her brain is swollen and pressing against her skull. She needs complete bed rest. I don't think she'll be going back for a few weeks."

I was so dizzy that this revelation didn't delight me the way I'd hoped it would. But I was still giggling whenever he raised his thirteen fingers. Dr. Smith wrapped a towel around my neck twice, like a brace, and tucked it in. "I don't have a neck brace with me," he said. "This will have to do for now. I'll bring a brace next time I visit. Keep her in bed. No walking around for you, missy. Tell your brothers not to threaten you with the Mummy anymore."

"It was the Wolfman," I replied.

"Okay," the doctor said, as he patted my arm and shook his head.

When Joey came home and my mother told him what happened, he actually looked sad. It upset him so much to think that he had caused me to almost kill myself that he came right into my room and made a solemn promise.

"Next time," Joey said to me, "I promise not to turn into the Wolfman while you're around any stairs. Okay?"

Maybe it was the concussion, but that sounded reasonable to me. It took me two more weeks to get over the concussion, sprained neck, and bruises that made me look like I'd just gone fifteen rounds with Muhammad Ali.

But even Joey eventually outgrew the worst of his big brother tendencies. Although he could be horribly embarrassed by my very presence when we were in high school together, he could also be very protective. When one of my fellow freshmen said something that Joey felt was disrespectful toward me, he confronted him.

"Did you just say something rude about my sister?" Joey said.

"So what if I did," the young boy said. "What are you going to do about it?"

Joey proceeded to run after this boy, who had no idea that someone as large and muscular as my brother could run so fast. They were about two miles from the school when the kid tore through someone's backyard, leaped over the fence separating the two gardens, and got away.

"Don't worry," Joey assured me. "I'll catch him later."

I hoped that Joey wouldn't turn into the Wolfman on him, because if he did that kid was in big trouble.

Joey ended up being much more loving and supportive than I ever expected him to be. He would come home from garage sales with stuffed animals or dolls that he thought I'd enjoy. When I got older, it was Joey who took me to buy my first car.

We drove to Brooklyn on a crisp March Sunday. He killed

the ignition and said to me, "Now don't say a thing. Let me do the negotiating."

There was the car I wanted: a completely beat-up, navy blue VW Superbeetle. All the upholstery inside the car was torn to shreds; all four tires were bald; it was a semi-automatic and I only knew how to drive an automatic. I did the math in my head; the owner wanted $500 for this car, and I had about $600 in the bank. This car was perfect for me!

Joey and I walked up to the owner and my brother began to hardball her. "Listen, this car is in terrible shape," he said, as he pointed out its many flaws. "The upholstery is torn, the tires are bald. You've got over 100,000 miles on the odometer. There's no way you can ask my little sister to pay you $500 for this hunk of junk."

"I'll take $450," the owner replied.

"Sold!" I yelled, as I grabbed the keys and jumped inside.

So perhaps my skills as a fierce negotiator were not honed that day, but as my brother drove my car home (I sure couldn't—it would take me weeks to get the hang of a semi-automatic transmission), I smiled gleefully.

"You asked Dad for permission to do this, right?" Joey said.

All the joy drained from my heart. "Ummmm, nooooooo."

Joey pulled the car into the driveway, handed me the keys, and took off with his girlfriend, Christine.

"Can't you help me with this?" I said, as Joey pulled away.

"I'm not a miracle worker," Joey screamed from his

window. "Good luck—you'll need it!" He burned rubber in his haste to drive away and leave me to my fate.

My father was inside the house watching golf when I came indoors. "Say, where did Joey and you go?"

"Joey helped me buy a car!" I said, hoping that my emphasis on the words "Joey helped me" would mitigate my punishment. I ran to my bedroom.

"What did you just say?" my father yelled behind me.

That Joey was always getting me into trouble!

Recipe: Wolfman Cupcakes

Joey's innate talent for turning into the Wolfman is one that I believe should be celebrated and immortalized in a cupcake. These are lots of fun at Halloween parties (just like Joey).

1 box of yellow cake mix

1 tub milk chocolate frosting

1 tube white decorative frosting

1 tube red decorative frosting

Candy corn or M&Ms

Following directions on box, bake cupcakes. Let cupcakes cool. Ice with milk chocolate frosting. Use a knife to make peaks with the chocolate frosting so it looks like fur. Make eyes with the candy corn or M&Ms. Make fangs with the white decorative icing and blood with the red icing.

Yield: 24 cupcakes

Chapter 9: Chris

Finally, there was my beloved twin brother, Chris. When I was growing up, I considered my five older brothers one unit, and my twin and me another one. It was us against them, and Chris was always my ally.

Unless, of course, he was angry with me and then we were mortal enemies. Let's say we were playing with our Barbie and GI Joe dolls. Chris would be busy planning an all-out attack featuring his Incredible Hulk doll and Mike Powers, Atomic Man. I would interrupt him by saying it was time for Malibu PJ to marry GI Pete.

"Don't you see these guys are busy?" Chris would say.

"I can see that," I replied. "But you promised you'd play with me. I have the bridal gown all ready and all the guests lined up. Can't you take a few minutes out before your attack to get PJ and Pete married?"

So, Chris would agree to participate in the marriage ceremony, and we'd have the cop from his motorcycle gang officiate (he was the closest thing we had to a judge, after all). The wedding would be fine, until GI Pete kissed the bride and tried to leave.

"But wait," I said. "There's supposed to be a reception."

"This is stupid!" Chris yelled. "GI Pete, GI Joe, Mike Powers, and The Incredible Hulk have got to save the world!"

Things would deteriorate from there. "You're just a dumb girl!" my brother would yell. "I'm never playing with you again!"

He'd stomp out of my room, run past the kitchen where Paul was playing with the waxed fruit, and try to find a quiet place to save the world. We wouldn't talk for a while, until he got over it and decided that GI Pete missed Malibu PJ. Then we'd be back to playing together again.

For all of Chris's anger management problems, he was really a very sensitive and loving person. He hated to disappoint anyone, especially my father.

One day, my mother came to our kindergarten class to help with a baking project. We made big soft pretzels, twisting the dough into fun pretzel shapes, brushing them with egg wash and butter, and adding big specks of kosher salt to the outside of them. Mom told Dad how fabulous they were and what a great job we did on them.

"I even brought one home for you," Mom said.

Too bad she didn't say that in earshot of Chris, who would eat that last pretzel later that afternoon and spend years feeling guilty about it.

Long after my father had forgotten about the Great Pretzel Incident, Chris was still racked with guilt. Blame it on us being Catholic, blame it on his tender-hearted nature, blame it on his desire to make my father happy—Chris needed to make things right. So imagine his glee when my mom brought home the pretzel recipe from one of her friends.

"Now we can surprise your dad," she said, and Chris was delighted.

While New York's Unemployed practiced "It's Only Rock-'n'-Roll" for hours on end, Chris and Mom spent that Saturday afternoon kneading the dough, watching it rise, shaping it like praying hands, brushing it with an egg wash, and then sprinkling it with coarse kosher salt while Dad sat in the living room and watched bowling with Joey.

A few hours later, Chris brought the pretzels out to Dad, still piping hot, with some mustard on the side.

"Hey! Pretzels," my dad said, as he chomped away blissfully, and Chris beamed.

Chris wasn't always so sensitive or prone to guilt. For instance, when we first moved into the new house, our grandmother stayed there with us for what seemed like an endless two weeks.

"When is she going to leave?" Chris asked me one morning.

"I don't know," I said. "But I wish she'd go already. She's such a pain in the neck! She never wants us to play with Goldie, she's always running around cleaning and telling us we're pigs, and she keeps taking my toys to donate at her thrift shop. Plus, you need to go back to your bunk. You keep kicking me."

A minute later, I stopped munching my cereal just long enough to hear Chris tell my grandmother, "Yeah, see, Maria thinks you should just pack up your valise and go home. She says you're a pain in the neck."

The next thing I heard was my grandmother's wracking sobs emanating from my back bedroom. It was hard to concentrate on my cereal with all that crying going on. Now my father was talking to his mother, and I suddenly lost my appetite. Dad came into the kitchen and sat down across from me.

"Maria, why did you say your grandmother was a pain in the neck?" my father said, barely suppressing a smile.

"I didn't tell her! I told *Chris*! He wasn't supposed to tell her!"

My father laughed. "Well, now she's in your bedroom packing and crying. Why don't you go tell her you're sorry?"

I pushed my cereal bowl away and made the now-long trek toward my bedroom. There was my grandmother, with tears streaming down her face, muttering, "I bet she'd rather be with her other grandmother!" as she crammed clothes into her suitcase.

"Nonnie," I said, "please don't leave."

"I thought you said I was a pain in the neck," my grandmother said, brushing away tears. "That's what Chris told me."

That's probably what Chris had been dying to tell her for years now, I thought to myself. But I said instead, "I didn't mean it. I don't want you to go."

My grandmother finally stopped packing. "But my valise is all ready to go," she said.

I walked over to her valise and pulled out her clothes. I put them back into the drawers and turned toward her. "Now it's ready to stay," I said.

My grandmother started to cry again, and she threw her arms around me as I got showered in blubbery tears and kisses. "I love you, Maria," she said.

"I love you, too," I replied. "It's Chris I hate."

My grandmother burst out laughing. We were okay again. But when I hunted down Chris, I wasn't sure he could say the same thing...

Chris was a lot of fun, but there were times when he couldn't help walking a little too close to the flames—and getting third-degree burns. Most of those times involved angering my father beyond human reason, a gift that Chris seemed to have in abundance.

One night, as Paul sat at the kitchen table reading *Mad Magazine* and my parents sat in the next room watching *The Cowboys* with John Wayne, Chris came into the kitchen. He couldn't help but see how absorbed Paul was in his magazine, and the opportunity to play a joke on Paul presented itself like a gift from the gods.

"Say, Paul," Chris said, "can you scratch my back? I've got an itch I can't reach."

Paul, always good-natured when he wasn't in full torture mode, happily complied. Unfortunately, he never took his eyes off his magazine.

"That's great," Chris said. "But can you just go a little bit lower?"

Paul did just that, until he heard Chris laughing. I peeked in from the dining room to see Chris laughing and holding his pants down while Paul scratched his backside.

"Hey!" Paul roared. This, obviously, was an offense almost greater than calling him Milk. "I'm going to tell Dad!"

Chris's face blanched. Dad was the last person he wanted to let in on this funny little episode. "Oh, come on, Paul," Chris said. "Don't tell! I was only joking!"

At this precise moment, my father came into the kitchen to get a glass of milk. "Hi, boys," Dad said, looking relaxed and happy. "What's up?"

Paul could have responded, "Not much. I'm playing with the waxed fruit and reading *Mad Magazine*!" Instead, he began his grave account of Chris's wrongdoings while Chris stood there, looking as if he was about to be led to his execution.

Now, it could've gone one of two ways. Either my father would see how utterly ridiculous this whole thing was, and he'd slap Paul on the back and laugh with Chris at his remarkable, eight-year-old wit.

Or, sensing that Paul, poor persecuted Paul, was being picked on by his younger brother, Dad would explode with an instantaneous rage that would leave no survivors in its path—much like the volcano erupting at Pompeii.

Of course, he reacted the second way.

Dad began to slap Chris, who covered his head and said, "But I was only joking! It was all in fun!"

I was laughing so hard at this point that I was afraid my father would hear me, so I ran for the safety of my bedroom. I just made it there when I heard my father, mother, and Chris hot on my heels. I dove under the covers, fully dressed, and buried my face in the pillow to keep them from hearing me laughing.

My father hurled Chris into the bed beside me while Chris cried. I peeked out from under the covers and saw my father in the doorway, with his comb-over now hanging long on one side, his face red with fury, wearing nothing but his sleeveless white T-shirt over his boxer shorts.

"And don't you ever make Paul scratch your backside again!" my father screamed while my mother hovered nervously by his shoulder.

I looked at him screaming like a lunatic and back at Chris's tiny, shaking form. My father slammed our door shut and walked away.

Chris finally stopped crying and turned to look at me. I burst out laughing.

"That was great!" he said. "But why did Paul have to turn me in?"

We looked at each other and laughed ourselves to sleep.

Three years and one unfortunate dirty joke later, my brother Chris would be banished from the bedroom we shared. The reason? He chose to share that joke with my grandmother, who thought it was getting high time that my weirdo brother and I didn't share a bedroom anymore.

So one Friday afternoon, without any warning at all, off Chris went to the lions' den. Gone were the days when Chris and I would tell each other tales of what had happened that day, which kids were being picked on—was it one of us? Jimmy? Anne? Roger the Janitor? In no time at all, we would be hysterical as our mother said softly outside our door, "Kids, go to sleep!"

No, now Chris would be sleeping upstairs, with Tony, Louie, Paul, and Joey. They got rid of Chris's bed and gave him a horrible plastic couch as his new bed. His new spot was right next to the door leading into the room; when you went up the stairs, you could see his space.

He thought it couldn't get worse, until my brothers moved the furniture around, placing his couch/bed between the two bunk beds. This allowed the older boys to use him as a stepstool, and they would make a point of stepping on Chris whenever they got up for any reason.

It was Animal House without the liquor or the fun. My brothers were always putting someone's hand in a glass of warm water while he slept; painting someone's fingernails a cherry-apple red and hiding the nail polish remover; or putting lipstick and eyeliner on someone's face and waking him up just minutes before he had to leave for school or work. Sometimes it was Chris, sometimes it was someone else. Chris looked shell-shocked.

"It's all Nonnie's fault!" he said.

Throughout those long growing-up years, whether we were in our tiny house, walking through the streets of Bayside, or making our way through Catholic school, public school, or college, there was nothing better than having my twin by my side. I mean that…even though he did eat all the pretzels.

Recipe: Oversized Soft Pretzels

These big, chewy pretzels are perfect for a Saturday afternoon, or any time you want to treat someone to something hot and delicious.

1 package dry active yeast

1 cup warm water

1½ cups flour

2 tablespoons vegetable oil

½ teaspoon salt

1¼ cups flour

4 cups water

2 tablespoons baking soda

2 eggs, beaten

2 tablespoons coarse salt

1. Dissolve the yeast in the warm water and let stand for 10 minutes. Add the 1½ cups flour, vegetable oil, and salt. Stir

together until thoroughly combined. Add remaining flour and knead dough for 5 minutes. Let the dough rest for 1 hour.

2. Divide the dough into 12 equal pieces and re-form them into small balls. Let them rest for 15 minutes. Roll them into 18-inch lengths and form them into pretzel shapes or cut each length in half to make sticks. Let the pretzels rise for 30 minutes. Preheat oven to 475°F.

3. In a large pot, bring the water and baking soda to a boil. Add the pretzels to the boiling water; cook for 1 minute. Remove; brush with beaten eggs. Place on a greased sheet pan. Sprinkle with coarse salt and bake for 12 minutes.

Yields: 12 pretzels.

Chapter 10: Uncle Sal & Uncle Don

No story of my family would be complete without an entry about two of my uncles. They were always around for every holiday or celebration, and ready to tell a story to make you laugh or make fun of you until you cried…well, uncle.

Uncle Sal was my great-uncle, and the baby brother of my grandmother. He was tall and thin, with big brown eyes and, once upon a time, brown hair. The big thing that happened when we were kids is that he showed up one day without his toupee on, and we thought something terrible had happened, because how could you go bald over night?

My great-uncle was a surprise, late-life baby who, according to my grandmother, was a little bit spoiled.

"He always got an Indian head penny on his toast," my grandmother explained. "We were dirt poor, and here my mother was, scrounging around so she could give my baby brother an Indian head penny. Do you know how much a penny bought back in those days?"

"Just get on with the story, Lena," Uncle Sal would say, rolling his eyes and dreading the rest of it.

So Lena got on with it. "One day, my mother was making breakfast when she realized she didn't have any more Indian head pennies. So she took another penny out of her pocket and placed it on the toast.

Well, don't you think Sally came walking in and started to cry: 'Bah bah, you didn't get me my Indian head penny! I'm not going to eat now!' he said, and he threw the penny to the ground.'"

Our crowd of kids, cousins, aunts, uncles, and my parents all went "Ooooohhhhh" because we understood that, in this family, doing something like that to your mother or father could result in an immediate execution.

"That was it! My mother slapped him across the face and said, "Now you get nothing. Eat your breakfast. I'll never give you any pennies again, you little ingrate."

Calling someone in our family an "ingrate" was hardcore. My great-grandmother must have been incensed! It couldn't have been worse, unless she called him *chadrool* (stupid), *stunad* (also stupid), *facce brute* (ugly), or just plain lazy. Ingrate meant you were disrespectful and possibly the worst person on the planet, because you didn't appreciate the great lengths your mother went to for you, and therefore, you made her so mad that she was forced to call you an ingrate.

My grandmother and everyone around the table laughed, and Uncle Sal just shook his head.

"I've been listening to that story for over seventy years," he said wearily. "I was five! Haven't I done anything else you can talk about at every single family party?"

This would crack my grandmother up, and everyone else at the table would laugh too. Then, since she was forever Uncle Sal's big sister, she replied: "Nope."

Of course, that wasn't entirely accurate. Uncle Sal left home when he was sixteen and joined Vaudeville. He worked as a comedian, singer, and dancer. He would show up at family weddings and parties with a showgirl on each arm and dance the night away. When all of our relatives were hard hit by the Depression, Uncle Sal was making great money doing his shows.

His album, entitled *"If I Insulted You, It Was Intentional,"* was a success and he got to rub shoulders with the likes of Lana Turner, Jackie Gleason, and Jimmy Durante. He used the money he earned to help his family.

When the time came, he helped my mother and father buy their first house in Queens…and then helped them again so they could buy their second house.

Uncle Sal was our angel, but he was not to be confused with Mother Theresa. He would sit quietly while everyone around him was shouting and waving their hands, and then he would deliver the funniest, most biting comments of the night.

When I was dating someone my uncle and grandmother

didn't like, they would sit and glare at him. Their biggest complaints were that this young man didn't understand respect, had no social skills, was not good enough for me, and was quite possibly an ingrate. I think some of those comments may have been true, but it wasn't enough to make me break up with him.

One time, a friend of my brother's dropped by and greeted my grandmother and uncle like they were visiting royalty. He stopped just short of kissing their rings as he threw his arms around them and told them how happy he was to see them.

When this friend left, Uncle Sal said to me, "Why don't you go out with him?"

I replied, "We're just friends. He's not really my type."

"You have a type?" Uncle Sal grunted. "Have you seen what you're dating lately?" he said, as everyone roared with laughter. Even I had to laugh.

No holiday was ever complete if Uncle Sal, Nonnie, and Uncle Don weren't there. They were like the fixtures that made our holidays extra special.

Now, as for Uncle Don....He was my father's brother, and he was always pretty lucky. Even in his middle seventies, he was long-limbed and handsome and, like his father before him, had a full head of sandy-brown hair.

My uncle's real name was Dominic, but we all called him Donny. Why? Because my grandfather wanted to name him Dominic after his father (an Italian tradition) and my grandmother wanted to name him Don after her father. So technically my grandfather won because my uncle's name was Dominic. But my grandmother and everyone else in the family called him Don or Donny throughout his life...so who really won?

Don Lagalante was the best dancer that ever did a tango, and he could lead any partner—even one who can't dance, like me—as if she were Ginger Rogers to his Fred Astaire.

My relatives came to our house a lot when I was little, and we were happy to see them all. But we always knew we were going to have fun when Uncle Don walked through the door.

Uncle Don owned his own furniture businesses when he was young and lived at home, where my grandmother catered to him the way only an Italian mother can. He was sixty-three before he ever learned that he needed to do laundry (now that his mother was eighty-three and couldn't do it anymore), and the only thing he knew how to cook was a cup of water for his instant coffee.

Even though he had a good life, Uncle Don hit some rough patches. One night in the 1970s, while running across a slippery Manhattan street on his way to the disco to shake his groove thing, he slipped, skidded, and rolled across two busy lanes of traffic until he crashed into a parked car. He tried to get up, but couldn't. His leg was broken in two places, and he had to get a cast that went up to his thigh.

That Monday, my uncle was supposed to start a new job.

Now, Uncle Don had to give up the new job, along with the brand-new car he'd just bought. What did that mean? It meant out with the Chrysler Cordoba, with fine Corinthian leather, and in with my grandmother's ancient, powder-blue Ford Fairlane.

Jude was supposed to inherit the Ford, but times were tough, and Uncle Don was the first son of the first son, which in an Italian family outranks God the Father, Jesus the Son, and The Holy Spirit combined.

So here was Uncle Don, with his cast up to his thigh, no job, and a car with no air-conditioning and a total lack of fine Corinthian leather. Most people would want to be by themselves, to gather their strength for the battles ahead. That would be normal. But Uncle Don was a Lagalante, and my grandmother thought it would be best if we had a party and fed him.

Coffee, cannoli, and crumb cake were loaded up on my grandmother's kitchen table while we filed past Uncle Don, who sat helpless on the couch. We signed his cast and laughed as he said over and over again, "I kept trying to stand up. I just wanted to get out of the way of oncoming traffic."

It took him awhile, but Uncle Don was finally able to stand on his own two feet again. The cast came off, and he rumbled off in that Ford Fairlane in search of a new job. After many days of searching, he finally landed a posh gig—as a waiter at one of the best country clubs on the famed Gold Coast of Long Island.

His first day was Mother's Day. The restaurant was packed, and the clatter of dishes clashed with the banging of the kitchen door as the waiters and waitresses rushed from the kitchen to the tables and back again. Uncle Don rubbed his aching leg in between running from the kitchen to his hungry diners. Tray after tray was loaded up, and Uncle Don held them high over his head as he rushed to get the meals, still steaming hot, to the tables.

It was a long, grueling day. Sweat poured off Uncle Don's Roman nose and through every strand of that wavy hair. All he could think was "Aren't these people full yet? I wish this day would end. My leg is killing me." And then, just as he was about to serve the last meal of his unbearable shift, the unthinkable happened: Uncle Don's leg gave out.

It is best described in Uncle Don's own words:

"I was struggling to carry this gigantic tray over my head, and I walked out to the main dining area. There were steps down to the sunken dining room, where I needed to go. The first step went fine, but as I felt for the next step, my leg refused to work and down I went. The tray, piled high with all the entrées and drinks, went crashing forward as I landed face down.

"As I lay there, with my eyes shut tight, I began to think, 'This isn't really happening. It's all just a dream, and when I open my eyes, I'll be at home in my bed.' So I opened my eyes and looked around me. It was so quiet that I was sure I had been dreaming. But instead, the nightmare was for real, and the entire dining room was silent, and I lay there with mashed potatoes on my head, dishes smashed beyond recognition, and food thrown everywhere."

My family got the bad news later that night, as we sat snacking in our living room, watching television. My father turned down the volume on *Mutual of Omaha's Wild Kingdom with Marlin Perkins* as he yelled into the kitchen phone. My father wasn't mad, but he has been stone deaf ever since a shooting accident in basic training left him that way. That's his story. His own mother said that he was just born loud.

When Dad came back out into the living room, he sat next to Chris. Dad was perched a little bit in front of Chris, while Chris sat back, seemingly out of my father's range of vision. As Dad told us the latest tragic chapter in Uncle Don's life story, my mother winced and clucked sympathetically.

At nine years old, I tried to follow my mother's lead, but I was much more amused by the sight of Chris, just behind my father, making believe he was carrying a tray loaded down with food—and crashing to the ground.

I was doing my best not to laugh when I noticed that my father was watching Chris and his shenanigans in the mirror right next to him. We always marveled at my father's apparent "eyes in the back of his head" vision. But it was the 1970s, and most houses were thoroughly carpeted in orange shag, slathered in dark brown paneling, and mirrored up to the gills. Our house was no different.

At first, Chris wondered why I wasn't laughing, so he redoubled his efforts to crack me up. I watched him as he threw himself into a mock nosedive and picked imaginary mashed potatoes from his hair and eyes. Then I watched my father as his forehead grew red and expanded like the Goodyear blimp. It seemed an eternity before Chris followed my gaze to my father and realized, with nothing less than horror, that Dad knew what he was doing.

"Do you think your Uncle Don's situation is FUNNY?" Dad said, in that "my vocal cords always sound like they're being dragged over broken glass" hiss he saved for angry occasions.

Chris sat up straight. "No," he replied. "Not at all."

Chris's own fall that night was not nearly as entertaining as my uncle's must have been to witness. Four or five skin-burning slaps and a whole lot of "Don't you ever laugh at your uncle's misfortune again" later, Chris and I disappeared into the relative safety of our back bedroom.

I handed him a cookie as I shut the door. Despite the lecture, despite the head-slaps and tears, we couldn't help ourselves. Chris said "Who am I?" as he put a toy tray over his head and fell to the floor. We laughed the night away. Nine-year-olds don't worry about the future—not when they've got a box of cookies and a funny story to share.

I wish I could say the same thing for Uncle Don. It took him many years before he could find that particular moment in time nearly as funny as we did. Needless to say, that was Uncle Don's first—and last—day as a waiter. Eventually, his leg firmed up enough so that he was able to land a job that made him really want to close his eyes and dream: he became a salesman in a ladies' shoe department.

Recipe:

Uncle Don's Peaches and Cream Upside-Down Cake

Since the only thing my uncle knew how to cook was water, this recipe is really from my grandmother. But the idea of Uncle Don upside down still makes me laugh.

1 box yellow cake mix

1 tub Cool Whip

2 cans cling peaches (or pineapple)

Bake cake according to box directions. When cool, slice in half lengthwise (if sheet cake) or use two 9-inch round cakes. Spread Cool Whip over the bottom layer. Drain the peaches and lay them on top of the Cool Whip. Put on the top layer, and spread Cool Whip on top. Use your knife to make swirls and designs in the Cool Whip frosting. This isn't exactly the kind of secret recipe that families hoard for generations; it's just a real quick, cheap, and easy dessert when you want to make something tasty but you're short on time and money.

Serves 6-8.

Chapter 11:
Weekends with Sarita and Louie

Being good Catholics, my parents believed that a weekend away spent in prayer and contemplation, once or twice a year, was essential to their spiritual well-being.

Or maybe, just being away from their seven children, two dogs, house that always seemed to fall apart without any warning, basement rock band, smoking green station wagon, and angry neighbors was too good a deal to pass up.

Whatever the case may be, every September my dad would go away on retreat. Mom would pack his suitcase, and off he'd go with four or five of our relatives for a weekend getaway to Pennsylvania.

When Dad left, Mom would send out for pizzas and take us for rides in the station wagon. She'd gun the engine and we'd go sailing over giant potholes as we came down off the two-block hill. Or she'd drive us to Bell Boulevard, where she'd do errands, and then stop at the ice cream store. We'd pile back into the station wagon and head home to watch *Sanford & Son*, *Love American Style*, and *Don Adams' Screen Test.*

On Saturday mornings, my mom would shut all our doors and quietly clean the house so we could sleep late. By the time we were up, she'd vacuumed, mopped, straightened, and folded five loads of wash. She smiled at us while we poured our cereal and she cut out coupons for her weekly shopping trip. On Sundays, she'd let us sleep until it was time for mass; then we'd jump into the shower, get dressed, and run off to church. By the time we got back, we could smell the spaghetti sauce and meatballs simmering in the Crock-Pot while *When the Saints Come Marching In* played on the radio.

On one of my dad's retreat weekends, Mom came to the terrible realization that she had lost her wedding ring. In her typical "no-worries" style, she summoned Jude's girlfriend, Cindy.

"Sweetheart, can you do me a favor?" Mom said.

"Sure. What can I do for you?" Cindy said.

"Here's twenty dollars. Go to Consumer's Distributors down Bell Boulevard and get me a new wedding band. Don't get anything too fancy. You can keep the change."

Cindy ran down to the store, bought my mother the best ten-carat gold-plated ring she could find, and kept eight dollars. My mother was delighted. She wore the ring until it turned her finger green several weeks later and she was forced to 'fess up to Dad.

Weekends with Mom were always carefree and fun. She didn't get upset when Chris inevitably knocked over the soda bottle, and she took Goldie's habit of vomiting pizza on the living room rug in stride. Mom could blissfully watch the movie *Sybil* while Jude's band, New York's Unemployed, played the theme to *Barney Miller* for the millionth time.

When Dad came home, the house was a bit of a wreck, but everyone was happy, well fed, and glad to welcome him home. He, in turn, looked rested and happy. Mom would serve him a home-cooked meal of spaghetti and meatballs or chicken cutlets with mashed potatoes, gravy, and green beans. Then they'd sit together at the big dining room table and catch up on their weekend apart.

The only weekend that wasn't fun or stress-free came the year that my grandmother ran away to Puerto Rico, leaving my early-Alzheimer's-ridden grandfather with a friend. The phone rang late Friday morning about an hour after my grandmother had gone, and all my mother could hear on the other end was panic.

"Sarita, you've got to come get your father. I can't handle him," my grandmother's friend said.

So Grandpa came to stay with us for the weekend, and possibly beyond, as my mother worried about how to tell my father.

Caring for seven children and a father with Alzheimer's was as much fun as tap-dancing barefoot on broken glass. My mother couldn't keep her eye on her father every minute, and the seven of us were equally hungry and demanding. By Friday night, my mother was exhausted.

"I don't know what to do," she said, as her eyes barely stayed open. "I'm so tired."

"I'll stay up with Grandpa," I said, hoping to give my mother a break. I was seven years old, and the thought of staying up all night seemed very exciting to me.

"Just for a little bit," my mother said, as she lay down on the couch. "I just need a nap."

I went back into my parents' bedroom and told Grandpa the deal. "I'm going to stay up with you," I told him.

"What do you want to do? Want to play a game?" he said. Grandpa loved games.

"Let's play poker," I said. My brothers had just taught me how, and since Grandpa was not himself these days, I thought I could make a little pocket change.

We proceeded to play poker, war, spit, gin rummy, and hearts. As the night wore on, I could hear my mother snoring in the next room, and I figured sleep wasn't in the cards for me that night. Neither was winning. Grandpa might've had early-onset Alzheimer's, but he could still play a mean game of cards. He beat me all night long.

When my mom woke up at dawn, I crawled into bed and fell asleep as my grandfather finally conked out on the living room couch.

For the rest of that weekend, my brothers and I kept Grandpa busy. We put him in charge of the roller-skate key and let him tighten our skates while we got ready to race up and down the block, then let him tag along, running up and down the sidewalk beside us as we shot down our long hill. We watched him smile with glee as he won several dozen rousing games of balloon volleyball. I sat up with him for another long night of cards until I couldn't keep my eyes open anymore.

I heard my mother comforting him when his screaming started. In his mind, Grandpa was a little boy in the hills of Puerto Rico again, his mother had just died, and his father was leaving him alone with eight little brothers and sisters to watch. "Daddy, please don't leave me!" Grandpa cried again and again, as my mother tried to convince him that he was not in Puerto Rico anymore and that he could never be alone in this house if he tried.

By the time my father got home on Sunday night, my mother was so strung out that she was waiting anxiously by the door, pacing like a caged lion. When Dad came in, I heard her telling him in hushed tones that her father was here and would have to stay until her mother came back. My dad didn't look too happy, but what could he do? It's not like we were going to put Grandpa on the front steps with a sign that said "Puerto Rico or Bust."

I turned to see my grandfather cutting my baked potato into several thousand pieces, even though I told him I didn't need it cut.

"Here's your potato," Grandpa said.

I would've needed a forensic pathologist to identify it for me; right now it just looked like a white-slivered mass. I looked up at Grandpa, who was smiling warmly at his potato masterpiece. "Thanks, Grandpa."

After two solid weeks of living with my demented grandfather and placing God only knows how many phone calls to her mother—who was not supposed to be demented—my mother was overjoyed when my grandmother and grandfather went home. So when October came, just as it always did, my mother packed her bags in preparation for her own religious retreat. It was then that panic filled our tiny hearts.

"Mom, do you need to go away?" I would say.

"Yes!" Mom replied. "Don't worry. You'll have fun with Dad. There are trays of baked ziti, eggplant parmesan, beef cutlets, and meatloaf in the fridge. All the laundry is washed and put away. There's even tons of toilet paper in the house! There's nothing for your father to get upset about. I left out all the board games so you guys can play together."

"Dad always gets mad at us," I replied.

"He works a long hard day. Just do your best not to set him off."

So my six brothers and I watched as my mother jumped into the car with our cousins, and we blew kisses to her as she faded from sight.

Usually, my brothers and I would go inside and wait for Dad to come home. But one year, Jude had another idea.

"Let's go for a ride," he said.

"But you don't have a license," I replied.

"Details, details," Jude said. "If we go now, we can be

home long before Dad gets back. Besides," he said, as he showed me his wallet, "I have my learner's permit, and since I'm supposed to practice, I thought we could all go for a ride. Just don't tell anyone. Got it?"

I agreed—since turning Jude in would be as wise as openly fingering a mob boss. My parents would never be able to hide me well enough, and Jude would find me, even if they placed me in the Federal Witness Protection Program.

All seven of us piled into the station wagon and went for a joyride. Like Mom always did, Jude gunned the engine as we raced down the two-block hill and practically flew over the potholes. We drove all over the borough of Queens. Jude pointed out some of his old friends' houses, noted the exact spot where he first saw Henry, and then drove past Mom's old house in Flushing.

"Let's turn off the radio and have a moment of quiet contemplation in thanks to our Lord," Jude said, as we passed by in silence. It was something Dad always did to poke fun at the home where my mother lived "BL" (Before Lou).

We'd been driving for over two hours when Tony pointed out the time. "Dad could be back already, you know," he said.

Jude gunned the engine and headed home. "Home we go!"

Jude would've repeated his "driving without a license in a stolen car" ritual every year except that our nosy neighbor, Mrs. Schmucker, mentioned it to my mother when she got home the next week. After that, my mom never left the car with any gas in it, which was a source of great annoyance to my dad, who would say things like "Why doesn't she ever leave me any gas?" while Jude would just shrug his shoulders and try to look innocent.

On most occasions, there would be nothing to do except get ready for Dad's imminent arrival. Once Mom faded from sight, we would go back inside to set the table and get ready for him. Jude went downstairs to practice his guitar while Louie, Joey, and Paul jumped onto the couch to watch *Bugs Bunny*. That left Tony (always a natural-born leader), Chris, and me to get the table set and put the dinner in the oven.

Usually, Dad came home from work and ate with Mom. We kids ate at 5 pm, a whole hour and a half before Dad even walked through the door. But when Mom was away, Dad came home early and ate with us.

When Dad did finally come home, it was clear that he was tired and cranky. The fact that my mother was sorely missed was amplified in the world-weary look on Dad's face. Still, he tried to be game.

"Hey, guys! Let's get dinner on the table! I can't wait to eat!"

We all ran into the kitchen and perched around our cramped, crowded little table. Tony pulled the food from the oven while Louie poured the soda and Dad made sure we all had napkins.

Dad had a great sense of humor and loved to do fun things with us. But children were always something of a mystery to him; he had very little patience for the kinds of things that children do all the time. Whereas Mom could glide through the trials and tragedies of living with seven kids with a great big smile on her face, my dad usually reacted with a homicidal rage that was hilarious to witness, as long as it wasn't directed at you.

Let's take spilled milk. Apparently, the person who said "there's no use crying over spilled milk" never met my father. In our house, spilled milk was not just a crying offense, but one that was punishable by immediate public execution. Ditto for dropped forks, food left on your plate because you were full, or refusal to eat anything that made you gag. Depression-era baby that he was, Dad could not tolerate throwing away food. The only acceptable excuse for not cleaning your plate was your death by choking, possibly by my father, since he believed wasting food was a sin and a crime.

So here we were, having dinner together, and so far, no one had done anything to set my dad off. I had a small sense of panic when I realized that Tony had cooked the eggplant parmesan, which was never one of my favorites, and he was handing out big heaping portions to everyone at the table. I looked at the wall of food now on my plate and realized I was in for a night of my father screaming "You've got five minutes to eat everything. NOW GO!"

Just as I wondered how I'd get out of this, God smiled on me. Chris knocked over the soda bottle.

Jude, Tony, Louie, Paul, and Joey jumped up and scattered like roaches when the lights get thrown on while Dad and Chris both lunged for the bottle so they could right it. Louie ran back to the table with a fist full of napkins and sopped up the mess. Meanwhile my father screamed, Chris cried, and I quietly called Goldie and Henry over and fed them as much eggplant parmesan as they could eat without my father noticing.

Once we were all settled back at the table, Chris hiccupped quietly while we ate. Just as Jude and Louie had managed to get my father laughing again, Chris knocked his fork to the ground. We all froze and looked at my father.

"Pick that up," he growled.

Chris picked it up and placed it by his plate.

"Get a new fork so you can finish," Dad said.

"I'm full," Chris said.

Dad looked at the clock and pointed to it. "You've got five minutes to finish. NOW GO!"

The rest of us blissfully deserted Chris at the table and ran for our lives. About half an hour later, I heard my father yelling from the living room.

"WHO FED THE DOGS EGGPLANT? THERE'S PUKE EVERYWHERE!!!"

I closed my door quietly, put the wooden plank I kept for just these occasions under my doorknob, and lay down. Just six more meals and Mom would be home…

As the sun started to fill up the morning sky, my father banged on my bedroom door and yelled my name.

"Get up," he barked.

"What's wrong?"

"Nothing's wrong. We're going to make believe we're in the army. Now help me clean the barracks."

I came out of my room to find a very sleepy-eyed Jude, Tony, Louie, Paul, Joey, and Chris already dusting, vacuuming, polishing, and mopping. Goldie and Henry looked disturbed; they never did get used to seeing the house clean.

I never realized how hard my mother's life must've been until my father made me start cleaning up after us pigs. The dog hair was about an inch thick; dust coated the knickknacks that lined our mantel; books, bags, and clothes were draped over every piece of furniture; and junk mail, bills, school notes, and books obliterated everything like a total eclipse.

With eight of us cleaning, it still took a few hours to shovel through the refuse and make the place look decent—all at decibel levels that rivaled a construction site. Every week, while we slept and my father was out golfing, my mother handled this job herself. How did she do it so quietly?

"We're done!" my father said, as the last pile of clothes found its way to the hamper. "And just think, we get to do it all again tomorrow!"

"Yippee," Jude groaned.

In Dad's defense, once Friday night and Saturday

morning cleanups were behind us, he too would throw us into the car and take us out for some fun. One Saturday, he surprised us all with two kites, and he could barely contain his excitement as we piled into the station wagon and drove to a nearby open field.

Dad raced like a little boy, showing us how to get the kites airborne. Then he watched with glee as his four youngest, Joey, Paul, Chris, and I, took turns doing it. Here, Dad was in his element. Whereas Mom was calm and even-tempered in any crisis, she didn't really like doing anything athletic with us. But while Dad was as quick to explode as a Roman candle when we were home, he had endless patience when it came to showing us how to play.

We took long walks around Kissena Park and Oakland Lake, with Goldie and Henry by our sides. We took early Sunday morning walks through Alley Pond Park, hiking on the dirt paths and scaling the heights years before hiking would become popular or fashionable. We had paddleball contests at P.S. 203, with my father's comb-over flopping over to the side while he played each of us in a fight to the death. If you beat my father, you really beat him—he was never one of those parents who let you win because you were a kid.

When we went home, we baked a tray of food for dinner and then broke out the Chinese checkers, Rebound, Monopoly, or chessboard for a night of heated competition. We would be locked in mortal combat until our favorite Saturday night lineup of shows, including *All in the Family* and

The Bob Newhart Show, demanded our attention.

We managed to have fun with my dad after all. Still, when Mom pulled up on Sunday night, no one was sorry. Dad practically knocked us to the ground in his mad dash to greet her.

"Thank God you're home," Dad said, as they hugged. "Want some eggplant?"

"Let's have the beef cutlets," Mom replied. "I don't like eggplant."

Recipe: Sarita's Best Beef Cutlets

My mother could slice beef cutlets to paper-thin proportions and fry 'em up like no one else on the planet. So what if her eggplant parmesan crashed and burned—her beef cutlets ruled!

2 cups Italian style bread crumbs

1 cup parmesan cheese

1 teaspoon salt

1 teaspoon freshly ground pepper

1 egg

1½ pounds thin-sliced beef cutlets

Cooking spray

½ cup olive oil

Combine bread crumbs, parmesan cheese, salt, and pepper. Dredge the cutlets in egg and then place in flour; lay breaded cutlets in prepared pan (with cooking spray and hot oil) to fry. Cook until golden brown on each side, turning after 3–5 minutes, depending on thickness of cutlet. When fully cooked, drain on paper towels. Serve with mashed potatoes, green beans, and beef gravy.

Serves 4-6.

Chapter 12: Halloween, 1976

When I was ten, almost nothing else ranked higher on my FUN-O-METER than Halloween, except for Christmas. Both holidays meant food, fun, and fabulous toys and treats. I loved them both with the fierceness of childhood and the utter abandon of a girl on a mission: to score more candy than anyone else and get the bag into the house without my brother Jude taking all the best candy bars.

Usually, Halloween fell on a weekday, so Chris and I would come racing home from Catholic school, shove down a chocolate chip cookie and a glass of milk so we'd have enough strength for the grueling march ahead, then rush to put on our costumes. By the time we bolted out our front door, we had only about one and a half hours of sunlight to guide us, along with my mother's famous words: "Have fun, and be back here before five for dinner."

But this year was different. This year, Halloween fell on a Sunday, and Chris and I had been planning our candy-hoarding route for so long that we were giddy with delight. The fact that it had been raining all morning was only a small setback; we figured rain wouldn't stop us. With any luck, the rain would stop and we would head out about 1 pm for four whole hours of sunlight before we had to come back for dinner! It was like being dropped into Disney World on a day without crowded lines, and every single ride was waiting just for us.

Usually, our mother helped us get into our costumes and painted our faces. My usual standby costumes, gypsy or bum, required some oversized clothes, dirt, and earrings, depending on my mood. Was I a dirty gypsy or a flashy bum? No matter, as long as I was ready to go get my candy.

Only this time, Mom was heading out the door at noon, without us.

"Mom," I said to her, as she gathered her things and strode toward the door. "Aren't you going to help us get ready for trick-or-treating?"

"I can't, Maria," Mom replied. "Grandpa is in the hospital and I need to get there."

I felt a jolt in my stomach. Grandpa had gotten skinnier and skinnier over the last year and a simple cold seemed to knock him to the ground. But he'd never been counted down and out before. Why should today be any different?

"But how will we get ready?" Chris replied.

"You two are big now," Mom said. "You know how to dress

yourselves. I left makeup on the bathroom counter. Just don't go crazy with the black paint—you know how hard it is to get off." Mom kissed us both and ran for the door. "And make sure you're home by five!"

Chris and I looked at each other.

"You think Grandpa will be okay?" Chris said.

I shrugged. "I'm sure he'll be fine."

The hour zoomed by as Chris and I got dressed and suitably painted. Chris looked like a cross between Groucho Marx and a bum; I looked like Lucille Ball in her gypsy costume. Our father met us at the door.

"Where are you guys going?" Dad said.

"Trick-or-treating," I replied.

"Oh damn! It's Halloween! Do we have any candy?" my father said, as he rushed back inside. "Jude," we heard him scream, "go down to the candy store and get some candy."

We walked outside and took a deep breath. The rain had stopped; weak sunshine greeted us as we ran to our neighbors' doors. Chris and I hit all the houses on our block and started on the next one, where a group of kids we knew from grade school had formed a less-than-harmless-looking gang.

This was not Spanky, Alfalfa, Buckwheat, and Butch to my Darla; it was more like The Bad News Bears after they'd just smoked a crack pipe. There were about eight boys who I wouldn't eat lunch with, much less go trick-or-treating with if I'd had my say in the matter. But Chris wasn't listening.

"Hey," Charlie said to my brother. Charlie was dressed as the Grim Reaper and waved his scythe menacingly as we walked up. Chris was oblivious to the weapon-wielding bad "juju" emanating from the group. "Want to go trick-or-treating with us?"

"Sure," Chris said.

"Do we have to?" I replied.

"It'll be fun."

Fun wasn't what I expected, but I swallowed my uneasiness and continued on with Our Demonic Gang.

Charlie rang an old neighbor's doorbell relentlessly. "Come on, old lady! Give us a treat or we'll have to trash your house!"

The old woman finally came to the door and handed out pennies.

"Pennies?" Charlie replied rudely. "We should wreck the house."

"Charlie, stop being an idiot," I said as I went to the next house.

This continued, with the boys becoming more and more desperate to destroy something. Finally, when we rang a bell and no one answered, Charlie got his wish.

"I'm going to trash this place!"

With a quick swing of his scythe, Charlie pulled down the Halloween decorations and smashed the pumpkins. His cronies put shaving cream all over the front door and two others smashed eggs on the hood of the car.

"We should get out of here," I said to Chris.

"Oh, what's your problem?" Charlie yelled. "You're such a Goody Two-Shoes. You never want to have any fun. Why don't you just get lost?"

"Why don't you just shut up?" I yelled back. "Chris, are you going to say anything to defend me?"

Chris shrugged. "No. You are no fun sometimes."

"Fine!" I shot back. "You stay with these creeps. I'm going by myself."

"You're going to get into big trouble! You know Mom doesn't let us go alone."

Chris was right; I was about to break one of the cardinal Halloween rules that my mother had set down when she agreed to let us go trick-or-treating without an adult. But as Charlie and his demonic pals were getting rowdier and rowdier, I figured we had to ditch them or I'd be going home in a cop car. Which, I had a feeling, would get me into even more trouble.

"I'm leaving," I said, fully expecting Chris to follow me as I broke free from the crowd. But Chris turned and left with Charlie and the other boys instead.

I turned up Bell Boulevard and continued toward our old house. I could see groups of kids ahead, and I latched onto one of them, figuring my mother wouldn't get too mad if I didn't go alone. One of the girls in the group was my old neighbor, Dawn.

I walked everywhere with this group of kids, who were

tireless and not at all disappointed when old ladies gave them pennies. My brown shopping bag was straining at the handles as I loaded up on Hundred Thousand Dollar Bars, Charleston Chews, Reese's Peanut Butter Cups, Pop Rocks, Wacky Packs, Pixie Sticks, and Candy Cigarettes. I was having so much fun that I never noticed the time.

I did realize, however, that it was pitch-black when Dawn's mother finally said to me, "Does your mother know you're with us?"

I shook my head. "No. My mother isn't home."

"Oh my gosh! It's almost 8 pm! Your parents will be frantic!"

I was more frightened of what my father was going to do to me for breaking the rules than I was of any evil monsters or demons that night. As Jeannette dialed my house, I overheard the conversation.

"Hi, Louie. This is Jeannette Roman. Did you know that Maria went trick-or-treating with us?"

Silence as Jeannette registered what my father was saying. "No, she's not at home, Lou. She's here on the old block. You'd better send one of her brothers for her."

Waiting for Jude and Joey to come get me was torture. Would my father hit me for being out so long? What would my punishment be? My father could be very creative when it came to punishments, as I'd learned just by watching him deal with Jude, who was always in trouble. What would he do to me?

I paced by the front door and wrung my hands. But when Jude and Joey finally rode up on their bikes, they didn't seem too mad at me. We thanked Mrs. Roman and headed home.

"Listen," Jude said, as we walked their bikes up Bell Boulevard. "Dad isn't going to hit you or anything because we got bad news. Grandpa died."

I didn't realize what he was saying. "Grandpa died when I was four."

"Not that Grandpa, you dope! Mom's father," Joey replied.

"Oh," I replied. Oh well, so much for telling Chris that Grandpa would be all right. It was my first lesson in knowing that you can't always be right about these things.

"Don't let him know we told you," Jude said, as we swung into the driveway. "He wants to break the news gently."

When we walked through the front door, my other four brothers and my father were waiting for me. My mother was not yet home.

"Okay, so listen, Maria," my father said, as he cupped my head in his hand. "So your grandfather's dead. Do you feel like crying? It's okay if you want to cry. Go ahead."

I looked around at all of my brothers, who seemed to want me to put on a show. "No, thanks, I don't want to cry."

"Okay then," my father said. And just like that, I was released from fear. My father never even realized I'd broken the rules, and for that, I would always thank my grandfather.

I walked into the kitchen, still heaving my candy bag.

Chris sat sprawled out at the kitchen table, crying.

"Want some of my candy?" I said.

"You don't even care! No one cares!" he wailed.

"Chris, I care," I said. "But Grandpa's been sick a long time. He's better off. Now have a candy bar."

"I don't understand you people," Chris said, as he ran from the kitchen.

"I'll have some of that candy," Jude said.

"Fine," I replied. "I don't want any now."

It was perhaps the first time in my life that I ever said that.

I tried to tell myself that it was better this way, that my grandfather had suffered long enough, and that there was no sense feeling bad about it. But then the memories flooded in. There was Grandpa pushing me on the swing at the park near the old house. There was Nonnie and Grandpa jumping off the Q27 bus. Jude named them "Nonnie and Grandpa on the Bus" because they took the bus everywhere. (This was not to be confused with our other grandparents, Nonnie and Grandpa on the Car, who obviously drove everywhere). There was Grandpa wearing the suit he always wore, clutching his gray fedora in one hand and a bag of candy in the other.

Here was Grandpa taking me out for an ice cream cone and laughing when I put a dab of vanilla ice cream on his nose. Or there was Grandpa carrying me on his shoulders to Coronette's, the local toy store, for a toy car. Even though I wanted a Dawn doll, he was so excited to be taking me for a

Matchbox car that I didn't want to spoil the fun.

But then there were the less happy memories too. Grandpa taking Chris and me for a walk and getting us all hopelessly lost as I cried, Chris paced, and Grandpa clutched his fedora in his hands and asked strangers for directions. There's Grandpa in the hospital, after he was hit by a truck following a long day of wandering, getting his broken arm set. Worst of all, there was Grandpa, sitting in a high chair with baby food all over his face and clothes.

The thing about memories was, once you opened that valve, they all just poured in and you couldn't stop the bad ones from joining the good ones. I wanted to remember Grandpa the way he was before the senility: playing ball with Chris and me, eager to buy us toys, snatching his false teeth from his mouth and chasing us with his dentures. It was this Grandpa that I figured would want to go trick-or-treating with me if he'd had the chance. He'd be disappointed to know that he'd wrecked my big day.

I came out of my reverie and looked at Jude. He'd emptied my bag on the table and had pulled out practically every decent piece of candy I had.

"Hey! Leave some for me!"

"I did! There's some right there!" Jude said, doing his best to look wounded. "Mom told me to check your candy for you," Jude said.

"When Mom said to check my chocolate for razor blades,

I don't think she meant you should inspect them by eating every last one of them."

Jude laughed and bit into a Krackel bar. "I'm only thinking of your safety, Maria."

That would've made Grandpa laugh. Come to think of it, it made me laugh too. I imagined him sitting right there at the table with us, dentures in place, about to enjoy some candy.

That's how Grandpa would've liked it.

Recipe: Grandpa's Bats

My grandfather was just zany enough to get a kick out of this recipe. Here's a recipe that celebrates two things that make me think of my grandfather: cookies and Halloween.

4 big, soft chocolate chip cookies

4 scoops of chocolate ice cream

Assorted candies for decoration, such as candy corn, M&Ms, licorice, or jellybeans

1. For the wings, place cookies on a cutting board. Cut cookies into halves. Using a teaspoon, make a slightly scalloped edge (like the curves on a bat's wing) on the straight side of each cookie; set wings aside.

2. For the body of the bat, place a scoop of ice cream on each of four serving plates. Using a knife, make a cut about ½ inch deep on each side of the scoops of ice cream.

3. To assemble the ice cream bats, insert ends of cookie wings into cuts on sides of ice cream scoops. Place so they look like

wings. Decorate ice cream with candies to create the bat's face. Use licorice pieces for the ears, jellybeans for the eyes, and candy corn for the fangs, or use your own imagination. Serve immediately or freeze for up to two hours before serving. Serves 4.

Chapter 13: Living in the Baked Apple in the Summer of Sam

For the most part, growing up in the 1970s was an innocent time. You could take your banana-seat bike out, ride down to the local pizzeria, and plunk down two quarters to get a slice and a Coke without your mother issuing an Amber Alert.

On a sunny, beautiful day, my parents would open the front door, lodge their feet in our behinds, and jettison us out the door. As long as it wasn't raining (and sometimes, even if it was), we were expected to go out. That was just the way it was.

But in the summer of 1977, our innocence was shaken. A lunatic bent on killing girls with long brown hair was stalking the streets of New York City. In one crazy letter, he claimed that he "loved Queens girls best." He also wrote to the local newspapers and asked to be called the Son of Sam. The Son of Sam claimed that a neighbor's dog was giving him implicit orders to go forth and kill some more. It was the mass murderer's equivalent of "my dog ate my homework" excuses.

I had a dog at that time. I could've called myself the Sister of Goldie, but if she ever issued an order, it would've been something like "Go get me another Milk-Bone. And I mean now!" Most dogs that I know aren't that knowledgeable about discos, but then again, I suppose the dogs in my life are more interested in eating than dancing. But in the summer of 1977, Son of Sam had struck close to home. He came to a disco— known as Elephas—in Queens, where we lived, and shot a young girl and her boyfriend, maiming them both.

This was a disco that we could—and often did—walk to. It was two blocks away from the local White Castle, where we spent many a sweaty summer's evening wolfing down sacks of cheeseburgers and giving ourselves headaches from the freezing cold milkshakes that were too thick to suck through a straw. We'd sit there and talk about the discos that were springing up all over the neighborhood. We'd laugh about the disco with the weird name (what does Elephas mean, anyway?) that we could see across the street on Northern Boulevard. This was a disco where Kathie, one of my future sisters-in-law, would burst through the doors and yell "Rather dead than disco!" before being tossed out the door by burly bouncers.

Elephas was in Bayside. The Son of Sam was lurking on the streets of my hometown, just a few blocks from my open window that sultry summer night.

After that, my parents dragged us indoors before the last streak of sunlight disappeared behind the shadows. In 1977, that meant that all of us—with the exception of Jude and Tony—would be confined to quarters. There would be no more lazy walks out-of-doors, counting and wishing on the stars. When the first fireflies started to glow and fly toward the sky, we were collared and yanked inside.

The sense of despair and anger hung as dense as the humidity that made our tube tops and shorts cling to our skin. Who could this madman be? Where did he come from? What did this monster look like?

Everybody was suspect—and I do mean *everybody*. Our elderly neighbor, Mrs. Schmucker, was busy watching the Lagalante household that summer, cataloging the comings and goings of my brothers. She just happened to notice that Jude was out on the nights when the Son of Sam struck. So it stood to reason that my brother must have been the murderer.

Apparently, neighbors across the city were coming to similar conclusions about the hippie freaks that lived near them. Jude was a rock-'n'-roller, and rockers didn't wear their hair like John Travolta in *Saturday Night Fever*. Jude did happen to be near the scene of the crime on June 26, 1977. He had just come back from a gig, playing the bass in his rock-'n'-roll band, New York's Unemployed. He stood at the intersection of Northern Boulevard and Bell Boulevard with his friend, Mike, the keyboardist. They were waiting for the Q13 bus to arrive. They stood there, eating some White Castles and talking about that night's gig—their outrageous costumes, the band's set, the girls who threw themselves at them. When the bus finally arrived at 2:30 am, Mike jumped on and waved good-bye as my brother started to walk home.

So there was Jude, wearing a pair of skintight white pants, high white go-go boots, and a red top that had lots of ties and fringe. His long brown hair hung straight down his back, and from behind, he looked like the prettiest girl in Bayside.

He was about two blocks into his walk when he heard a BANG BANG, followed by the screech of tires and sirens from the nearby 111th Precinct. Jude looked around and saw a flash of red lights and heard the screams and commotion of a nearby shooting.

"It could have been me," Jude said later. "He could've been walking behind me for all I know."

After that, Jude and his first girlfriend, Cindy, started tucking their hair up and hiding it in skullcaps. Both Jude and Cindy wore their hair long and straight, and if you were a deranged, dog-driven killer, you'd be delighted to find them. They would be a big-time score for a tiny little mind.

At eleven years old, I was younger than any of the girls who had been killed or maimed by the Son of Sam. But that didn't make me any less afraid. As temperatures soared that year up to a whopping 104 degrees, I convinced my mother that it was the heat that made me want to shed my waist-length brown tresses.

Out with idolizing Cher and Crystal Gale hair: in with the pixie look, Dorothy Hamill, even Joey Heatherton. If my mother had let me, I would've gone blonde a whole lot sooner. Of course, that was before the Son of Sam widened his net, killing blonde Stacy Moskowitz in Brooklyn. I guess the dog was not so choosy after all.

Fear clung to the streets and stuck to the mist in the nighttime hours. We closed our windows and locked our doors, and for the first time in…well, *ever,* my parents let us run the air conditioner. *Baretta, Barney Miller, The Rockford Files*, and *Starsky and Hutch* held us captive as we sweated out the capture of a killer who was stalking the streets of the Bronx and Queens.

There was only one thing that kept us all from going crazy during that time of confinement: the ice cream man. My brother, Louie, had a pal named Bobby who drove an ice cream truck through the deserted streets of Bayside. When his bell chimed, we ran outside, en masse, sure that even a mass-murdering, dog-listening lunatic would not step out of the shadows and whack us while we licked our Firecrackers and Chocolate Éclairs.

The Good Humor man's bell was our siren song, and we ran to it, embraced it, and thanked him for giving us a reason not to be afraid. As we huddled around the truck, we'd chat with our young neighbors, who were also stuck indoors until the madman was caught.

Some nights, when my mother felt really sorry for us and

her pocket change was almost gone, she'd make us a special treat. With a fistful of bananas in one hand, the ice cream scoop in another, my mother would whip up a batch of banana splits that made us forget for a moment that we were trapped inside against our will. She'd pull out her special banana split bowls, which were long and thin and built just with this treat in mind, and she'd get to work. Toasted peanuts, gooey chocolate syrup, rainbow sprinkles, and a shot of whipped cream made a cheap thrill...well, thrilling.

Ice cream sundaes aside, the summer seemed endless until 2:30 one fateful morning, when my brother Paul burst into my room.

"They got him! They got him!"

I wiped the sleep and the fear from my eyes and ran out to watch the news with Paul. I didn't need to ask "Who?" I already knew.

My dog, Goldie, told me.

My brothers and I sat around the living room, chomping on ice cream cones and watching the details of the Son of Sam's capture unfold. David Berkowitz, mail collector. Someone I'd walk by in the street and never dream of fearing; someone who let his neighbor's dog push him around. My brother Jude remarked that Berkowitz was so incredibly plain that it made him think of the phrase "the banality of evil." Here it was, in human form.

Jude, Tony, Louie, Paul, Joey, Chris, and I all breathed a sigh of relief that early summer's morning. We were free again.

The monster couldn't prey on us anymore.

Ice cream for breakfast never tasted so good.

You Know You Grew Up in Queens in the 1970s if...

You knew people who lived on Archie Bunker's block.

Your teachers referred to their students as "sweathogs."

You thought Huggy Bear's clothes were stylish.

You still remember that the Son of Sam thought Queens girls were the prettiest prey.

You cut your long brown hair short and dyed it white.

The headline "Ford to Mayor Beame: Drop Dead" still makes you mad.

Recipe: Sarita's Banana Splits

Perfect for a summer night, or any time you want to enjoy a special homemade treat. My mother could make any occasion (even forced indoor imprisonment) better.

4 bananas, split lengthwise

Vanilla ice cream

Chocolate ice cream

Toasted almonds or peanuts

Rainbow sprinkles

Hot fudge syrup

Whipped cream

Place ½ split banana in bowl. Add one scoop of vanilla and one scoop of chocolate ice cream. Shower with nuts and sprinkles.

Zigzag chocolate syrup over ice cream; finish with whipped cream on top.

Serves 8.

Chapter 14: Manorhaven Beach

For some people, summertime conjures up memories of running after the ice cream truck, playing baseball, and firing up the hibachi for an outdoor cookout. I did all those things back when I was a kid, but my fondest summer memories come from a tiny little beach on Port Washington Bay: Manorhaven Beach.

My family was the annoying crowd of immigrants who got up before dawn and hogged all the barbecue grills. My Nonnie and my Aunt Mary would get there just as sunlight started to shimmer on the murky green bay water, putting their coolers, blankets, and chairs across any and all working hibachis to claim them as our own. When the nine of us would finally totter in from the "long" drive from Bayside, dozens of members of our extended family would be there, firing up the grills and getting ready for some serious eating.

But you have to remember that this was a first-generation Italian family. Sure, we had hamburgers and hot dogs, macaroni and potato salad and cole slaw. We also had things like sausage and peppers on crusty Italian bread and my Aunt Mary's unforgettable peppers and eggs on rolls. A casserole dish filled with lasagna was sure to be found if you just looked hard enough. We also had meatball heroes, mozzarella and tomatoes, ice cream from the nearby stand. I'd run to the water's edge to wash the stickiness away, never wondering what that brown foam was all about.

Some of the men would get together to play softball, while the rest of us would go for a swim, if the bay wasn't off-limits due to an oil spill or bacteria. If the water was off-limits, we'd run to the bocce courts, where Uncle Sal and Uncle Pete would give us lessons on how to throw the *ballino* (the little white ball) to get the most balls close to it. My twin brother, Chris, was a seasoned pro at this game by the time we were ten. I used to just throw and hope for the best.

When we weren't eating, we'd team up with the cousins we only saw at these family functions. My cousin Lisa was about a month older than me and I really enjoyed her company, even though my Italian grandmother liked to tell me how wonderful she was, how much thinner she was than me, how straight and perfect her teeth were, and how she could walk on water.

I didn't hold this against Lisa; it wasn't her fault she was perfect. I just enjoyed being with perfection. Chris teamed up with our older cousin Johnny, who would run and play with him until he would run off to play with some of the older boys. Then Chris met up again with our cousin Tommy, Angela and Pete's grandson. Tommy was about the same age as us and could see Chris's inherent coolness.

Tommy was funny, and smart, and was always ready to conspire with Chris to have a good time. Between swimming races at our cousin Eleanor's pool and bocce tournaments here at Manorhaven Beach, Tommy was great company. Chris and Tommy ran all over that beach together, swimming, playing, laughing, and eating, all day long.

Meanwhile, I was busy hatching a plot to ditch one of my younger, more distant cousins, Amelia. Amelia was a whiny little creature whose acid tongue made my relatives laugh, but who made my mother arch her eyebrows and say things like "Don't you ever say something like that" while she took a swipe at me. Amelia was trouble, and I thought trouble should be dealt with. Unfortunately, Lisa balked; perfection never can see the whole picture. Eventually, Amelia got wind of my diabolical plan and, since no one would help me hoist her into the garbage dumpster, she got away.

My six brothers and I would run to the swings, where we would launch ourselves higher, higher, higher into the sky until, inevitably, one of us would fall off. Paul was usually the victim. No matter where you were, you could hear Paul's screams amid the "caw caw" of the seagulls. He'd land with a thud on the sandy beach below, crying and holding out his often-injured wrist, and my mother or father would kiss it... and send him back to play. If he couldn't be consoled, they'd feed him.

Some summer days, my father would try to teach me to swim while my Uncle Bob would say encouraging things like "She'll never learn if you go easy on her" right before he'd shove my face down into the water and hold me under. I'd sputter and kick and scream and he'd laugh. My cousin Lorraine would make believe she'd sneezed, only to unravel seaweed the length of her arm and yell, "I need a tissue!" Our cousin Richard would throw his mother into the water—"Protest is futile!" he'd say—while Aunt Eleanor kicked and hollered and begged for mercy and rolled beneath the waves.

My Puerto Rican grandparents and uncle joined us on more than one occasion. As a result, we'd get to feast on *platanos* (fried plantains), *bacalaitos fritos* (fried codfish), or hot dogs. Hey, they were as American as the rest of us.

A day at the beach was, well...a day at the beach. We'd eat and play and come home sticky, sandy, and satisfied. If only every day could be like the ones we shared at Manorhaven Beach.

The Top Five Horrifying Sights, Smells, and Sounds for the Rich Folks Driving by the Beach:

Codfish frying on the hibachi

400 people packed into 30 square feet

Queens residents playing in the park

Dean Martin singing "That's Amore" over the loudspeaker

My family

Recipe:

Aunt Mary's Unforgettable Peppers and Eggs on a Roll

There was nothing like Aunt Mary's peppers and eggs. Lucky for me, she had an amazing sense of humor and always loved to share.

8 eggs

Red, green, and yellow peppers

Butter

4 club rolls

Salt and pepper to taste

Scramble the 8 eggs. Slice peppers lengthwise and remove the seeds. Add salt and pepper. Roast sliced peppers under broiler until tender (5-7 minutes). Butter the club rolls. Mix eggs, salt, pepper, and roasted peppers together. Place on bottom of sliced rolls; then put the top of the roll on.

Serves 4.

Chapter 15:
Wednesday Afternoons *con mi abuela*

If you went to a Catholic school in Queens during the 1970s and 1980s, chances were good that you got out of school on Wednesdays at 12:45. Classes in Catholic Church Doctrine (CCD, as it was known then, or Faith Formation, as it is known today) were held on Wednesday afternoons for the poor, hopeless souls that attended public schools.

The afternoon was yours to do what you pleased, provided it pleased your parents. When I was very young, my mother would take me to visit her mother in nearby Flushing. It was a quick car-ride in our lime-green Buick station wagon to her house, where we'd spend an hour or two with her before rushing home so my mother could get to work cooking dinner for the seven hungry monsters that would soon be banging on the table.

My happiest memories of those Wednesday afternoons came when I got a little bit older. My mother went back to work at a local high school and couldn't get home as early as we did. Since Chris and I were eleven years old, she thought it was high time we started taking the bus to meet her at my grandmother's apartment. So my twin and I would scrape together enough change to cover the seventy-five-cent fare, and off to Grandmother's house we'd go. The buses would be jam-packed with students, housewives with carts and strollers, and senior citizens. We'd hop on the bus three blocks from our house, cram ourselves inside with the other sweaty locals, and hang on for dear life to the slippery metal strap that hung a bit too high over our heads. Then we'd laugh and snort as the bus swung around corners and we slammed into fellow travelers.

Chris and I would bargain about who got to pull the cord that let the bus driver know we wanted to get off. One week it was Chris's turn; one week it was mine. Except we couldn't always keep track, and lots of times Chris got to do it because I didn't want to walk back from three stops away by the time we decided which one of us could ring the bell.

We would take that bus to Flushing because we knew what would be there when we got off: lunch! Our Puerto Rican grandmother was not a great cook, but she was determined to please, and since she knew we took a long bus ride straight from school to spend our afternoons with her, she went out of her way to make it special.

Chris and I would yank on the bell rope to signal for our stop, then jump clear of the last step just as the bus tore away. We'd race each other up the block from Kissena Boulevard to 140 Beech Avenue and ring the bell marked "1D" inside the vestibule of our grandmother's building: *The Yorklyn*. It sounded fancy, and maybe it was once, before Puerto Ricans like us moved in.

We'd jump onto the elevator for the ride up one floor; even though the stairs were faster; there was something fun about taking an elevator when you were a kid who lived in a house. As the doors of the elevator opened, Chris and I would breathe in deeply, knowing that the salty, chicken broth smells that greeted us were meant FOR US. Then we'd rush to 1D and start pushing the bell.

Our grandmother—Nonnie, as we called her—would open the door with a big hearty laugh and a bear hug and kisses to match. She was a tiny woman, barely 5'2", and round all over, with big, thick glasses and lots of wavy brown hair. She smelled of Jean Naté perfume and lavender soap, both gifts bought by us at the local drugstore.

"What's for lunch?" Chris or I would yell, even though, most days, we knew what the answer would be.

"Come and see for jor selfs," Nonnie replied, in her endearing Spanglish. She may have lived in this country for some fifty years, but English was clearly her second language.

There it was: a repast that only we could get giddy about. On the table lay two steaming bowls of Lipton Chicken Noodle

Soup, two plates of perfect, pink ham on crusty bakery rolls, lots of spicy brown mustard, and several six-packs of Coca Cola.

Okay, so we're not talking about an ethnic feast to make Puerto Ricans everywhere proud. What we are talking about was food that was too expensive for our parents to buy if they were going to feed all nine of us at once. But Nonnie *wasn't* going to feed everyone—just Chris and me. So she could splurge on us, spoil us, make us glad to be spending an entire afternoon with her when we could be at home riding our bikes or roller-skating with friends. Nonnie was grateful to be chosen, and she rewarded us with the greatest gift she could afford: food. And just to show us how hip she could be, she made sure to buy the most American fare she could lay her hands on.

Week after week, Chris and I would hop on that bus, brave all kinds of weather, race off that elevator—just to get to Nonnie's and share lunch with her. After we ate, our grandmother would turn on Channel 4 and we'd spend the afternoon watching her favorite soap operas. First, we'd watch The *Doctors* and *Days of Our Lives*. Then we'd switch off to Channel 2, where we'd watch *As the World Turns* and then *Guiding Light*. Channel 4 again, for *All in the Family, Mary Tyler Moore*, or *Bob Newhart* before the day was through.

Nonnie would share chocolate and vanilla cream cakes with us while we chewed on plotlines. Would they really kill off Missy on *The Doctors*? Would Don ever find out that Marlena's twin sister, Samantha, had kidnapped her and taken her place? Did Nola Reardon *really* think she could get pregnant by Floyd and convince Kelly that it was his baby? Was Chuckles the Clown the best *MTM* episode ever, and didn't Mr. Carlton in group therapy look just like our sixth-grade English teacher?

By this time, my mother would have arrived. She and her mother would speak in pure, unadulterated Spanish. Since Chris and I didn't speak Spanish, we could only guess what my mother was saying to her mother. We would let them talk while we caught up on our favorite shows.

Sometimes, in the summer or on vacations, my grandmother would want to go shopping on Main Street in Flushing. My brother, mother, and I would join her as we walked down Kissena Boulevard toward the heart of our shopping universe. Nonnie, Mom, and I would walk, three across, with our arms linked. Chris would walk behind us, saying things like "You three look like monkeys in a barrel!"

We'd go to Bang! Bang!, a clothing store that had things that were way too cool for the likes of me, while my grandmother vainly tried to talk me into wearing leopard-skin T-shirts and short skirts. Then we'd hit the stand under the train trestle, looking for off-price goodies like leather moccasins for only $5. Next, it was off to Alexander's, where my grandmother and mother would ransack the bins in search of discounted treasure. If today was Chris's day, we would even go to Korvette's (which later became Gertz, and one day became Stern's—but that's another story), where my brother would be allowed to choose a Tom Jones record while I looked through the toy department in search of Cher, Baby That-a-Way, or the Bionic Woman.

We were in Gertz the day we found my communion dress. A salesclerk refused to help my grandmother because, the clerk said, "I can't understand a word this lady is saying." My grandmother was embarrassed, but my mother went right up to the manager and told him how rude his salesclerk was being to her mother.

"I'm sorry," the manager said. "What can I do to make it up to you?"

My mother got a discount on my dress and a discount on my brother's suit, which was purple (maybe the manager was just happy to actually sell that). Then she and my grandmother sought out the rude saleslady and made her ring it all up.

My brother said, "I love this suit! Isn't it great?"

My mother replied, "As long as you're happy. I'm just glad I don't have to wear it."

Sometimes, when we were all worn out from our shopping and hungry beyond belief, my grandmother would say, "Sarita, let's go to the Long Island Room."

At that moment, I would hear a symphony of angel's harps playing "Glory Be." Located at the top of Gertz Department Store, the Long Island Room was, in my child's mind, the most glamorous place on earth.

We'd get onto the elevator, where my claustrophobic

grandmother would fasten her vice-like grip on my hand (years later, when that elevator got stuck, I would learn firsthand why the escalator was a better choice). Once we got off the elevator, my grandmother would laugh—a great, boisterous laugh that began in her belly and rumbled up her throat and out her mouth like a faraway clap of thunder—when she saw the look of delight on our faces. Mom, Nonnie, Chris, and I would follow the waiter to our table and to the delights that our meals held for us. Eating out was a rare treat in our world, but my grandmother liked to spring for it every once in a while.

Chris and I would look around, wide-eyed. There were crystal chandeliers, linen tablecloths, and real silver on the tables! This was a far cry from our regular haunts, where a paper plate and a plastic cup were standard. Plush burgundy draperies lined the windows, and the mirrored walls let us see ourselves wherever we looked. The room was as multifaceted and as shiny as the whitest diamond. To offset the brightness, the linens were burgundy-colored and the dishes were translucent and creamy, with a small flowered border. Whether the glasses were Waterford crystal or Crystal d'Arque, it didn't matter. This was fancy living to us!

"Order whatever you want," my grandmother said, in her broken English. It really sounded like "Oder whatever jou wan," but we knew what it meant, and we smiled.

I always ordered chicken croquettes with mashed potatoes, gravy, and corn on the cob. My grandmother would smile with pleasure as Chris and I clinked our glasses and watched the other "fancy" folks in the restaurant. Chocolate pudding with whipped cream on top was our final reward. Chris would tell Nonnie jokes just to hear her big, boisterous laugh. When we weren't laughing with her, we listened to the steady cadence of her Spanish chatter with our mother, who sometimes would pepper the words with English so we could follow along.

"Mira, mama," she would say, pointing to her fancy drink. "Un cherry!"

This broke my mother and her mother up, and Chris and I laughed along too, not knowing what on earth they were laughing about but enjoying ourselves all the same.

"Les go home," my grandmother said finally. Mom, Nonnie, and I linked our arms together like monkeys in a barrel and headed out. Chris walked behind us and laughed.

Nonnie loved treating us to lunch at the Long Island Room. On days when she was feeling less extravagant, she'd take us out for pizza, Chinese food, or Kentucky Fried Chicken. She never really cooked for us, except for one tragic time that included chicken thighs, brown sauce, and Spanish rice.

It wasn't really her fault. She'd grown up rich and spoiled on a ranch in Puerto Rico before her parents died and her older sister tried to press her little sister into household servitude. That was it for her. She ran away to New York, where she met the hillbilly grocery boy that used to deliver food to her door: my grandfather. He became the cook in the family.

But grandpa was gone now, and Nonnie could do what she did best: treat us to a special meal, whether it was fancy or fried, and throw in some laughter on the side—no charge.

I can still hear my grandmother's laugh even though it's been almost 30 years since I last heard it. While she may be long gone, I can always think back to those lazy summer days or those wonderful Wednesdays, when our grandmother made our time with her rich and satisfying.

Recipe: Maria's Quick and Easy Arroz con Pollo

Even if my grandmother couldn't cook, I still learned how to make a tasty (and quick) chicken and rice dish from my mother.

2 tablespoons extra-virgin olive oil, divided

1 bag (16 oz.) yellow Spanish rice

1 pound thin-sliced chicken cutlets, cubed

1 bag frozen vegetables

(broccoli, carrots, peas, green beans, etc.)

Bring 4 quarts of water to a boil in a large pot with a tight-fitting lid. Add 1 tablespoon olive oil and let boil one minute. Add rice. Turn heat down and simmer for 20–25 minutes. Stir occasionally to make sure the rice doesn't stick to the bottom of the pot. Meanwhile, put the cubed chicken into a frying pan coated with another tablespoon of olive oil. Cook until nicely browned. Place vegetables in microwavable bowl and cook for approximately 5 minutes. When there's about 10 minutes left on the cooking time for the rice, add the chicken and vegetables. Stir well. Heat through and spoon into warmed bowls.

Serves 4-6.

Chapter 16: Hey, Mom, What's for Dinner?

My mother was a constant and steady presence, and at times a wonderful cook. For years, she cooked our evening meals with a precision that would've made Donna Reed proud. She never, ever used bottled spaghetti sauce—only homemade gravy in this household.

I would rush home from school at 3 pm, eager to get a snack and wait for my 5 pm dinner. I was never sure what Mom had on the menu, but I did know that there would be something good and hot.

But then the unthinkable happened. My mother got a job outside of our home, and the effortlessness with which she ran our completely insane household began to unravel. Now, after working all day, she would have to come home and cook dinner as well. What on earth could she cook when she was tired, didn't always have food on hand, and didn't have hours in which to prepare it?

No problem, Mom decided. She would concoct a weekly recipe routine that would give her hectic world structure and get us fed every single night. My mother called tons of relatives to get quick and easy recipes, turning to anyone who could give her a fast, hearty meal that required little or no prep time but delivered big on taste. My mother hoped to discover our likes and dislikes and find a few staple recipes that she could rotate in order to keep the hungry masses happy. The problem was that, when she hit on something we liked, she'd feed it to us until we thought we'd vomit at the sight of it.

Monday night was pot pie night. I'd run into the kitchen, provided there was nothing really compelling on the 4:30 movie on Channel 7, and help my mother carve letters into the pot pies. B was for beef, C was for chicken, and T was for turkey. My mother would make nine pot pies, and I'd make sure to get my order in early; otherwise I'd be stuck eating that god-awful beef pot pie.

We had a brief respite from the pot pie night when my mother bought some Jimmy Dean sausages, figuring she'd make sausage and eggs to break up the monotony. We knew we were in for a strange evening when a smell that would make a skunk cry started emanating from the frying pan. The sausages had gone bad, and Mom had to toss the whole pile of them straight into the garbage. We ate our eggs with our noses pressed closed and all the windows open. The following Monday, it was back to carving B, C, and T into tiny frozen pies.

Tuesday nights were tuna casseroles. Actually, it was only tuna casserole night for my brother Paul and me. This happened because, on the first night that my mother decided to try Tuna Helper, Hamburger Helper's sickly and disgusting little cousin, my other brothers rioted. My mother was able to figure out, somewhere in the din, the shouting, the crying, and the cursing, that Tuna Helper was no help whatsoever, and she should cease and desist from ever tormenting us with that slop again.

Notice that I said five of my six brothers reacted this way. Paul hummed happily through the meal. My mother adored Paul, because if she served him dog food on shoe leather, he would've eaten it greedily, with a smile on his face. Paul didn't care what you gave him, as long as it resembled food.

My own undoing came about because I felt sorry for my mother. Poor Mom, who was as kind and bighearted as the great outdoors, didn't really deserve to be treated like a wayward scullery maid working in a prison. While my brothers gagged and complained, I said, "Oh, don't feel bad, Mom. It's actually very good."

My mother smiled at me and pinched my cheek. I was really pleased with myself...until the following Tuesday, when she served something edible to my five brothers and Tuna Helper to Paul and me.

Her exact words were, "You two enjoyed this so much that I made it special for you!"

My mother had nine people to feed every night. How

could I not eat something that she made special for me?

Paul and our two dogs, Goldie and Henry, ate most of my Tuna Helper on Tuesday nights. We continued to eat this movable feast until the night that Paul said, "Mom, I'm tired of Tuna Helper."

My mother knew it was time for a change.

Wednesday nights were Prince Spaghetti nights. My mother enjoyed the commercial showing the Italian momma yelling out the window "Hey, Anthony! It's Prince Spaghetti night!" so much that she made it our night for macaroni. This was back in the day when you "stuck a feather in your hat and called it macaroni." Not pasta. Pasta became the name of ziti, spaghetti, lasagna, penne, and linguine in restaurants that wanted to sound fancy. But in my house in the 1970s, we called it macaroni.

My mother would start her sauce in her Crock-Pot and let it simmer all day long. Sweet Italian sausage, firm round meatballs, and homemade tomato sauce bubbled and cooked slowly. Spaghetti and meat balls in my mother's kitchen was magic, and she was more powerful than Samantha from *Bewitched* and Jeannie from *I Dream of Jeannie* combined. More beautiful, too.

In this case, the Crock-Pot was our friend. Good things emanated from the Crock-Pot at these times. During the winter, though, when my mother felt like branching out into unknown Crock-Pot terrain, there would be some scary, Crock-Pot-inspired meals, like beef stew (did you know that really bad cuts of meat don't actually soften much even after cooking for twelve hours?) or chicken legs, thighs, and butts with peas, carrots, and egg noodles ("I went looking for a noodle, a different kind of noodle, that was gold and light, tastes so right"). My mother was an advertiser's dream come true.

Thursday nights were chicken or beef cutlet night. My mother would cut a piece of chicken or beef paper-thin and then fry it up—simple, hearty, and good. She'd make mashed potatoes and corn on the cob to go along with it. Nobody complained on Thursday night, unless you count Jude saying that Tony's cutlets were golden brown while his were charred and edged in black. This was proof positive to him that Tony was her favorite. My mother should've just given Paul all the burned cutlets. He wouldn't have complained.

Friday nights were La Choy nights. My mother was once again inspired by a commercial ditty, the one that said "La Choy Makes Chinese Food That Swings American." So she rushed out to the store and bought enough La Choy to keep us in sesame noodles for decades to come. Joey hated La Choy nights. However, in my parents' home, this was not a problem. No separate meal would be made for him. He could have the Tuna Helper leftovers or the La Choy, or he could eat nothing. So Joey ate the La Choy with the rest of us, until a new commercial ditty won my mother's heart.

Saturday nights were the one night a week that my mother didn't cook. Like her recipe routines, my mother would insist on one type of fast food for weeks and weeks, until someone complained or the line was too long or the teenage clerk was too rude; then we'd move on to other fast-food pastures.

We enjoyed sacks and sacks of White Castles, which couldn't be beat for a family of nine. Each mini-burger cost a quarter, and even if each child asked for a cheeseburger (which was twenty-nine cents), you could be the big spender, get them four each along with fries, thick milkshakes, and onion rings, and still get change of a twenty-dollar bill. Now that was my parents' idea of fine dining! Only pizza came close to being as economical.

When the gastrointestinal toll from the Murder Burgers, as we affectionately called them, began to get too high, we switched off to Burger King: "Hold the pickles, hold the lettuce, special orders don't upset us, all we ask is that you let us have it your way." My mother was right there, clutching handfuls of coupons, asking for two-for-one Whoppers with free bonus fries, hold the pickle, can the lettuce on some, extra ketchup on the others. Burger King was the new fast-food joint in town, and as long as they were giving out freebies, we were there for the taking—that is, until we fell under the spell of "two all-beef patties, special sauce, lettuce, cheese, pickles, onions on a sesame seed bun." The Big Mac was the *new* new kid in town, and we lined up like the hopeless lemmings we were.

As a change from hamburgers, Kentucky Fried Chicken, original flavor and sometimes Extra Crispy, with extra mashed potatoes and gravy and a boatload of biscuits, ruled in our house until a nasty teenage clerk ignored my mother and lost millions of dollars in Saturday night revenue.

Sunday dinner was a midday meal, served at about 2 pm. That was when we were all finished with mass, and we could really enjoy sitting around the dinner table and eating a heavy, carbohydrate-laden meal that was sure to put everyone in a coma for the rest of the afternoon.

Lasagna or baked ziti, lots of crusty Italian bread, salad, and homemade sausage bread (bread with mild Italian sausage baked right into the middle) were terrific to start. We followed that up with chicken or ham, potatoes, two or three vegetables, and more bread, and ended it all with lots of cake, some doughnuts, Munchkins, cannoli, napoleons, or Carvel's Flying Saucers.

My father's mother, her brother Sal, and my dad's brother Don were usually in attendance for the Sunday meal. Of course, this meant that my mother was actually cooking and serving three meals, because Uncle Don would drop off his mother before work, and that meant that my mother should have a sausage biscuit and a cup of coffee waiting for them. Oh, and pick up Uncle Sal at the Long Island Rail Road. My grandmother and her brother didn't like cheese, so my mother had to cook separate trays of cheese-less lasagna or ziti to make them happy. Then, at about 6 pm, they'd all be looking for ham sandwiches and more coffee—"And say, do you have any more cake left?"

If my grandmother, great-uncle, and uncle were there, chances were good that our extended family would call for dessert: Angela and Pete with their grandson, Tommy, Eleanor and Bob, Aunt Frances, Aunt Mary, Uncle Pete, Lorraine, Angela, Aunt Tessie, Auntie Anne, Diane, Gina, Dominic, Greg, Marcia, Peter, Jan, Bobby, Cindy, and our little dogs too. Everyone was welcome, and everyone was eating on Sundays in our household.

My mother ran herself ragged and did it all with a smile on her face. Back then, I always wondered, what is she so tired for?

Now, I wonder, when did she sleep?

What I learned from my mother about cooking:

Watch lots of commercials. You never know when a jingle will solve the age-old question, "Hey, Mom, what's for dinner?"

Buy in bulk. A twelve-year supply of La Choy, Jimmy Dean Sausages, and pot pies will never go bad.

A Crock-Pot can be your best friend…or your worst enemy.

Make out a recipe plan and NEVER, EVER deviate from it—except you can adjust it accordingly when even your child who would eat garbage (and sometimes does) complains.

Consider loyalty to fast-food restaurants as flexible. If the management offers only one coupon per customer, hand out nine coupons to your family members (even if they are only five years old) and send them each in with part of the order.

When your husband's family calls and asks what's for dinner, tell them, "I don't know. Where are you taking me?"

Recipe:

Auntie Anne's Fast-'n'-Easy Eggplant and Linguine

My brother Paul's godmother, Auntie Anne, gave me this recipe when I told her I was writing a book. She said it was quick and delicious—so enjoy!

1 pound Italian sausage

½ cup olive oil

1 medium eggplant, diced

½ pound linguine

¼ cup fresh minced Italian parsley

Italian grated cheese, to taste

Remove sausage meat from casings. Brown sausage in hot olive oil. Remove and drain. In drippings, cook eggplant and 2–3 tablespoons of water until eggplant is very tender (10–15 minutes). Meanwhile, cook linguine until it is *al dente*. Add sausage to eggplant and toss mixture with linguine and parsley. Sprinkle top with cheese.

Serves: 4-6.

Chapter 17: The Great Spaghetti and Meatball Fiasco

Being a mother is often a thankless job. You try to explain to your kids that no matter how many children you have, your love is limitless and infinite, and just because you love a brother or sister doesn't mean you love each child less. Of course, when you're a child, you don't buy any of that. You look for clues or signs that will show your mother's overwhelming favoritism for your brother or sister, justifying your own fears of being loved less.

My own mother faced just such a dilemma. It was accepted in our family that her favorite child was Tony, followed by Chris, with the other five of us fighting for her attention and love. She denied this vehemently, especially to me. How could she not favor me, she'd say, when all she'd ever wanted was a little girl? Of course, I knew that she wished that her little girl loved frilly, lacy things and tea time, instead of beat-up clothes and rolling in the mud.

My oldest brother, Jude, saw signs of favoritism for Tony everywhere. Each night, he'd find evidence: the steak that was grilled to perfection for Tony while everyone else's was burned at the edges. The French fries that were golden brown and crispy on the outside, soft on the inside, that lay on Tony's plate, while Jude's were blackened and tasted like soot. The pop tarts bought in Tony's favorite flavor and never his. In a court of law, this evidence wouldn't have been enough to convict anyone. But in the curious world of the Lagalantes, this was enough evidence to hang someone. And that someone was Mom.

Never mind that Tony was always kind and helpful to my mother. Never mind that he'd clean, do the dishes, or help out by babysitting for us younger kids so my mother could get a much-needed break. Never mind that Tony had been sick often and my mother probably worried a lot about him.

Jude still held a grudge against Tony for showing up less than a year after him and taking away some of his glory. Jude was quite sure that my mother would throw herself in the path of an oncoming train for Tony, without a moment's hesitation. But if it was Jude standing there, well...let's just say that he hoped the train wasn't traveling at top speed.

There was one day in particular when my mother's dedication to Tony seemed clear. It all started as we huddled around our kitchen table, reading a magazine. By today's standards, the kitchen was approximately the size of a walk-in closet. There was just enough room for a refrigerator, a stove, a table with six chairs (whichever child got there late had to eat alone, after everyone finished), and a sink. Naturally, since it was so cramped in there, we were all drawn to that exact spot.

My mother cooked while we sat around and talked. Jude, Louie, and my father were in the living room watching baseball while Tony, Joey, Paul, Chris, and I looked at the pictures in a magazine and laughed. My mother finished rolling the last of her meatballs and threw them into the big gray pot to simmer. She walked over to see what we were laughing about, and she laughed too.

A little while later, Tony got up to get a drink from the refrigerator. As he passed the stove, his flannel shirt caught onto the pot handle and yanked the entire pot of simmering meatballs and gravy down to the floor.

"Tony!" my mother yelled, as she sprang into action. Tony. The son she'd seen through infancy with colic, the preteen years with pleurisy, the teen years with colitis, ileitis, and assorted other -itises. The child that she and my father had to race off to the hospital one early April morning, when they feared his appendix was about to burst and he was in mortal danger. Tony needed her, and quicker than Lindsay Wagner in *The Bionic Woman*, my mother jumped into the path of that oncoming train with no thought of the consequences.

A tsunami of spaghetti sauce splattered everywhere as Joey, Paul, and Chris leaped from the kitchen and ran for the living room. Since I was sitting between the kitchen table and

173

the sink, I was trapped. As the floor turned into a sea of lava-like goo, I hoisted myself onto the kitchen table to save my one and only pair of white Keds.

My mother feared that the pot handle had adhered to Tony's skin and burned him, so she leaped across the room to pull it off him. She landed with her legs akimbo, her backside straight down into the crimson tide. Tony wasn't burned, but my mother sure was. My father raced her into the bathroom, where she had to sit down in a tub filled with ice-cold water to alleviate the pain.

By the time the screaming died down, the laughter began. Our dogs, Goldie and Henry, made themselves sick eating as many meatballs as they could before being banished to the yard.

When my mother emerged from the bathroom, she checked Tony over for burns while Jude got to clean the kitchen.

Even Jude had to laugh.

Recipe: Sarita's Homemade Gravy
(Spaghetti Sauce, for the Un-Italian)

My mom's sauce was always so delicious! I've tried for years to recreate it, and thanks to my cousin Angela, I finally realized the one ingredient I was missing: fennel!

Olive oil spray

Enough olive oil to coat the pan (drain off any fat from the meat)

4 cloves garlic, crushed and chopped

1 can (28 ounces) crushed tomatoes

1 can (6 ounces) tomato paste

1 can (14.5 ounces) stewed tomatoes with onions, celery,

    and green peppers

½ cup water

¼ cup sugar

1 tsp. fennel seeds (optional)

Dash of Italian seasoning

Salt and pepper to taste

4 bay leaves

1½ pounds chopped sirloin (optional)

Spray pan with nonstick spray; add light coating of olive oil and heat. Cook garlic until golden. Add all tomato products and water. Add sugar and stir. Add all seasonings. Let simmer for one hour (at least—the longer you let this cook, the better). After one hour, taste the sauce and adjust the seasonings.

Brown chopped meat. When meat is cooked, drain off excess fat; then add to sauce. Allow meat and sauce to simmer together for at least another hour.

Yield: 4 cups

You can also add meatballs to the mix.

1 pound chopped meat

2 cups Italian bread crumbs

salt and pepper to taste

1 tablespoon Worcestershire sauce

1 egg

¼ cup milk

¼ cup water

Mix ingredients together, roll into balls, and fry in another pan that's been coated with olive oil. When fully browned, toss into the meat sauce and let everything simmer together. For added flavor, buy freshly made pasta from your supermarket or make your own.

Yield: About 12 meatballs

Chapter 18:
Dining and Driving Adventures

The best part of having so many brothers was sitting across from them at the table. Each night at 5 pm, our mother served dinner for us kids, and every one of us was expected to be there. As the youngest and the oldest, Jude and Chris had assigned seats, but the rest of us were on our own. Tony, Louie, Paul, Joey, and I would tear into the kitchen, desperate to fit at the cramped little table.

Since my father didn't usually eat with us on weeknights and our mother waited to eat until he got home, dinner was usually a free-for-all. Mom would put dinner in the middle of the table and we'd dig in. The older brothers would help us younger ones serve ourselves the meat, vegetables, bread, and drinks.

Usually, my older brothers were very helpful. But some

nights, their patience would be severely limited. One night in particular, as I lunged across the table for a biscuit, Jude plunged his fork into my hand.

"Ouch!" I yelled, as I pulled the fork out of my hand. "What did you do that for?"

"It's time you learned some manners," Jude said, in his haughtiest older-brother voice.

"That's right, Jude," Mom replied. "Why don't you teach her manners right after you teach her how to survive a knife fight?"

My mother and Jude were forever locked in battle. In many ways, my mother was Czar Nicholas to Jude's Rasputin; revolution was always just around the corner.

Mostly, dinner was a noisy, raucous, and fun time. Every one spoke over every one else. We laughed, we argued, we spilled drinks, dropped forks, and shared jokes. On some nights, when dinner conflicted with the airing of a really great show on *The 4:30 Movie*, we would abandon the kitchen to eat at the dining room table and swing the television around so we could watch it.

We chewed on lasagna and Italian bread as we watched *The Great Escape*. We hoped that this time, oh maybe this time, the prisoners of war would make it out at last. I secretly swooned over James Garner while Jude and Louie admired Steve McQueen's superior motorcycle skills. I cursed Donald Pleasance for his blindness; James Garner would have been skiing in Switzerland instead of recaptured by the Nazis if it weren't for him. Tony would yell "The tunnel is too short!" as if

The Lagalante Kids
Left to right:
Back Row:
Tony, Louie, Jude, Joey
Center Row:
Maria & Chris
Seated: Paul

Nonnie and the kids
Left to right:
Back Row:
Joey, Nonnie, Tony, Jude, Paul, Lou
Front Row: Maria, Chris

Goldie and Henry,
best friends to all.

Glamour shot of Mom

Big sister
Nellie, middle
child Mom,
and baby
brother, Nick.

Grandpa,
Nonnie, Uncle
Don, Junior
(Lou). Easter
Sunday,
early 1940s.

Grandpa (Mom's father). Best
balloon-volleyball player ever.

Nonnie and
Grandpa, 1920s
Coney Island

Family Get Together:
Standing: Auntie Ann
Seated, Left to Right: Cousin
Dominic, Lou Sr., Lena,
Grandpa's sister Tessie,
Tessie's husband Tony,
Lena's sister Tessie, her
husband Nick, Lena's niece
Mary and her husband Pete.

Uncle Sal

Uncle Don

Mom and Dad

The Honeymooners

Macy's Herald Square:
Mom, Dad, Maria and Santa

Mom and Maria. Photo shoot
at Gertz Department Store.

Dad's High School Yearbook Photo

*Mom's High School
Yearbook Photo*

*Uncle Don's High School
Yearbook Photo*

Mr. Reines and Maria

All the Young Dudes:
Left to Right:
Mike, Gerry, Jude
Seated: Gary G.

Prom Night!
Left to right: Frank, Denise, Chris, Lisa, Tommy, Maria

Joey sings at Maria's wedding; Jude, Chris, Louie, Paul, and Tony on backup

Nonnie (Mom's mother), Maria, Mom   *Chris and Maria*

Early parenthood for Joe, Tony & Lou

Maria & Mom

Mom

Tony and Kathie

Nonnie and Maria

The Lagalantes welcome Gary to the fold

Uncle Don & Maria

Standing, left to right: Dad, Mom, Uncle Nick, Uncle Don, Aunt Nellie, Uncle John
Seated: Uncle Sal, Aunt Tessie, Nonnie, Mary, Pete

Gary's and Maria's Wedding Day

The Schulz Family
Standing: Paige & Maddie
Seated: Maria & Gary

Mom and Dad dancing at Maria's wedding

The Next Generation
Left to Right: Back Row:
Dan, Sara, Louie, Melissa, Tom, Gina, Joe Jr.
Front Row: Paige, Maddie, Kate

Seven Siblings all in a row:
Left to right: Joe, Jude, Tony, Maria, Lou, Chris, Paul

they could hear him and he could save them from their grave disappointment, or "Why doesn't everyone just ride a bike like James Coburn?"

My brothers and I wolfed down burgers and fries while we watched Chicken Charlie and his wife jump the broom in *Roots*. We discussed deep philosophical ideas, like "Do you think Kizzie really spit in the water that Sandy Duncan drank?" We also wondered, did they have to kill off James in *Good Times* so that he could play the mature, half-footed Kunta Kinte? How many days would it take to watch this miniseries (which I thought was pronounced "minisery") when you could only see it in 1½-hour increments, and most of that time was taken up by commercials—so you were really only seeing about forty minutes each day?

We also discussed the pointlessness of horror movies like *The Blob*. Really, how terrifying was a big, messy blob of goo that couldn't run and could easily be avoided if you just walked around it? If Steve McQueen was such a great motorcycle rider, why didn't he just pop a wheelie over it and ride away?

Yes, these were the great existential thoughts that we pondered as my mother heaped steaming mounds of food on our plates. Dinner's end would coincide with the end of the movie, and Tony would command us all to "clean, clean, clean!" before we could scatter to the four corners of the universe.

It was the best of times; it was the worst of times. This

would sum up all those years when I was growing up with my brothers. Seven very different personalities in one tiny house, with a father who made Joseph Stalin seem like a softie and a mother who could teach Santa Claus a thing or two about benevolence, made life interesting, to say the least.

But no matter what, I always knew that my parents and brothers had their hearts in the right places, even if the facts seemed to contradict that idea.

Take, for instance, St. Patrick's Day. My mother decided to treat us to corned beef and cabbage, with boiled potatoes and biscuits. She cooked, she slaved, and when it was all done, we held up our plates in eager anticipation. Mom served everyone and then got to me. As I held my plate out to her, she ladled the meat onto my plate—and dropped steaming hot grease onto my hand.

I screamed as the hot liquid bit into my flesh. For a moment, my mother looked around, as if one of my brothers had done something to me. Then she dropped the platter of meat and whisked me off to the bathroom.

"Hold your hand under the cold water," she said, as my finger and hand proceeded to morph into one big, angry-looking blister.

I knew that my mother didn't do this to me on purpose. It was an accident, and nobody felt worse about it than my mother. She was inconsolable every time she looked at my hand.

A few days later, as I sat at the table with my hand wrapped in gauze, my mother smiled at me. "I have a surprise for you!" she said.

For dessert, my mother brought out a cherry cheesecake that she had obviously slaved over for hours.

"Uggh," Jude said. "I hate cheesecake!"

"I'd rather have brownies," Tony said.

"I can't eat that," Chris blurted.

Louie and Joey seconded that emotion.

Even Paul shook his head. "Cheesecake's not really my thing."

My mother frowned. "I didn't really make it for you guys anyway. Here, Maria, have a slice."

I kept my hands away from the table as she served me, just in case.

Up to that point, I had never had cheesecake and I had no great desire to have any that night. But my mother was clearly trying to do something nice for me, so I smiled and dug in. When it was clear that no one but me was going to eat that cheesecake—my brothers had long since abandoned me at the table—I looked at Mom. She was so disappointed that no one wanted any.

"Have some more," she said, as she placed another huge slice on my plate.

I didn't want any more, but she looked happier when I ate it, so I smiled and had another slice.

When Dad came home later, she gave him a slice and implored me to have another. "You like it so much!"

I didn't have the heart to tell her that no, I really didn't like it. The cherries tasted weird and my taste buds were more attuned to the joys of Twinkies than cheesecake. But she had worked so hard and she was clearly pleased by the fact that I was enjoying it.

"Thanks, Mom," I said, smiling. Just a few more bites, and I'd be done...

The next morning, I woke with a start. My father was hovering over me, staring at me like he had just spotted the bearded lady at the circus.

He whistled. "Whooooo," he said, like an amazed owl.

"What?" I said, through lips that felt oddly misshaped. I lifted my unburned hand to my face and touched my mouth. My lips felt about a hundred times bigger than I remembered them being; my eyes felt like tiny slits.

"Nothing," my father said, as he walked to his room to summon my mother. "Just don't look in the mirror."

With those words ringing in my ears, I shot out of bed and lunged for my mirror. There I was, in all my misshapen glory. My head looked like someone had come into my room in the middle of the night with an air pump and blown me up bigger than a Macy's Thanksgiving Day Parade balloon. Kermit and Snoopy had nothing on me! My entire face was red and blotchy, my eyes were almost completely shut, and my lips could hardly open.

My mother came into the room and leaped back when she saw me.

"Do you think she has the German measles?" my father said.

"I don't know," my mother replied. "But I think we have to go see Dr. S."

So off we went to see Dr. Smith. Mom would shepherd whoever was sick off to see him, and we'd sit in big, overstuffed red leatherette chairs and couches in his office waiting room, watching the other patients and hoping Dr. S. would get to us eventually. You'd make a mental note of who was there when you arrived, and then when it was finally your turn, you'd stand up triumphantly when Dr. S. came out of the examining room and said, "Who's next?"

So that day, after we lunged to our feet like the happy contestants who get told to "Come on down" on *The Price Is Right*, my mother and I followed Dr. Smith to his examining room and I climbed up on the table.

Dr. S. looked a bit frightened when he looked closely at me. "What the heck happened to you?"

That's what I'd like to know, I wanted to say, but I didn't want to anger my curmudgeonly, needle-owning doctor. "I woke up like this," I said through my now huge lips.

"We thought maybe she has German measles," my mother explained.

Dr. S. nodded. "What color is your mucus?"

No matter what was troubling you, Dr. S. would inevitably say, "What color is your mucus?" It didn't matter if you were there with a sprained knee, flea bites, or a ruptured aorta. Apparently, the color of your mucus was the key to deciphering any and every medical mystery.

I shrugged. I hadn't made a mental note of my mucus that day, which was a shame, since I knew it would be the first question he asked me and I liked to get the answers to things right. "Um, white? Yellow? Green?" I said, searching for the answer that he wanted.

He stuck his ice-cold stethoscope on my chest and tried to open my eyes with his pudgy fingers. "What did she eat last night? Anything new?"

My mother shifted uncomfortably. "Well, I did make her a cherry cheesecake."

He had his "aha!" moment. "That's it! Were they maraschino cherries?" Dr. S. asked.

"Yes," my mother replied.

"She's having a severe allergic reaction," he said. He handed her a packet of Benadryl. "There's water right here. She needs to take one of these now, before her tongue swells up and she chokes to death."

My mother, clearly shaken, raced to give me a paper cup with water and shove that pill down my throat. Once it was down, she held up my hand and asked Dr. S. to look at it. "I was serving her corned beef and cabbage, and I ladled some grease on her hand," my mother explained.

The doctor gave her a withering look. "What are you doing to this poor child?" he exclaimed.

My mother was on the verge of tears. "I was trying to do something nice!" she blurted.

Dr. S. patted her on the shoulder. "Oh, well, no sense getting crazy over it."

He looked at my hand, changed the dressing, and handed my mother some ointment. "Make sure you change this dressing a few times a day and keep reapplying this ointment. She's going to have a nasty scar. And please, no more maraschino cherries," he said, as if this was something that any moron should've known, even before yesterday.

"Okay," my mother sniffled. "When can she go back to school?"

"Oh, forget it!" Dr. S. exclaimed. "The swelling will subside, but those blotchy red marks may be there for a while. I doubt they'll let her back in until those clear up, because they'll think she *does* have the German measles. I'd say she'll be home with you for a while."

My mother was clearly not pleased, but I couldn't have been happier if he'd told me I'd just won The Showcase Showdown from *The Price Is Right*—and it included two brand-new cars, a trip to Paris, and a boatload of cash!

I may have looked like the Elephant Man, but I didn't mind. For two solid weeks, I got to sleep late and then relax in my pajamas while my brothers pulled on their Catholic school uniforms and got ready for school. I blew them kisses from my enormous lips and waved from the window while they scowled at me.

For days on end, those red blotches were my ticket to some serious Mommy & Me time. Since it was early spring, Mom took me to Kissena Park and we fed the ducks almost every day. We went shopping with my grandmother on Main Street in Flushing. We cooked dinner together and Mom told me stories about her dating days and how she and my dad met. My mom showered me with gifts; paper dolls, craft kits, and Dawn dolls littered my dresser as Chris looked on jealously.

"I should've had some cheesecake!" he wailed.

At the end of the two weeks, my mother had an even bigger surprise in store for us.

"Tonight you're going to the circus with Father O'Leary!" she said.

Father O'Leary was a priest that had befriended my parents. With a shock of white hair and an Irish brogue that was thicker than the yellow pages, the good Father seemed like a fun and playful figure in our lives, and our parents were happy to have him take us places like a devoted uncle.

About this time, it was starting to dawn on me that Father O'Leary was more like a funny uncle than a devoted one. I had plenty of uncles, and while most of them didn't mind taking us here or there, to the dairy to get milk for their coffee or to the candy store for their cigarettes, none of them begged my parents to let them take us places for more than ten minutes at a time. But Father O'Leary acted as though the idea of spending countless hours with young, bickering children was the answer to his prayers.

For some reason, Father O'Leary was the only person that our two dogs, Goldie and Henry, despised. When he walked through the door, the dogs would swing into action. Every hair on Goldie's long head would stand on end; Henry's normally placid demeanor would change and he'd become Cujo on a bad day. Both dogs would lunge at him and try to place themselves between him and us kids. My parents thought this was funny; I began to believe that the dogs were the only ones with brains in that house.

Recently, Father O'Leary's jaunts with us had been becoming increasingly bizarre. One Palm Sunday, he came over and asked our parents if he could take Joey, Paul, Chris, and me to Coney Island to have fun at the amusement park. My parents said sure!

So off we went to Coney Island, where everyone but us was having fun. Father O'Leary nursed a beer while his face grew darker and darker. He made us stand there and watch the other children playing games and shrieking with delight on the rides.

"Are we going on the rides?" Chris asked.

"Whaddya think, I'm made o' money?" Father O'Leary growled.

We stood there for another hour until he threw his cup away. "I'll be taking you home now."

The winter before, he piled the four of us, plus four other young kids, into his Grand Le Mans sedan and took us to a rectory in Westchester. We were supposed to go sleigh riding, but once we were there, he couldn't find any sleighs. This filled Father O'Leary with incredulity; I mean, doesn't every rectory keep sleighs in case he decides to bring a carload of children over for a day of sleigh riding?

The eight of us kids ran up and down the hills, throwing snowballs at each other and making snowmen while Father O'Leary stood there, looking annoyed.

"I'm hungry," Chris said.

"Don't you worry," Father O'Leary said, about three hours into our little odyssey. "We'll be getting pizza in a bit!"

Hours later, as darkness filled the sky, Father O'Leary put the eight of us in his car and started driving around the neighborhood, in search of a pizzeria. We were cold, tired, and soaked.

"Do you think he'll let us go in and eat at the pizza place?" I whispered to Chris.

"Whaddya think, I'm made o' money?" Chris said in his best Father O'Leary voice. I stifled a laugh.

Father O'Leary did find a pizzeria, but when we got there, he left us in the car and ran inside. He emerged ten minutes later with one pizza for the nine of us.

"Are we going to eat here?" Paul said.

"Now don't you worry," Father O'Leary replied. "I've got friends nearby."

We drove about five more miles to a tiny house on the side of the road. As all eight of us kids stumbled from the car, we rang the bell, unsure of who we were going to meet.

"Father O'Leary?" our reluctant hostess said as she

pushed the door open just a crack. Her husband and children sat at the kitchen table, eating dinner.

"Helllooooooo!" Father O'Leary yelled, as he pushed his way past the woman. "You won't be minding if we use your dining room table for dinner, now, will ya?" he said, as he cleared some papers away and dumped us at the table.

"Uh, no, sure," the lady stammered.

Chris and I giggled nervously as the children who lived there watched us eat. When the pie was done, Father O'Leary jumped up from the table and waved.

"Thanks!" he yelled, as we marched out of the living room and back into the car.

So, as thrilling as going to the circus may have been, going anywhere with Father O'Leary had the potential for disaster written all over it. It wasn't really my parents' fault that we kept going places with Father O'Leary; we were so young that we didn't understand how bizarre his behavior was or that he was slightly dangerous, especially after downing a few beers. We never told our parents what was going on because I, for one, thought it was perfectly clear that Father O'Leary was insane. Even Goldie and Henry knew it!

"He never lets us get anything," I warned my mother.

"Oh, don't worry," Mom replied. "I'll give him enough money so you can get something to eat and maybe some small souvenirs. Dad has to work tonight and I can't go. Trust me, you'll have fun!"

I was stir crazy and sick of sitting in the house every night. The daily excursions had been great, but I was tired of not being around other people. I didn't need much convincing to go to the circus, even if it was with Father O'Leary.

That night, as Father O'Leary drank his beers and refused to buy us one single thing, Chris, Paul, and I somehow managed to enjoy the show. There were the amazing acrobats, the roaring lions, and the silly clowns who pretended to fall from the high wire. Paul would point to one ring; Chris would point to another. Meanwhile, I tried to watch all three rings, as well as Father O'Leary, from the corner of my eye. Later that night, Chris defended me as little girls pointed at me and whispered.

"Her blotches will go away, but you'll always be ugly!" he said to one redhead.

We left Madison Square Garden and made the trek home. We just needed to make it back to Queens without any incidents for the night to be a complete success…

And that's when Father O'Leary did the worst thing possible. He asked Paul for directions.

"How d'ya get to yer house from here?" he said.

Paul got confused since we were going east on the Long Island Expressway; we usually came from the west. "You need to get off at the next exit," Paul said.

"No, Paul," I said, as I turned around to face him in the backseat of the car. I'd somehow gotten the dubious honor of riding shotgun. "You need to get off at this exit because there's construction on the next one. It's closed."

"No, Maria, you're wrong."

"No, Paul, she's right," Chris chimed in.

"WHYDDYA ALL JUST SHUDDUP?" Father O'Leary exploded. "Paul is the oldest—I'm sure he knows a thing or two about directions. Certainly more than the likes of you."

I looked at Chris in the side-view mirror; he stuck his tongue out at me and nodded ominously. I could feel the laughter bubbling up. "Okay," I said, as I fought off the urge to put my head down and laugh until I cried.

About twenty minutes later, when Father O'Leary realized that he'd shot past Bayside and we were now in Douglaston, he started cursing and pounding the steering wheel. Of course, this set Chris and me off on an explosive bout of laughter. Father O'Leary responded as befitted his station as a drunken, psychotic man of the cloth: he slammed on the brakes so hard that I went flying forward and banged into the dashboard.

"Now get out!" he roared at me.

I looked at him in horror. There was no way on earth I was going to step one foot out of that car door. It was 11 pm and pitch-black out there; I couldn't walk home from Douglaston if I tried.

"No!" I yelled, as I tried to hurl myself over the bench seat and into the safety of the backseat, where my frightened brothers were watching the scene unfold.

In a blinding series of moves, Father O'Leary grabbed me

by the collar, unlocked my door, hurled me out to the side of the road with a swift kick in the rear, and started screaming at Paul, "Now get up front and help me find the way home!"

I rushed to get back into the car—since being abandoned there seemed all too likely—and I crunched down as far as I could in the backseat beside Chris. We were shaking with laughter and quite sure that if Father O'Leary heard us, he'd kill us, while Paul gave him directions that drove him further and further away from our house.

When we got home an hour later, our mother greeted us brightly. "Where were you guys? I was starting to get worried. Did you have fun?" she said.

Chris, Paul, and I burst out laughing.

"SHUDDUP!" Chris responded, in his best Father O'Leary impersonation.

Recipe: Corned Beef and Cabbage (no burns required)

Remarkably, I like Corned Beef and Cabbage. I cook it every year on St. Patrick's Day and really look forward to it. I make sure to wear baker's mitts and I never have cherry cheesecake afterwards.

1 medium onion, cut into wedges

4 medium new potatoes, quartered

1 pound baby carrots

3 cups water

3 garlic cloves, minced

1 bay leaf

½ teaspoon pepper

1 (3-pound) corned beef brisket with spice packet

1 small head cabbage, cut into wedges

Place the onion, potatoes, and carrots in a 5-quart pot. Combine water, garlic, bay leaf, pepper, and contents of spice packet; pour over vegetables. Top with brisket and cabbage. Cover and cook on low for 2–3 hours or until meat and vegetables are tender. Remove bay leaf before serving.

Serves 4.

Chapter 19: Walking with My Father

When the days began to get longer and sunlight promised more hours of fun, my father liked to go walking after dinner. Some nights, he would go alone; some nights, he'd ask my mother to join him. Then, some nights, he'd ask me.

"Re-re," my father said. "Want to go for a walk?"

"Yes!" I said, jumping up quicker than either of our dogs ever could.

Walks with my father were special. Mostly, they were great fun because I rarely got one-on-one time in our household. But on a sultry summer's night, my father would take my hand in his, and he'd be mine and mine alone.

Once, when Chris and I were about four years old, my father took us both out for a walk. Dad thought it would be fun to ask us some questions.

"So," Dad said. "Who do you love more—your mother or me?"

I was horrified. I did not like having to choose between the two people I loved most in the whole world. As I stood there, panicked, Chris smiled the smile of someone without a care in the world.

"Mom," he replied.

My father laughed, and he didn't ask us that question anymore.

But a few short years later, my father and I would take a walk without Chris or my mother coming along. We'd stroll through the streets of Bayside Hills, peering into windows just starting to light up as shadows engulfed the dimming sunlight. My father and I would make up stories about the people inside, about how many children lived there, the pets they might have, and what color the rooms were painted.

Sometimes, we'd peer into the windows of a house whose occupants I really knew, and then the truth would be more amusing than the made-up stories. I'd tell my father about the creepy bullies, the nasty popular kids, or the shrinking violets that lived behind the curtained windows, and he'd laugh.

"Why don't you tell me what you really think?" he'd say.

But that was just it. On those long walks with my father, I could be whoever I really was and I knew it would be okay. That's what life was supposed to be like with your parents.

Once the lights shone through the windows and the sun sank into the night sky, my father would turn me toward Mecca.

No, not the spiritual city of Mecca. Not even home. My Mecca was Joe's Pizzeria, dubbed "Joe's Sleazeria" by us neighborhood kids. Joe's pizza had enough grease in it to keep the gears on a Long Island Rail Road train running smoothly. But it wasn't the pizza I was interested in, and my father knew it. It was the Italian ices.

Now here was my dilemma: do I choose cherry, the forbidden fruit of my allergic youth, or lemon? The red dye 40 in the cherry ices was enough to turn me into a giant cherry. If my mother was along, she would never let me get cherry. But my father believed you had to take your chances and live with your choices.

"You'll be the one with the hives," he'd say, as I slurped away.

But then, what if I longed for lemon? The sweet and tart sting of a lemon ice was perfect on a hot summer's night.

The lemon and cherry ices called to me, each with its own particular siren song. What to do? How to choose?

"Get rainbow," my father said, as he handed me an enormous rainbow ice.

Red, white, and blue! Cherry, lemon, and blueberry too. My father knew everything and could solve every problem. Once he opened the door to rainbow ices, I never looked back.

Why choose when you could have it both ways?

Sometimes, our walks would take us to Alley Pond Park. My father's family had gone there for summer barbecues many years before, and my dad liked to walk through the woods, looking at the birds, squirrels, and rabbits that darted past us. Nestled on the eastern edge of Queens, this huge park was ringed by towering oaks, steep hills, and ponds across miles and miles of woods.

We'd go out early on a Saturday or Sunday morning for a brisk walk in the winter or an early morning stroll before the sun got too high on summer mornings. The prize for heading out so early was breakfast at the International House of Pancakes, for a pancake sandwich (three pancakes, two eggs sunny-side up, bacon and sausage, with lots of maple syrup) and a big steaming cup of hot chocolate with whipped cream on top.

My brothers and I would have liked to have ordered orange juice with our breakfasts, but my father had imposed a prohibition on OJ many years ago. It dated back to 1955, when his then-girlfriend—my mother—had the audacity to order orange juice for an extra fifty cents. My father would try to get my mother to have coffee or tea since it was included in the price, but my mother would politely decline as she sipped her Mercedes-Benz of morning beverages.

This transgression on my mother's part had kept us all from ever enjoying orange juice if it wasn't included in the price of the breakfast special. My father was the only person I ever met who let his six-year-old child drink coffee because it was included in the price of breakfast.

So with breakfast as our ultimate goal, we'd walk long and far. One time, my father, mother, and I scaled a hill whose vertical drop rivaled that of Mount Everest. Climbing up was hard, but doable, because pushing my weight forward seemed to stop me from falling. But when it was time to head back down, my father had a bright idea.

"I think we can climb back down. Don't you?"

My mother, who had wisely run for the stairs hewn out of the mountainous rock, shook her head violently. "Louie, this isn't a great idea."

But I was so thrilled that my father thought that I could accomplish this feat that I rushed ahead to beat him down the hill. With six brothers, I was always the one chosen last for softball and football, and no one thought I could do much of anything when it came to sports. My mother spent most of my childhood fearing that I would be killed or would kill myself, since I always tried to keep up with stronger, faster, more capable people.

So, I figured, if I could do this, my father would see what an incredible athlete I was. Of course, there was this little thing called gravity that I had to contend with, but I was quite certain that I could defy it, if I just tried really, really hard.

"Sure!" I replied.

So while my mother yelled to us to stop, my father and I ignored the voice of reason and began to trot down the cliff. At first, it wasn't too hard to keep my footing steady. But I began to realize that I was moving slightly faster than the Road Runner with Wile E. Coyote hot on his heels.

My dad kept saying "Steady now. Steady," as if this could slow me down. Instead, I continued to gallop at neck-breaking speeds down the side of Mount Alley Pond Park. Then I tripped on a stick and did the unthinkable: I began to fly.

I'd gained so much momentum careening down the hill that by the time I tripped over that stick, I was able to launch myself off a nearby rock and go soaring through the air with the greatest of ease. The problem was there was no daring young man with the flying trapeze waiting to scoop me up at the end. There was just hard, solid ground.

As my body plummeted back to earth and my ribs and spine became conjoined, my head smashed into the ground with a solid THUNK that I'm sure some rabbits and squirrels still laugh about to this day.

I could hear the sound of my mother's consoling voice, shrieking from the top of the hill, "SHE'S DEAD! SHE'S DEAD!"—along with my father's encouraging "We're coming, Re-re! Hold on!"

As if I was going anywhere.

I lay in a heap on the ground, hearing my mother's frantic cries coupled with my father's cheery voice, and I tried to lift myself up so that they wouldn't worry. But falling from the sky and getting intimate with gravity had taken its toll on me. I decided to just lie there and wait for them to reach my side.

When my parents finally reached the valley floor, my father rolled me over and slapped my face. I tried to push his hand away.

"See?" my father said to my mother. "She's not dead."

"Maria," my mother said, "speak to me."

I grunted and sat up. "Can I have orange juice with my breakfast today?"

My father grunted back. "I suppose," he said, as he dusted me off. "Just this once."

Twenty-five years later, when I shared that memory with my father, his only reply to me was "I think if we went back there, we could get down that hill."

"Sure, Dad," I replied. "I've always wanted to wear a body cast."

I suppose the farthest I've ever walked with my father in order to get a treat was the three miles we walked from our house in Bayside Hills to Korvette's Department Store in Douglaston. The buses were on strike, and the recent high prices of gasoline made my father think that a three-mile walk to buy back-to-school supplies was the perfect prelude to a root beer float and a Yankees–Red Sox baseball game.

The year was 1978, and every game that season held a special significance to me. I had watched Ron Guidry strike out eighteen batters. I'd watched him win most of the twenty-plus games he'd pitched that year, pulling his listless team from certain extinction to the role of David to Boston's mighty Goliath. I wasn't sure if the Yankees could pull it off. But I didn't want to miss a single inning of it now that September was here.

There was a game on that night, and my father had bought vanilla ice cream and A&W root beer for that "frosty mug taste." We were going to settle in and enjoy a night of baseball and ice cream…until I realized that I still needed to buy a school bag.

"It's early yet," my father said to my mother. "Let's walk to Korvette's."

"Korvette's!" my mother said. "It's three miles away. You want to walk?"

"Sure! It's nice out. We'll have ice cream when we get back."

So, since it was my school bag we had to buy, we set out. Like the pioneers before us, we had high hopes for the journey and never dreamed that our destination could be so far away.

Getting there wasn't too bad. Whenever we drove there in our car, it took ten minutes—tops—to get there. But I'd never realized how many hills there were in Bayside Hills, how long the side streets seemed, or how hot and sticky your mouth could get when you were too far from home to turn around and too far from the beaten path to buy a soda. That frosty mug taste had better be worth it, I muttered to myself, as my parents and I trudged on. Still, we enjoyed the walk. Finally, we ambled down the enormous hill that separated Bayside from Douglaston, gaining a bit of speed with our descent. Korvette's was just around the corner, and when we got there, my father and mother bought up all the supplies they could carry for all of us.

The problem was…we had to carry them home. Up that gigantic hill we climbed, loaded down with notebooks, folders, pencils, pens, and schoolbags. My father had the bright idea of buying an electric pencil sharpener. It seemed like we needed one, before I started climbing the hill from hell.

"Just a few more miles," my father said, as we huffed and puffed up that hill, loaded down like the jackasses we were.

My mother wiped her sweaty brow. "We should've driven," she said.

"You should've said that *before*," my father snapped back.

When we got to the top of the hill, I leaned against the overpass railing and looked down on the Long Island Expressway below us. Cars sped by, and I imagined that not one of them would be missing the first pitch of tonight's game. But as twilight descended and Korvette's shone below us like a wad of aluminum foil under a heat lamp, I faltered. With only 2.7 miles to go and the big hill behind us, I sat down on my new book bag and shook my head.

"What?" my father said. "We're almost home! Don't quit now. The Yankees are on in half an hour."

I got up, cradled that overstuffed bag in my arms, and continued to trudge along. I was hot. I was hungry. I was thirsty. I was mad. Suddenly, I understood what my sixth-grade teacher had meant when he described what turned the Donner Party into cannibalistic death marchers. Only the promise of baseball, ice cream, and the total annihilation of the Boston Red Sox kept me going.

It took us three hours from start to finish. We left the house at 5:30 and made it home by about 8:45. I'd missed an inning or two, but when my parents and I unloaded our cargo and sat down for our ice cream, I smiled.

I had been to hell and back. And now, as I watched Ron Guidry pitch and drank my root beer float, I knew what heaven must taste like.

Recipe: Louie's To-Die-For Root Beer Float

When you're walking six or seven miles and carrying enough packages to load down a donkey, this is one treat you can allow yourself! It's a fun treat on a hot summer night, perfect when watching a baseball game.

½ gallon vanilla bean ice cream

2-liter bottle root beer

Put 4 beer glasses in the freezer to frost for at least an hour. Fill the frosted glasses with root beer. Add two scoops of vanilla ice cream to each glass, and *voilà!* You've got yourself a frosty mug of sheer delight.

Serves 4.

Chapter 20: Holidays with the Relatives

When I was growing up, I didn't worry about cholesterol, dieting, or how fat I was getting. That's probably because I was usually running after my brothers, trying to seem athletic, or walking miles and miles, trying to impress my father.

In an Italian household, you don't serve diet cookies, diet soda, and fresh fruit at a party. Oh, maybe there's a small section on the table where you can find that stuff, but it's only meant for your ninety-year-old, diabetic grandmother (the one most Italians call Nonna).

If you're standing by that table, nibbling on a dietetic cookie and nursing a diet Coke, someone is going to make fun of you. Or they are going to harass you until you eat three cannoli, a cup of gelato, and ten or twelve zeppole.

These parties from my childhood resembled Roman eating orgies, without the vomitoriums. We believed in eating, laughing, and then eating some more. If my grandmother or aunts thought you were going outside to throw up, they'd have pinned you down to the table and force-fed you. I can hear it now: "Maria, you don't eat? After all my hard work? Whatsamaddawidyou?"

My Aunt Tessie's eightieth birthday party was one of those times. I remember climbing down her basement stairs into an enormous, wood-paneled room, where table upon table was loaded down with trays and trays of food.

My grandfather's sister, Tessie, may have been only five feet tall, but she held herself tall and straight and seemed queenly in her deportment. Her hair was always perfect, her clothes were tailored and classy, and her home was beautifully appointed with all the most modern appliances. Aunt Tessie was the closest thing my family had to royalty, and when she summoned you to the ball, you came...with or without the help of your fairy godmother.

It didn't matter that it was Aunt Tessie's eightieth birthday. Aunt Tessie could cook, and she knew it, so she cooked most of that food on those tables. Homemade manicotti, meatballs the size of your head, sausage and peppers, prosciutto- and mozzarella-stuffed calzone, and lasagna trays perched atop Sternos, bubbling to perfection.

The next table had twelve different types of bread, all of them crusty and hot from the oven. The table after that held desserts: Italian pastries, rainbow cookies, chocolate-fudge seven-layer cakes, biscotti, cannoli, and zeppole that were puffy, light, and coated with just the right amount of powdered sugar. Grapes, figs, melons, apple slices, peaches, and cherries were on the table with the coffee, espresso, and hot water urns.

Perry Como, Dean Martin, and Frank Sinatra blasted from the stereo speakers while shouts of dirty jokes mixed in with peals of laughter. Donna Summer's "Last Dance" was snuck in on the turntable when our Bronx disco-loving relatives thought that their rock-'n'-roll-loving cousins couldn't stop them. Well, we couldn't stop them, but my older relatives could: they broke out even older records and started singing "Funiculì Funiculà" and dancing the tarantella.

Aunt Tessie's family made my family seem quiet and reserved. They could out-eat, out-drink, and out-dance us any day of the week, and that was saying something. When my cousins talked, it always sounded like they were fighting. It didn't matter what the topic was. It could be as innocent as this:

"Hey, Louie!" cousin Sammy said, loud enough for the neighbors three blocks away to hear. "How come you keeping this pretty little girl all to yourself?"

Now, Sammy was about six decades older than me, and I was only twelve at the time, but Sammy felt it was never too soon to flirt with a girl—even if that girl was still playing with dolls and just happened to share a family connection.

"Sammy," my father replied. By comparison, he sounded quiet. "If you're looking for a child to play with, go find your wife."

Everyone roared with laughter, slapped backs, and drank

another round of anisette. Sammy faded into the background, and another roughish relative stepped up.

"Say, Louie," cousin Domenico said. "Introduce me to your little girl."

My father introduced me to Domenico, who looked just like my now long-departed grandfather and, by extension, my dad.

"Say," Domenico said to me, in that shout that my family mistakes for a whisper voice, "why would you want to go home with this guy when you could come home with me? Wouldn't I make a better father?"

"Nah," I replied. "My father's better looking."

Everyone laughed and ate some more. Cousin Dominic told his usual tale of catching a fifty-foot-long great white shark, which had become his favorite story since *Jaws* was released. Aunt Tessie kept coming down the stairs with more food; my grandmother, Lena, kept cheating by eating "just one cannoli" when she should have been eating those dietetic cookies; and cousin GiGi (pronounced GeeGee, and short for Luigi) explained why another set of cousins, brothers Dominic and Nicholas, were both known as Nicky.

When we finally rolled out of Aunt Tessie's house, our sides ached from laughter, our ears rang from singing, and our stomachs were distended. All in all, the party was a hit!

Sometimes, our family celebrations took on a more routine flavor. My grandfather's family was bawdy and loud. My grandmother's family was...bawdy and loud, but imagined themselves not so bawdy or loud. While I was growing up, it was my grandmother's family that gave most of our holidays their distinctive flavor.

Christmas Eve for many years was spent at my cousin Eleanor's house. My twin and I would wake up early on Christmas Eve morning, shower our mother with her birthday gifts (poor Mom always had to share her special day with Jesus, who got a lot more attention), and then count the hours until we could all pile into the car and go to Franklin Square.

Eleanor and her husband, Bob, always threw the best parties. Whether it was a pool party in the summer or a Christmas Eve celebration, we knew there would be tons of food served up with a whole lot of laughter.

My grandmother was one of six children. They, in turn, had a few kids apiece, and they all seemed to show up at Eleanor's every Christmas Eve. The relatives all crowded in, bringing the total up to about thirty assorted cousins and friends rockin' around the Christmas tree.

By the time we arrived and piled out of our lime-green station wagon, loads of food were already piled on the tables. We feasted on baked ziti and lasagna, or the manicotti made famous around Corona by my grandmother. Mozzarella and tomatoes with a little olive oil, a tossed green salad, some fresh melon, and make sure you leave room for dessert.

When the goodies were finally rolled out on our version of a Viennese table, there was so much to choose from: cheesecake and profiteroles, Italian pastries and cookies, lemon meringue pie, apple pie, napoleons, angel food cake, and layer cake galore.

My family started going to Eleanor's house when I was still young enough to believe in Santa Claus. In honor of this tradition, a neighbor or friend would always drop by in a Santa suit, handing out gifts and chatting to me and any other little kids that were around. My twin, Chris, had already begun to doubt the existence of Santa by the time we were nine. So when Santa called him to his lap for a toy and a chat, Chris eyed him warily.

"Don't you think Santa would be a little too busy to come here?" Chris said to me, as I waited my turn.

"Maybe he's just being nice," I replied. I was so desperate to still believe.

But when I walked in on Santa getting changed in the downstairs den and realized that he was really my cousin Richard's friend, I was shattered. I ran to my brother Tony, who was busy playing pinball (yes, a real, live pinball machine— no wonder we loved going there!) in the downstairs game room. My other brothers were huddled around Richard's television, playing Atari, but I knew I'd find Tony right there.

"Tony," I said, near tears, "is it true? Is there no such thing as Santa Claus?"

Tony turned from the pinball machine and shrugged. I didn't know then that he was practicing for his future as a school psychologist.

"Maria," he replied, "there's always a Santa Claus if you

keep him in your heart."

I walked up the stairs and thought about what Tony had said.

So they were *lying* to me all those years!

I found my mother eating a cookie and sipping a cup of coffee.

"Ma," I said, "is it true that there's no Santa Claus?"

"I hope not," she said. "Or he won't be giving you anything this year."

I nodded. "I guess it's a good thing I still believe in him."

My mother smiled. "That's right."

Invariably, after my grandmother coaxed me to eat three platefuls of pasta, drink a gallon of soda, and eat enough Italian pastry to feed an entire village, I would get *agita*. This is the Italian term for a tummy ache. *Agita* can also be used to describe how you feel when someone is annoying you or telling you that there's always a Santa Claus if you keep him in your heart.

"Nonnie," I would say, as I steadied myself on the dining room table, "I don't feel so good."

"Poor baby," Eleanor said. "Go upstairs and lie down."

"It's because she eats too much!" my grandmother would say, not exactly diminishing my *agita* pangs.

It's been a lot of years since Santa Claus took up residence in my heart, but one thing has never changed. I have never forgotten how much fun the holidays can be when you cram a hundred people into twenty square feet.

For me, Christmas isn't just about getting presents. It's about eating, and laughing, and surrounding yourself with people who make you smile. Whether it's one person or a hundred, as long as we're eating and laughing, it's a holiday.

We would usually spend Christmas Day with my mother's family. We would wake up at 4 o'clock in the morning to open presents (we had to wait for Santa to come and go, and boy was he slow). We then had a few hours to play with our toys before heading over to my Aunt Nellie's house for a Christmas feast.

Christmas in Commack was filled with the sounds of my mother, her sister, and her brother-in-law talking in mellifluous Spanish, while my Italian father would crack them all up with his very bad Spanish. Sometimes, my mom's brother, Uncle Nick, would show up with his two kids, and my grandparents would be there too. We couldn't really make out what they were all talking about because:

1) We didn't speak Spanish

2) They were talking about people and places we didn't have the slightest interest in

3) They sat at the adult table, with my older cousins Nancy and Sue, and my older siblings, Jude, Tony, and Louie.

The rest of us (cousin Greg, my brothers Joey, Paul, and Chris, and I) sat at the kids' table in the kitchen. Years later, little John, Nancy's son, would join us at the kids' table too. We could see and hear the grownups at the adult table, but we were so busy laughing at each other's jokes that we didn't care what they were up to. In between all the yelling and the laughing, we also managed to eat. There were trays of lasagna, turkey or ham, mashed potatoes, corn on the cob, glazed carrots, baked ziti, meatballs, and salad. When dinner was finished, we'd exchange gifts with each other, then head back to the table for dessert.

When dessert was over, we went downstairs to my Aunt's basement, where my father had a surprise in store for us. Since he worked for a major motion picture company, he owned a big screen and a projector, so we would watch reel-to-reel movies like *The 101 Dalmatians* or *Cinderella.*

Of course Christmas was fun, but it was just the warm-up to New Year's Eve. My parents realized early on that they weren't going to be able to find a sitter for all seven of us on New Year's Eve, so they decided that the party would have to come to them. My mother would start cooking a couple of days before so that she had everything she needed to feed the relatives and friends who would be stopping by. There was more lasagna and baked ziti, antipasto, roasted chicken, and of course, my mother's Quiche Lorraine.

You knew it was New Year's Eve when you woke up to the smells of bacon sizzling in the kitchen. Mom put together her quiche like she was painting the Mona Lisa; it was a thing of beauty, and she took her time with it. She cooked the bacon to a crispy brown, and then she chopped it up and added it to the eggs. After that, she poured the whole mixture into her pie shell and layered shredded Swiss cheese on top. Then, she put the quiche into the oven and let it bake until it was golden brown. We knew the end result would be worth it, but it was hard waiting another twelve hours to eat something that smelled so good. When the party finally began, it seemed like a busload of relatives and friends came through the door.

Music blasted from the stereo as my grandmother and Aunt Frances did the chicken dance or showed off their legs. Eventually, someone would yell, "Hey, Louie and Sarita, sing 'That Old Black Magic,'" and my parents would swing into action. Someone would pop on the Louie Prima album, and my father and mother would stand in the center of the living room, mouthing the words to the song and hamming it up for the crowd. Everyone would laugh and clap as my parents danced around the room and pretended to be singing. When it was done, the others would jump up and dance too.

My brothers and I would try to insert new albums into the mix, but the old folks would say, "Who is this?" and very often the album would be removed immediately. Only The Beatles, Billy Joel, and Meatloaf (yes, Meatloaf) got the thumbs up. "Play that funny song," my father would say, and someone would pop on *Paradise By the Dashboard Light*. No one would laugh harder than my father when Meatloaf sang, "I was swearing to my God and on my mother's grave that I would love you 'til the end of time, I swore I'd love you 'til the end of time…. So now I'm praying for the end of time…." My father loved a great punch-line, so we got to listen to the whole album while they talked about Phil Rizzuto's voice-over and the rest of the song.

Later, we gathered around the television as Dick Clark counted down and the ball dropped in Times Square. Everyone was kissing everyone else, as I sought out my mother, father, brothers, grandmother, and all of the aunts, uncles, cousins, and friends who made each New Year worth celebrating. At 12:05, we ate…and the Quiche Lorraine was worth the wait!

Recipe: Quiche Lorraine

10-slices bacon

1 cup shredded Swiss cheese

$\frac{1}{3}$ cup diced onion

9-inch single pie crust

4 eggs, beaten

1½ cups light cream

1 teaspoon salt

¼ teaspoon sugar

$\frac{1}{8}$ teaspoon cayenne pepper

$\frac{1}{8}$ teaspoon nutmeg

1. Preheat oven to 425° F.

2. Place bacon in a large skillet, and cook until crisp. Drain on paper towels, then chop coarsely. Sprinkle bacon, cheese, and onion into pastry shell.

In a medium bowl, whisk together eggs, cream, salt, sugar, cayenne pepper, and nutmeg. Pour mixture into pastry shell.

3. Bake 15 minutes in the preheated oven; then reduce heat to 350° F, and bake an additional 30 minutes, or until a knife inserted 1 inch from edge comes out clean.

4. Allow quiche to sit 10 minutes before cutting into wedges. Serves 6-8.

More Holiday Recipes

These holiday favorites came from my cousin, Gina— granddaughter of Aunt Tessie.

Manicotti

For the crepes:

2 eggs

½ cup water

½ cup flour

(some people add pinch of salt)

Cooking spray

Preheat oven to 350°F. Whisk ingredients together by hand. Spray a crepe pan with cooking spray. Using a coffee measure spoon (approximately 1 tablespoon), pour batter into a crepe pan. Cook for about 2 minutes. Watch for the edges to firm up, and then flip. Cook the other side for about 2 minutes; remove from pan. Stack crepes and continue until all the batter is used up.

For the filling:

32 ounces ricotta

1 or 2 eggs (depending on how watery the ricotta is)

1 cup grated cheese

16 ounces mozzarella, shredded

4 cups tomato sauce

Mix ricotta, eggs, grated cheese, and mozzarella together. Place a heaping tablespoon of the mixture in each crepe, and roll the crepes, tucking in the ends. Place in baking dish and cover completely with sauce. Cover dish with foil and bake at 350°F for 30-35 minutes; remove foil for the last 5 minutes. Remove from oven. Let stand with foil loosely over the dish to keep warm 5 minutes before serving.

Serves 4-6.

Torrone

The best candy you've ever eaten. This is always made for Christmas. You are guaranteed to burn your fingers, but it is worth it.

16 ounces slivered almonds

8 ounces honey

Lightly toast almonds in a 350°F oven for 3-5 minutes. Cook honey on the stove on low heat for 5-10 minutes. The honey is ready when it starts to stick. Mix the almonds into the honey until they are coated well. Drop one-inch candies with a spoon onto wax paper and let them harden overnight. Makes about 1-1½ dozen candies.

Chapter 21: The Blackout

Sticky. Sweaty. Thirsty. Those were just a few of the feelings I remember from the summer of 1977. There were also the fear and the nervousness that went with knowing that the Son of Sam was still out there…somewhere…and here I was, with my shoulder-length brown hair.

There was the endless, convection-oven heat of summer days that reached as high as 103 degrees and newspaper headlines that read "The Baked Apple" to describe New York City's sweltering heat. There was just the hint of promise that my father might come home early and take us out for Italian ices. But mostly, there was the constant feeling of being slow-cooked in the hazy summer sunshine.

We didn't have air-conditioning in our house. Well, we did, but it was confined to two window units, one in my parents' room and one in my bedroom. But we were only allowed to turn the air conditioners on when the nighttime temperatures rose above 80 degrees. So when the heat became unbearable, sheets and pillows would be strewn across the floor, with lanky boys lying this way and that, and a dog or two curled up beside them on my bedroom floor.

1977 was the hottest summer I had ever imagined or experienced. Of course, it would follow that the family of my only friend in the neighborhood with a pool would choose that summer to dismantle their above-ground pool and dig a built-in pool to replace it. Which would've been great, mind you, if they had it ready for the summer. But as the sun continued to shine relentlessly, the pool installers took their time putting in the closest thing to an oasis that we had in Bayside Hills.

So on top of being hot, sticky, and bored, I had to endure a whole summer without swimming in my friend's pool or enjoying her mother's home cooking. This summer was too cruel.

Meanwhile, my father took off two weeks so we could spend some lazy summer days together. Of course, his idea of "lazy" was jamming all of us into the station wagon and heading off on some crisis-fueled adventure.

One of those adventures included a ride on the Circle Line, where Chris went ballistic after Paul licked his ice cream cone. When my mother finally managed to tear Chris and Paul apart and we got off the Circle Line, we headed for the Statue of Liberty.

Back in 1977, most self-respecting native New Yorkers that I know never actually climbed the Statue of Liberty or went to Ellis Island, which was not the lovely, renovated museum it is today. Back then, it was just a rundown old building that hinted at its glory in earlier times, when the immigrant really sweat it out in order to get into this country.

My father kept pointing to Lady Liberty, saying "This is where my father first came to America!" He couldn't wait to drag all ten of us (our family of nine, plus Jude's girlfriend, Cindy) up to the very tippy top of the lady's crown so we could peer down on the harbor below.

Which was a very cool notion, except…my father feared only three things in life: his mother's left hook, heights, and tight spaces. Without my grandmother there to punch his lights out if he didn't continue to climb, my father began his long climb into all-out panic attack as we got about halfway up into the tall green lady's head, surrounded by about a million other hot, anxious New Yorkers.

"I can't do this," he said over his shoulder to my mother, as we continued our march single file up the long, narrow, winding stairway. Sweat poured off him, and not just because of the sweltering heat.

"Louie, you have no choice," my mother said, as we marched on. "There's only one way down, and that's after we get to the top! Just keep walking and don't look down."

That was apparently the wrong thing to say, because no sooner did she say "don't look down" than my father peered down the winding metal staircase and decided it was time to abort.

"That's it! I have to get down!" my father roared. He did an about-face and began pushing his way down to the safety of the ground floor. Now, one thing you've got to say about New Yorkers…they aren't exactly the friendliest bunch when it's hot, sticky, and you're going the wrong way down a one-way street, or staircase. People shouted, they cursed, but they had never encountered the wrath of Lou, and although they thought they could stop my father's untimely descent, they were wrong.

Since no one would ever mistake the rest of us for bleeding hearts or sympathetic types, and since we were already halfway up, we forged on to the top of the stifling hot staircase. When my mother, brothers, Cindy, and I finally got to the top of Lady Liberty's crown, we peered down. We gazed out at the New York skyline, saw the steam rising off the blue-green waters of the Hudson, and marveled at the steel and glass spires that dotted the nearby shore.

"Hey, look!" Chris said, as he pointed at someone hundreds of feet below us. "Isn't that Dad?"

Of course, there was no way of knowing if that man lying on the grass was my father, but since he was either passed out from the heat or dead from exertion and panic, it could very well have been. We all laughed. And ten seconds later, we were pushed back down the stairs to make the long, noisy, sweaty, and cramped descent to Lady Liberty's feet—and my still panicked father.

That summer, we also went to the Feast of the Giglio (which is the Feast of the Lily, dedicated to honoring the Blessed Virgin Mary). At this celebration, hordes of young, strapping Brooklyn boys hoisted a five-hundred-pound statue of the Virgin Mary over their heads while a twelve-piece brass band played, singers belted out hymns, and they all marched down an avenue crowded with vendors hawking sausage and peppers, flaky zeppole with airy powdered sugar, frothy cotton candy, and homemade crafts like dolls in billowing gowns that came on a stick. "The Tarantella" and "That's Amore" rang through the sultry air from vendors' radios as we stuffed our faces.

My mother bought me a doll on a stick, dressed in a pink billowing skirt. I waved it around, hoping to create a wind to fan myself with. My brothers ran to different vendors and brought back sausage and peppers, calzone, pizza, and fresh zeppole dusted liberally with confectioners' sugar. We broke the hot pastries open and breathed in the fragrance of soft, sugary dough baked to perfection. We washed it all down with lemonade and my parents gave us a taste of cappuccino and espresso.

The festival was a crush of people pressing against each other but smiling still the same, the blaring of Italian music and laughter, the smell of too many people in too small a place, and always, always, the aroma of freshly baked bread and sausage sizzling somewhere nearby. In many ways, this was an Italian freak show—and in others, it was a party that could've happened in my Aunt Tessie's basement (except her zeppole were much better).

But the one thing that I remember most of all that summer was the night the lights went out in Georgia…er, Bayside.

My brothers and I sat in our stifling little living room (we were under Son of Sam lockdown, remember), watching a rerun of *Baretta*. It was a critical episode: Baretta was finally in love. This was long before Robert Blake, the actor formerly known as Baretta, would end up charged but not convicted of murdering his wife. As Baretta looked into the eyes of what could be his one true lady love…

ZAP!

The lights went out.

We sat there for a moment, dazed by the sudden quiet. Then Tony stood up and said, "Where's Paul? Was he running the hair dryer and the air conditioner again?"

But when we stepped out onto the porch, we saw complete darkness. No street lamps were on, and a hot, sultry silence blanketed the streets of Bayside Hills. This time, even Paul wasn't to blame.

"It's a blackout," Jude said, holding his AM radio to his ear. "Everybody in New York is blacked out."

"Where are Mom and Dad?" I asked.

"They're having dinner in some German restaurant in Ridgewood. It's called Zoom Stampdish or something like that," Tony replied. "Don't worry. They'll get home soon."

So we sat on our front porch and waited. Finally, my parents pulled up in the station wagon and honked the horn.

"All the street lights were going out as we drove home," my mother said. "I didn't know if we'd make it."

"I knew we would," my father said.

Jude held up his radio. "They're looting the Consumer's Distributors on Bell Boulevard! Do you know what great stuff you could get there?"

"You leave this house," my father snarled, "and I'll kill you."

So much for that big plan.

We moved back indoors and fanned out across the house. Since we had no fans or air conditioners, we threw open the windows and prayed for the slightest summer wind. I lay in bed, sweating and sticking to my sheets, searching for a cold spot on my pillow—but there was none to be found.

Dawn finally came and I got up to join my father for the seven o'clock mass. We trudged up the block to church, where we prayed for electricity. Then we came home and stared at each other.

Without electricity, the daily hum and rhythm of life was altered beyond recognition. We couldn't have eggs for breakfast because we had an electric stove. Between the heat and the blackout, our refrigerator had been under siege for at least twelve hours, and our milk was beginning to look and smell a lot like cottage cheese.

Even worse, without electricity, we would have to forgo the one thing that bound us like superglue…television! No reruns of *I Dream of Jeannie* or *Bewitched*. No *F-Troop* or *Hogan's Heroes*. If the juice didn't come back soon, we would miss our 12:30 pm ritual…*The Gong Show*! There'd be no Jean Jean The Dancing Machine, no surprise visits from the Unknown Comic. And a day without *The Gong Show* was like a Twinkie without the cream.

As 12:30 came and went and I realized that the *Gong Show* host, Chuck Barris, and I would have to live without each other for at least today, I turned to my father and Chris.

"Want to play something?"

They, too, were bored and defeated.

"Why not?" my father replied.

That afternoon, we played, and played and played. Battleship. Life. Monopoly. Gin rummy. Rebound. Several rousing games of hearts later, the living room lights flickered once…then twice…and then stayed on.

"We're back on!" Jude cheered, as he raced to the basement to play his electric bass and listen to some Johnny Winter music. Tony and Louie rushed out to find friends, Joey and Paul disappeared upstairs, but Chris, my parents, and I stayed in the living room and shot more rounds of Rebound. My father and mother looked sweaty but happy and more relaxed than I had seen them in a very long time.

"I had sauerbraten with dumplings," my mother said of her German restaurant dinner the night before. "You know, it's just pot roast."

"I had jaeger schnitzel, which is a veal cutlet, and it was the size of your head!" my father said.

I didn't know it then, but the *J* in *jaeger schnitzel* is pronounced like a *Y.* I'd only learn that many years later, when my Lagalante name would give way to Schulz.

"I'm going to see if I can get some groceries and cook something for dinner," my mother said.

But Chris, Dad, and I stayed in the living room, playing our games.

Too bad there weren't blackouts more often.

Recipe: Mom's Blackout Cake

Chocolate is required, and the darker, the better.

1 box chocolate cake mix

1 tub chocolate icing

Hot fudge sauce

Chocolate chips

Oreo cookie crumbles

Bake cake according to directions. Cool. Ice and then drizzle with hot fudge sauce. Be creative—lacy, web-like designs make this cake a stunner. Add chocolate chips and cookie crumbles. Enjoy!

Serves 6-8.

Chapter 22:
The Yankees Win! The Yankees Win!
Or, The Year Bucky Dent Broke a Million
Red Sox Hearts

For me, autumn always conjures up memories of itchy new uniforms on the first day of school, crunchy brown leaves under my feet, and the sweet smell of apple pie wafting from open windows as I walked home from school.

It's also the time when the Yankees captured my attention—and my heart—for good. In the summer of 1978, the Yankees were languishing fourteen games behind Boston in the pennant race, and the Red Sox were laughing all summer long at my hapless, hopeless Yankees.

But Ron Guidry (Louisiana Lightning, as WPIX play by play sportscaster Phil Rizzuto called him) kept winning, and soon the rest of the team followed. When autumn came, the

Boys of Summer were tied for first place.

I watched every single game that summer that I turned twelve. I was too young for boys and too old for dolls; baseball became my life. I could watch the Yankees on Channel 11 and the Mets on Channel 9, alternating between the two camps that my family set up. On the Yankees side were Dad, Louie, Chris, and me. On the Mets side were Joey and Jude. Paul, Tony, and my mother were Switzerland—they insisted on neutrality because they really didn't care.

The Mets weren't a lot of fun to watch in 1978. This was long before Joe Torre made crying in autumn a yearly ritual; at that point, he was considered mortal and a terrible manager. While the Yankees were exasperating early in that season, they still could be exciting. Ron Guidry threw an amazing eighteen strikeouts in one game. Reggie Jackson blasted homers right and left. Graig Nettles smoked the ball and snagged vicious liners from frozen ropes. I knew my boys would rally, so I was one of the few who wasn't surprised when it all came down to that fateful playoff game on October 2, 1978.

My stomach churned all afternoon long while Sister Anne Kathleen droned on about the Israelites and the Philistines. When school was finally done, I raced outside to walk home with Chris.

"The Yankees' luck ends today," our classmate, Debbie, said in singsong.

"Says who?" Chris replied.

"My dad," Debbie said. "The Red Sox are the better team

and the Yankees know it! And soon you'll know it too."

We crossed the street in silence. It was never my way to gloat before a game. My words didn't taste so great when I had to eat them later.

My dad was home that afternoon, waiting for us to get there to watch the game with him. We parked ourselves on the couches and loveseat and took a deep breath. One hundred sixty-two long, grinding games had come down to this. Only one team could go on to meet the Kansas City Royals. Please, Lord, I said to myself. Let it be mine.

Ron Guidry was pitching on short rest and the Red Sox jumped out to an early lead. The Yankees looked like they were sleepwalking and burned to a crisp.

"They can't lose," Chris whispered.

I clutched the pillow to my stomach and prayed.

Mike Torres was always blowing leads to the Yankees. So why did he look unbeatable while Guidry looked shaky?

By the time the Yankees came up in the top of the seventh, I felt my heart sink to my feet. Even if two men got on, it's not like Bucky Dent could do anything about it. Bob Lemon usually pinch-hit for him in these situations anyway. So what was he doing coming to the plate?

"There goes the inning," I said.

I broke out my rosary beads. It was my firm belief at that time that God had to pick a winner, so why not get his mother involved and have her see things my way? I said a quick string of Hail Marys, then broke into the Memorare: "Remember,

Oh Most Gracious Virgin Mary, that never was it known that anyone who fled to your protection, implored your help, or sought your intercession, was left unaided. Inspired by this confidence, I come to you, oh Virgin of Virgins, my mother. To you I come, before you I stand, sinful and sorrowful. Oh mother of the Word Incarnate, do not ignore my petitions, but in your mercy, hear and answer me. Amen."

I thought the part about "never was it known that anyone who implored your help was left unaided" was a nice touch. If I had to guilt Mother Mary into helping us out, well, then, so be it! This was the Yankees and the Red Sox! "Let the Yankees win," I pleaded.

And boy, did Mary ever come through!

As I watched Bucky Dent connect with the ball that would define his career and break a million Red Sox hearts, it was as if everything went in slow motion.

My father jumped up into the middle of the living room, screaming.

"It's a home run! A home run over the Green Monster! He did it! Bucky Dent did it!"

Chris and I let out loud whoops and danced around the floor, clapping hands, hugging my father, and laughing until the tears ran down our cheeks.

"Now," my dad said, "we can eat."

"But the game isn't over yet," I said.

"Oh, the Yankees will win now. I guarantee it."

We pulled the TV around so it faced the dining room and

sat down. My mother made foot-long hot dogs piled high with sauerkraut and mustard, along with crispy steak fries. This was my mother's nod to the national pastime.

I chomped on my hot dog, mumbling a silent prayer to Mary, thankful that I got there first. Please, please just let the Yankees hold on!

But my father never doubted that the Yankees would win. Even when the Red Sox pulled within two runs, we just laughed—because Mr. October, Reggie Jackson himself, smashed a two-run homer that put the game out of reach.

My mom served up apple pie à la mode while we watched our beloved team soak themselves in champagne. And while Carl Yastrzemski cried on the dugout bench, my brothers, father, and I ate and celebrated.

"I don't even care about the game," my mother said, "but I'm glad you're happy."

And was I ever.

Best of all, I could eat to my heart's content since I didn't have to leave room for any gloating words.

"I can't wait to see Debbie tomorrow," Chris said, in between bites.

Recipe: Apple Pie

Baseball and apple pie always marry well. I wish I had learned how to make pie from scratch from my grandmother (the world champion of pie making), but since I didn't, two 9-inch pie crusts do the trick nicely.

6 cups sliced, peeled apples

(Granny Smith, Rome, Cortland, Jonathan)

2 tablespoons lemon juice

¾ cup white sugar

¼ cup brown sugar

¼ cup all-purpose flour

1¼ teaspoon apple pie spice

2 9-inch pie crusts

2 tablespoons butter

1 egg yolk

1 tablespoon milk

Sprinkle of cinnamon sugar

1. In a large bowl, toss the sliced apples with lemon juice.

2. Combine sugars, flour, apple pie spice; add to apples and toss well to coat.

3. Line a nine-inch pie pan with bottom crust. Fill with apple mixture. Dot with butter. Place second crust on top of pie filling; cut slits in top of crust to vent. Seal the edges of the crust with a fork or by hand.

4. In a small bowl, beat the egg yolk and milk. Brush mixture over top crust. Sprinkle with cinnamon sugar.

5. Bake at 425°F for 15 minutes. Reduce heat to 350°F and bake 40–45 minutes more or until crust is golden and filling starts to bubble.

Serves 6-8.

Chapter 23: Kathie Comes to Stay

It seemed like we would always be sitting there in that little house on 214th Street, sharing big meals with extended family, asking Jude's band-mates to stop eating the sandwiches we had made for ourselves, and enjoying take-out pizza, hamburgers, and fried chicken. But something incredible happened that changed our lives forever: Tony got a girlfriend.

Her name was Kathie, and the first inkling I had that she existed occurred when I saw my brother walking down the street with a giant stuffed dog and a bag of presents. Since it was Christmas time and the only girl I thought he bought presents for was me, it seemed strange that he made no attempt to hide anything. Instead, he waved hello to me as he hauled the bag full of booty that was for some other girl into his bedroom downstairs.

Of course, Jude had been dating Cindy since we were all very young, and in my mind she was more like another sibling than a future in-law. Cindy had shown up looking like just another male band groupie, wearing a knitted cap and a bulky sweatshirt that covered her from neck to hips.

Sometime over the years, the cap came off, revealing long brown hair, and the sweatshirt was replaced with a tube top, and it became obvious what Jude saw in her. She was pretty and had more curves than Marilyn Monroe. But by then, she was just Cindy and I never thought about her as a potential in-law.

Cindy came along with us when we went on family outings and was always at every band gig. She kept an eye on me when my mother didn't want to go to the local street fair to watch Jude play again; she held my hand and walked with me down to Carvel, where we enjoyed Cherry Bonnets, Flying Saucers, and soft ice cream drizzled with sprinkles and hot fudge sauce. I no more perceived Cindy as a threat than I would've had Santa Claus arrested for breaking and entering.

But Kathie was a different story. The first time I ever saw Kathie, she was a volunteer at a program for the mentally retarded and deaf that my father helped run, along with Kathie's mother, Pat. My brothers Tony, Joey, and Paul were also volunteers. Kathie's brother, Jimmy, was one of the program participants.

Kathie had a short brown bob, a cute button nose, and the map of Ireland across her face. Her laugh was easy and infectious, but she was also feisty and combative. Kathie was cute and Tony definitely liked her.

Tony and Kathie were ancient as far as I was concerned; at nineteen years old, they were entering that weird, almost adult age that meant ankle bracelets and claddagh rings, with the next logical steps being engagement and marriage. I wasn't sure I was ready for this.

Luckily, after Tony and Kathie exchanged Christmas gifts, it was clear to me that she didn't like him nearly as much as he liked her. Tony left with three large bags of gifts and came home with one vinyl record. I breathed a sigh of relief.

But a funny thing happened...Kathie liked him after all. Soon, they were dating all the time, and Kathie was even willing to spend time with Tony and his friends, a gang of hooligans who made the Son of Sam seem like a fun guy with just a few odd quirks. Kathie was definitely a keeper, and I imagined my brother leaving us behind for a normal life, far away from 214th Street.

To Kathie's credit, she didn't ignore me like so many other girlfriends who came and went did. She shook my hand the first time we met and asked me what I liked to do.

"I like the movies," I said.

"Let's go together!" Kathie said. "We can go on Wednesdays, when you have a half day at school."

"Okay," I said.

Kathie didn't forget like some other girlfriends might have. For quite a few Wednesdays to come, as well as Friday or Saturday nights when she could've easily left me behind and just gone with Tony, we went to the movies together and saw such unforgettable hits as *The Main Event, Ice Castles, Every Which Way But Loose, Grease, Polyester* (with fun-filled Scratch-o-rama cards...watch out for #9!), and *9 to 5*.

While I never had enough money for the movies and popcorn, Kathie showered me with popcorn, M&Ms, and even a burger afterward. She bought Chris and me birthday presents when our parents forgot, and she was the first to invite us to the local street carnivals and fairs.

Tony and Kathie were always happy to let us bring along our friends; as many people as we could fit in Kathie's green Ford Galaxy were allowed to come along. Along with our friends John and Maureen, Chris and I would push our way into the back of the car, while Tony and Jimmy (Kathie's brother) would sit up front. Kathie would slam her foot down on the gas pedal (gaining her the nicknames "Leadfoot" and "Ice Breaker") as we barreled off to another adventure.

By the time Kathie had been around for a year or two, it was clear that she was here to stay. Although she and my father did not get along—shouting seemed to be their preferred method of communication—my mother liked her and Kathie became the new fixture at family gatherings while Cindy slowly disappeared from our lives, in search of new, band-free relationships.

Kathie was such a good sport that she did not run and hide like she should have when my father took up a new hobby.

"I'm going to start cooking," he declared one day, much to our collective horror. Not that we didn't think my father could do it. I was pretty sure he could, but the amount of time and energy it would take to endure the days leading up to his ingredient-gathering mania, then the screaming and insult-throwing that would accompany the preparatory craziness, followed by the actual meal (God forbid if it was terrible) and the hours of congratulations that would be necessary afterward seemed daunting.

Still, when my father latched onto something, resistance was futile. My mother would walk out the door with his ingredient list in hand, looking like she was off to buy the executioner's noose that would be used on her. Then, on Sunday mornings, the screaming would begin.

"I need chops that are three-quarter inches thick!" or "I need amaretto!" would ring out from the kitchen, while my mother would apologize for not getting everything exactly as he needed it to create his masterpiece. It was on days like these that I wished we could go back to the relative peace of his AM radio blasting *Jonathan Schwartz in the Mornings* on Sundays while he read the newspaper and my mother prepared her homemade sauce.

Like survivors hiding from a marauding army, my brothers were smart enough to stay in their rooms until there was absolutely no choice but to come out. At 2 pm, we would gather around the table and…wait. Usually, dinner prepared by my father was not on time. There was still plenty of screaming and crying going on in the kitchen, while we sat at the table and waited for the dinner to come out.

Since Kathie was not an official family member, she could have (and should have) stayed home and seen Tony afterward. But my father almost dared her to join us, and Kathie could not stay away.

As a result, it became something of a challenge for my father to prepare something really fantastic not just for us, but for her. That first week, he and my mother came out of the kitchen about an hour late with gigantic veal chops that were still very undone. My brothers, Kathie, and I pushed the chops around on our plates until my father pulled them all off and disappeared back into the kitchen to cook them some more. When it became clear that we wouldn't be getting anything for dinner that day, we made an emergency visit to the one place guaranteed to satisfy every last one of us—White Castle.

The following week, my father tried his hand at French onion soup. Much to our surprise, it was really delicious. But we should have paid attention to our Catholic school upbringing and realized that just as the Lord giveth, the Lord taketh away. Within an hour, all ten of us were experiencing horrific stomach pains and gastrointestinal distress that hinted at my father's use of TNT as the secret ingredient in his soup. The sight of each of us banging on the bathroom door with all the quiet good manners of Jack the Ripper alarmed Kathie, who politely asked Tony to drive her home…and fast.

Week #3 found Kathie still steely-eyed and determined not to be bested by my father's determination to kill us, her first of all. The gods smiled upon her that day, because my mother decided to help my father along and bake sausage bread, with him giving minimal assistance. The sausage bread was a big hit and it accompanied a lasagna dish that even my father could not destroy. Everyone breathed a collective sigh of relief until my father pulled out his dessert—an apple turnover flambé that had been torched beyond recognition.

"Too bad it doesn't have dental records," Louie said. "Maybe then we could identify it and give it a proper burial." We each took a little bit and congratulated my father on his valiant attempt at apple burnovers.

The weeks went on, with my father having some successes and some disastrous failures. Finally, with Kathie in attendance, my father served spaghetti carbonara with sausage bread and apple pie for dessert.

The spaghetti carbonara had great potential for success. It was just spaghetti with heavy cream, eggs, bacon, and mushrooms. How wrong could you go with that? My father followed the directions exactly and, with my mother's help, created a dish that everyone enjoyed.

Kathie enjoyed it too…at first. But poor, Irish Kathie was not used to the fare that was thrown out on our table week after week. Our stomachs had been hardened to the consistency of a cast-iron skillet from run-ins with my mother's and father's cooking, and strengthened by a love of White Castles and Kentucky Fried Chicken that could have undermined entire civilizations.

Even though my father tried his best, he had added a little too much fat and had not drained off enough of the bacon grease, thinking it would make the sauce richer. Well, it certainly was rich. So rich, in fact, that poor Kathie had to ask to be excused so she could go into the bathroom and throw up.

"I thought it was good," my father said, as we all laughed.

Later that week, Kathie's mother confronted my father.

"Are you trying to kill my daughter?" Pat said. "She was sick for days."

For once, my father paused, then looked at Pat. "Want to come over for dinner some time?"

Recipe: Pasta Carbonara à la Chris

Chris recognized the great potential of this dish and started cooking it more than twenty-five years ago.

Here's his recipe:

1 lb. bacon

1 onion, chopped (optional)

1 garlic clove, minced

2 tablespoons olive oil (enough to coat the pan)

1 lb. pasta (spaghetti, linguine or fettuccine)

2 eggs, slightly beaten

2 cups Parmesan cheese

1-cup heavy cream (optional)

Black pepper to taste

2 tablespoons parsley (optional)

1 jar (12 oz.) mushrooms (optional)

½ cup wine (red or white, optional)

Put on a pot of water to boil. Meanwhile, cook the bacon until it's crispy. Drain the fat as you go, but reserve ¼ cup to coat the pasta when you mix all of the ingredients together. Chop and mince the garlic, then sauté till golden brown in olive oil (along with onion, if using). Toss in a splash of wine to coat garlic (if you like). A little splash of the pasta water also works well—a tablespoon's worth as the garlic sizzles with the wine. Boil pasta water so when the bacon is finished it doesn't have to sit around too long. Pour ½ of the eggs into bottom of large bowl. Coat the entire bowl. Put cheese and black pepper into bottom of bowl.

Salt the water and then throw the pasta in. When the pasta is cooked, take half of the pasta and put it in the bowl. Continually mix all of the ingredients (pasta, eggs, cheese, pepper, repeat) so you don't cook the eggs (you don't want fried eggs). Add a little bit of the bacon fat, half of the bacon, drizzle half the garlic and olive oil on, add some grated cheese, add some the other ½ eggs, then some black pepper. Garnish with parsley on top. Repeat with what you have left. Make sure the dish is not too dry.

To quote Chris, "for your future culinary exploits, vary it up, MARY! It is a dish that is delish even with fish! Capice?" By that, he means you can change things up by using prosciutto instead of bacon, add peas, use fettuccine or penne, or do any number of things that suit your own tastes.

Serves 4-6.

Chapter 24: Lunch Breaks With Borah

Sometimes, you meet a person who changes everything about your world, and you end up with a friend you never expected. Until I was thirteen years old, I went to a Catholic grammar school. I thought everyone on the planet was Italian, Puerto Rican, or Irish, and everyone was Catholic. But when I went off to a public high school in the fall of 1980, I got an education on a whole lot more than reading, writing, and arithmetic. I didn't know it yet, but I was about to get a crash course on Jewish food.

One early morning in the summer between tenth and eleventh grades, I lay in bed wondering what I was going to do with myself that day. It was so unbearably hot that sweat trickled down my back as I fanned myself with a magazine and dreamed of winter. Just then, the phone rang.

"Hello," I mumbled, as only a sweaty, bored, disengaged

teenager can.

"MARIA DARLIN'!" a voice boomed. It was a voice from my not-so-distant high school past. This wasn't a relative. It wasn't a pal. Who the hell was this?

"Oh, man, who the heck is this?"

"Hah!" The voice cackled. "Have you forgotten me so soon?"

I sat up in bed and stared at the phone. Could it be? Was this really happening?

"Mr. Reines?" I said. Was I dreaming, or was my high school English teacher really calling me?

"The one and only," he replied. His voice dripped with mischievous glee, just like old times.

"What on earth are you calling me for?" I said, in the most thoughtless and impolite way possible. I mean, I loved this teacher, but the school year was over. Sure, I was grateful to him for bringing Shakespeare, Wilde, Malamud, and Thurber into my pop-culture-soaked mind, but I couldn't figure out why he would call me.

Borah Reines was tall but pudgy, with a sandy-brown mop of curls and hazel eyes hidden behind eyeglass frames and lenses that could have brought outer space into focus. His clothes used to scream "Lost in 1972!" even though it was 1982. He should have set off geek alarms wherever he went. But his wild sense of humor and infectious joy made me adore him.

"I've got a proposition for you!" Borah replied.

Now it was my turn to laugh. "I've got a proposition for

you" was what he always said when he had me run some slave's errand for him. Maybe he needed me to run down three flights of stairs to get him his lunch. Perhaps he wanted me to run out to the parking lot, root around in his car, and get him a book. Or maybe he needed me to type up ten or twenty pages of lesson plans. Mr. Reines had a heart condition, so if he asked me to do him a favor, I did it. I figured the world was a far better place with Borah Reines in it, so I ran, typed, and carried anything, anytime he called.

"Haven't you learned the words to that Alice Cooper song yet? 'School's out for summer!' My slavery ended in June!"

Borah laughed. It was a loud, booming chortle packed with delight, as refreshing as the Nestea Plunge. "I heard you'd do anything for money," he teased.

"How would you know? You never paid me a penny," I shot back. But then I softened. "All right, what do you have in mind?"

"My wife runs a medical records business from home," he replied. "She needs help, and she said she'd be willing to pay you $5 an hour."

Now, that summer I was working as a deli cook, making $3 an hour to do hot, sticky, miserable work. Office work, off the books, for $2 more an hour was like hitting the lottery.

"All right!" I cheered, while Mr. Reines laughed. "When do you need me?"

"Now," he replied.

Now was 8:30 am.

"You really are a slave driver, you know that?" I said, as he whooped with delight.

Borah Reines was many things: funny, vivacious, quick-witted, and mischievous. But he was not punctual, at least where I was concerned. When he finally rang my doorbell at 11:30 am, I had actually convinced myself that our early-morning phone call had been a heat-induced hallucination.

But no, there he was, in all his nerdy glory. He was wearing a "#1 DAD" T-shirt, plaid shorts, and black socks with his sandals. He burst through my front door like the long-awaited prophet Elijah in goofy summer gear.

"Sorry I'm late," he said.

I shook my head. "*What* are you wearing?"

"Why? Don't you like this shirt? My kids got it for me."

"The shirt's not the problem," I said, as I pointed to his feet. "What are you, eighty? You gotta ditch the black socks."

"I see you're just as bossy as ever," Mr. Reines replied.

"I'm happy to see you too," I replied, as we set out for his house.

We drove from Bayside to Great Neck, while Borah flicked on the radio to a station playing opera.

"What on earth is this?" I said, as I slapped my hands over my ears. "Please make it stop!"

"Would you rather I put on The Cops and Wasp?" Borah yelled over the aria.

"You doofus," I giggled. "You mean The Police and Sting!"

He smiled and continued to sing along with the radio.

"Please stop the car and let me out!" I begged, but Borah just ignored me.

As if his singing wasn't bad enough, his driving put the fear of God in me. Red lights, stop signs, crosswalks—Borah was so busy tormenting me with his singing that he blissfully drove through them all while I clutched the armrest and prayed. Miraculously, we made it to his house with the only damage being to my poor tortured eardrums.

He led me into his home. I was surprised to see a large, airy kitchen with cheery blue and white wallpaper and gleaming copper pots hanging from the ceiling.

"Your house is so nice," I said.

"Why do you sound so surprised?" Borah replied.

"Don't you remember what your classroom looked like?" I said. "I figured you lived in a shanty on the side of the expressway."

"HA!" Borah laughed. "My wife keeps me respectable. Speaking of my wife—" Borah swept his hand to the side as his wife, Miriam, walked in.

"Miriam, meet Maria."

Miriam Reines was taller than me and thin, with jet-black hair, high cheekbones, and big brown eyes. Geek alarms would definitely not go off when she entered a room. She was dressed in a navy-and-white-striped T-shirt, khaki shorts, and sandals. Right behind her came their twelve-year-old daughter, Sarah. She looked just like her father, although she was blessed with her mother's fashion sense.

"Isn't this great?" Borah boomed. "I'm in the room with the three women I love most in the world!"

I looked at his little family and arched my eyebrow. He was so full of it.

"Now, Borah, stop tormenting Maria," Miriam said. "Come downstairs with me and we'll get to work."

Borah smiled and winked at me. "I'll make you lunch. Come back up in an hour."

So, after an hour of filing medical records, I climbed those stairs and saw Mr. Reines foraging in the refrigerator.

"Maria darlin'!" He said. "Come and enjoy a feast!"

I looked at the table and saw rolls, tuna salad, a tossed green salad, and iced tea on the table. I slid onto the bench and dangled my legs like the little girl I was.

Here I was, about to have lunch with my favorite teacher. We had spent the last two school years having lunch together at school, but there were always other students or teachers around. I could be rude, unpleasant, ornery, or outrageous, because when we were together, I enjoyed making Mr. Reines laugh. In turn, he would make fun of me, say mean things, torment the other students, and I would laugh so hard that sometimes I'd choke on my Coca-Cola. I think Mr. Reines's real goal was to see the soda shoot out of my nose.

But school seemed to be another planet entirely. I was out of the safe confines of a world I knew and plopped down as a stranger in a strange land. What if I said something and he didn't laugh? What if I couldn't think of anything funny to say? What if Mr. Reines realized that I wasn't amusing, delightful, charming, good company, or smart after all?

How on earth did I end up here? Most teachers were as approachable as rock stars. You knew that they had lives— spouses, children, pets, homes—but you never expected to actually meet any of them. So here I was, about to have some Surreal Tuna Salad prepared for me by my English teacher.

I twisted my napkin and swung my legs, harder this time, until Mr. Reines broke the silence.

"Why are you so quiet today? I could never shut you up in class," he said, as he swung into the chair across from me.

I could've told him the truth. I could've told him that I was nervous, or that I wasn't sure how to act because I was just a little kid and what did he want from me anyway? Instead, I thought of a funny comeback and went with it.

"I think you traumatized me with all that opera singing."

Borah laughed. He jumped up, pulled out a Tupperware tin with some white fish in it, and dug into it with gusto. He tried to pass the fork to me, but I thought the food looked nasty. I pushed his hand away

"If this is how you thank me, then I'm in trouble," I said.

"Oh, come on, don't you like Jewish food?"

"I don't know. But if you come to my house, will you eat pig's knuckles? My Puerto Rican grandfather loved them."

"You used to eat bagels and cream cheese every day at school. That's Jewish."

"Okay, so I like some Jewish food."

"Ever have matzo ball soup? Ever try lox? Still not going to try the herring?" he said, as he offered the fork my way again.

"Yes, yes, and no. Have I passed the audition yet?"

"You're impossible," Borah said, as he passed me some rolls and tuna salad.

"I am a product of my teacher," I replied as we smiled and dug in.

Finally, I began to relax. Apparently, Mr. Reines hadn't realized that I was not nearly as much fun here as I was at school, and I supposed that was a good thing.

"Maria darlin', I've been thinking," Borah said, in between mouthfuls.

Now I knew I was in trouble. "Stop thinking," I replied. "That's never good news for me."

"No, really," Borah said. "I've been thinking about your friends, and I think you should branch out a little. You're too wonderful to spend your whole life with just your current batch of friends."

"What's wrong with my friends?" I replied. "You like Dorothy." My friend Dorothy was my best friend in high school, and she worked with me when I was Mr. Reines's service aid. "Yes, Dorothy is a great girl, but you should make additional friends, people who can help you become a better reader and writer. What about Evelyn? She's a lovely young girl."

Now, I didn't let my parents choose my friends, and I sure wasn't about to let Mr. Reines choose them either.

I sneered. "Evelyn? No, thanks. I don't like Evelyn."

"Oh, no, she's perfectly lovely. She always had something witty and wonderful to say in class."

I arched my eyebrow and swallowed. "Evelyn is not lovely or witty. She never even read the books you assigned! Boy, did she have you fooled."

Borah smiled. "Don't get so testy. I didn't say she was my favorite student."

Now I smiled. "That's good, because I'd have to kick you in the shins if you did."

Borah burst out laughing and slammed his fist on the table. He laughed so hard, I thought he just might shoot some iced tea through his nose.

Things were going well.

Lunch that day passed quickly, with Borah constantly refilling my soda glass and booming with laughter every five minutes. Every time I'd try to go back downstairs, he'd say, "Don't worry! I know the boss!"

It was the first of many lunches with Borah Reines. His wonderful wife kept me busy with the best job of my entire teenage life. Here was a job that paid well *and* included the added perk of lunch with my mentor.

But lunch with Borah was NOT *Tuesdays with Morrie*. Our conversations did not shed any significance on the meaning of life or our roles in the universe. Instead, they went something like this:

Borah: How could you be from Queens and root for the Yankees?

Maria: Because I believe in winning and tradition. And the Mets are losers.

OR:

Borah: How can you not like opera? Aren't you Italian?

Maria: So? Just because I'm Italian doesn't mean I have to love opera. I don't sit around making spaghetti sauce all day either.

OR:

Borah: You're Italian and Puerto Rican, right?

Maria: Can't you tell by my moustache?

Sometimes, we would talk about books, and these were the conversations that I really enjoyed. From *Arrowsmith* to *The Catcher in the Rye, Pride and Prejudice* to *A Member of the Wedding*, it was fun to talk about the authors, the books, the plot twists, and the things I saw coming from a mile away with my insightful English teacher. There was one thing, though, that Borah Reines insisted on that started to give me a sense of what I might do with myself in that faraway time and place called "being a grown-up."

"You are going to be a writer some day," Mr. Reines said.

"I don't know," I replied. "I'm not very good."

"What are you talking about?" he replied. "You won that essay contest earlier this year! I know it actually happened—and you didn't just make it up—because I was at the awards night!"

I smiled. I had indeed won an award in an essay contest titled "The Day Vandalism Ended."

"You just came because you had nothing better to do," I said, and laughed.

"Do you think I would've gotten up out of a sick bed to come to the awards show if I didn't think you were any good?" Mr. Reines replied.

It was true; he wasn't supposed to show up that night because his heart condition made him too sick to leave his bed. Still, that night he bundled up even though it was already April (he was always cold and wore more clothes than the Michelin Man) and surprised me by bursting through the doors and waving to me right before the awards were handed out.

"I didn't even take first place," I said. "So how good could I be?"

"Your essay was the best one," he replied. "One of the judges told me he didn't like it because instead of talking about how there was a parade and the world was clean and beautiful, you decided to go all 'Brave New World' on them."

He had a point. The girl who won first place wrote an essay about how happy everyone was in a graffiti-free world; my essay was about the stifling of creative expression, living in an antiseptic world, and graffiti artists being shot in the streets.

"Believe in yourself, Maria," Mr. Reines said. "You can write. You should write!"

"Okay, okay." I waved him off and said it like I was annoyed, because what teenager wants to tell a grown-up: "Hey, you're right!"

"You'll thank me one day," Mr. Reines said.

In the years that followed, over matzo ball soup, herring with cream sauce, bagels with lox, tuna sandwiches, Coca-Colas, and ice cream cones, I learned a thing or two about friendship and confidence from my mentor and friend.

When my first boyfriend broke my heart and I was reduced to tears, Borah Reines gave me a hug and told me that, someday, someone would come along, see me as the treasure I was, and snatch me up.

And when Borah's heart gave him trouble and he got too sick to ever return to work, I told him that if I could have my way, he would live forever. Even though he did give me a lower final grade than I deserved.

No, lunch with Borah was not *Tuesdays with Morrie*.

It was better.

Recipe: Matzo Balls à la Reines

Mr. Reines passed away over thirty years ago, but I still remember him fondly. Miriam Reines, Mr. Reines's lovely wife and my former boss, gave me this matzo ball recipe to help me celebrate the memory of a truly unique person and mentor.

1 dozen eggs

1 teaspoon salt

3 cups matzo meal

Boil water in a large pot. Separate the eggs; beat the whites stiff and add salt. Beat the yolks. Fold the whites into the yolks. Fold in the matzo meal. Moisten your hands with water and roll the batter into small-sized balls (they will expand in water). Immerse in the boiling water. When they come to a boil, cover the pot. Check them after 30 minutes by cutting one ball to see if it is done.

The amount of cooking time will vary depending on the size of the matzo balls. They swell during cooking so they will be larger than they are when you are rolling them. Matzo balls can be frozen in zip-lock bags and used at a later date.

Makes about 24 matzo balls.

Chapter 25: The Fortunate Deli Worker

Perhaps it was destiny that my life-long fascination with food would translate into an occupation. When I was sixteen, my mother announced that she had gotten me a job at our local deli.

My brothers Louie, Chris, and Joey all worked in local delis. But I didn't see any girls working slicers or ringing up customers.

"Oh, no," my mother said. "You're going to be Nancy's new cook."

A cook. A COOK? There was less chance of me harming someone while working on the old-fashioned meat slicer than there was while working with fire and grease.

"Ma, why on earth did you get me a job as a cook?" I said, in my most ungrateful teenager way.

"You need a job, and Nancy at the deli needs a cook. She

said she'd teach you everything you need to know. Besides," my mother smiled, "she owes me."

That was true enough. My mother shopped at the deli even though she could've easily gone across the street to C-Town, where she would save loads of money. But loyalty had to be good for something, and my mother figured this was it.

I trudged into Nancy's delicatessen hoping for the best. And as long as my mother was there, my new boss, Nancy, could be quite pleasant. She would smile often and clap me jovially on my back as she explained the intricacies of delicatessen cooking. The problem was that my mother didn't intend to stay with me during my shifts. Once my mother was gone, Nancy's smile left too and those jovial back slaps sure did sting.

"No, no, no!" Nancy said, as sweat dripped from her forehead into the cole slaw. Note to self: tell Mom no more cole slaw if Nancy makes it.

"What? What's wrong?" I muttered.

"You need to chop the cabbage this way!"

"Okay," I said, not quite understanding why it mattered. "But if I slice it in quarters and put it in the food processor anyway, who cares what the first slice looks like?"

"I CARE!" Nancy roared.

Lesson #1:
Accept instructions from boss, no matter how pointless.

Now that I knew how much cole slaw meant to Nancy, I tried hard to hold the knife at the same ninety-degree angle as she did, making sure all four triangles were perfectly symmetrical. Once I displayed this talent to her satisfaction, she uncreased her brow and let out a sigh of relief. It wasn't exactly "Snatch the marble from my hand, grasshopper," but it was close.

So the dog days passed, and even though Nancy's scowl didn't fade, it did seem as though the bad smell she always sensed in my presence was lifting a little bit.

Each day at the deli, I learned a new way to bake, roast, broil, mash, fry, slice, or dice. Nancy showed me how to crisscross and glaze a Virginia ham with the perfect amount of brown sugar and cloves, sprinkle the turkey with paprika, and roast the beef to medium-rare perfection every time. She taught me the secrets of making great potato salad, slicing potatoes until my knuckles bled, which gave the salad a lovely rosy hue. She showed me how to make a macaroni salad that was firm to the bite ("Throw the macaroni at the wall!" she'd holler, even though my own mother told me that a simple timer would yield the same results). The rice pudding recipe she taught me brought tears to the locals' eyes and gained me a legion of deli admirers.

Once I'd proven that I could actually be trusted (sort of), Nancy handed me a sheaf of recipes, written out in a painstaking print that looked like a cross between Old English, Chinese characters, and hieroglyphics.

"Now," she said solemnly, "you must make me a solemn vow that you will never share these recipes with anyone! Not a soul! Do you hear me?"

I wanted to bend over with laughter. Instead, I said, "Even if the Galloping Gourmet begs and pleads, I will never turn them over."

I was hoping for a laugh. Instead, Nancy scowled.

Lesson #2:

Do NOT make fun of boss unless you're sure she won't get the joke.

Working at Martinelli's Deli was hot, sweaty, disgusting work. It had all the allure of a cold-water enema without any of the obvious benefits...and I often ended up feeling like I was covered in excrement.

The deli was air-conditioned...up front. But the kitchen was an inferno, my own personal hell that Nancy said "wasn't meant to be air-conditioned." Her thought process was, why turn on the air conditioner in a room with an oven? Of course, this rule only seemed to apply to me. The air conditioner worked overtime when she was in there.

So on most mornings, I would stand in that cramped, tiny kitchen with the ancient gas oven and broken, leaky faucets, listening to WNBC-AM radio drone "Every Breath You Take" and "Baby Jane" until I thought my ears would bleed. The only thing sweatier than that leaky faucet was me as I chopped, boiled, baked, and fried until I was sure it was blood, and not sweat, pouring down my forehead.

Working there alone was bad enough, but on days when Nancy was by my side and we fumbled for something to say to each other, it was torture. I imagined there had to be a better way to make $3 an hour.

"Do you believe how bad the Yankees have gotten so fast?" I said.

"I hate baseball," she replied.

I fumbled with some sticky pots and pans as my mind frantically searched for something—anything—to say.

"Did you always want to own a deli?" I managed.

"No." Nancy frowned. "I was never any good in school. Working hard and cooking is all I know. How about you? Are you good in school?"

"I'm okay," I said, sensing that announcing I was a straight-A student would not endear me to her.

"There is one thing I'm pretty good at, though."

"You mean, besides cooking?" I said, hope filling my heart like air in a flat tire.

"Yes." She flipped on the small TV that sat on a shelf above the kitchen table. "*Wheel of Fortune*." She finally smiled. "I'm great at solving the puzzles."

"Really," I said, as I slid into a chair and started to peel the potatoes by her side. "Me too!"

I was too young to realize that letting Nancy win might have gone a long way toward breathing life into our respirator-bound relationship. But I was great at *Wheel of Fortune*, and without even realizing it, I pulled the plug once and for all.

"Ask for an N!" Nancy yelled, but then she couldn't guess the name of "Famous Woman."

"Nancy Reagan!" I blurted.

Three puzzles later, when I yelled out "Mississippi Mud Pie" with only M_ _ _ _ _ _ _ _ _ _ M_ _ P_ _ showing on the board, Nancy's red face made me wonder if at long last she would be forced to put on the air conditioner while I was in the kitchen. Or maybe she was about to die of heat exhaustion. Either way, I win!

"Are you all right?" I said, as she flicked off the TV.

"Fine," she yelled. "I think you're finished here. Why don't you go home?"

Not quite realizing that she meant that in more ways than one, I yelled "See you!" and bolted out the door like a sailor on shore leave.

I thought it was strange that Nancy was never around anymore during any of my shifts. And I really thought it was bizarre when she hired Jenna, the oldest living high school student at my high school, or anywhere for that matter, to help as a cook. Jenna was sweet, but dumb as a brick and only half as functional. But she and Nancy clicked. Jenna never yelled out the answers to *Wheel of Fortune*, even if they looked like Mississippi Mud Pie.

My shifts at the deli started earlier and earlier, while Jenna's were always from 11 am to 3 pm, which gave her plenty of time to sleep, not read, and be completely unproductive, as usual. On most days, I had to work from 6 am to 11 am. Of course, this meant that all the filthiest, hardest work was over by the time Jenna got there, but Nancy preferred it this way. It gave her more time to bond over the latest *Archie* comic books that Jenna was reading for her third crack at twelfth-grade English.

Meanwhile, I kept telling Nancy that making me come in so early was just asking for disaster, but she didn't listen.

One early Saturday morning, I stumbled into the sauna/kitchen, preheated the archaic oven, sprinkled a turkey with paprika, and turned to put it into the oven. Nancy had taught me the secret of opening the broken door and getting the food safely inside. "First," she said, as she pulled the door off by three of the hinges, "you slap the turkey inside; then you kick the door shut before the last hinge comes undone. But watch the grease, or you could start a nasty fire."

So that morning, I pulled the door open with one hand, slapped the turkey into the oven, and tried to kick the door shut. But that turkey refused to cooperate. It was hanging too far out, and instead of the door banging shut, turkey fat and grease sloshed into the gas flame—creating a conflagration (another great word for *Wheel* lovers that Nancy would never get) that rivaled *The Towering Inferno*.

A responsible person would have tried to put out the flames with the fire extinguisher that hung next to the TV for just this purpose. A responsible person might have even warned her coworkers that a fire was raging in the kitchen and, since Paul Newman was nowhere in sight to save anybody, they had better hightail it outta there and fast.

But I was not that person.

Sensing imminent death in a turkey-grease fire inferno, and since I never really liked my coworkers anyway, I dropped that oven door like the lead weight it was and tore out the back door to safety.

I was a good three or four blocks away when I realized that I'd left my purse behind. So I went back to Martinelli's Deli, where Bob, Nancy's partner, was waiting for me.

"Hey," he said, as he sucked on a stogie. "The next time you start a grease fire, can you at least warn me so I can escape too?"

"Sure," I said, because that was, I suspected, the right answer. What I really thought at that moment was, don't let that fire extinguisher out of your sight, because if you're counting on me hanging around to save you, you're toast.

Once word got around that I'd torched the kitchen and run away without a word to anyone else, I realized that I'd probably better start looking for a new job. Nancy wouldn't fire me, although I knew she would've loved to put up a big puzzle that said Y_ _ 'RE F_ RE D! and tell me to go solve it. But I knew Nancy would keep me just as long as my mother continued to be her benefactress. We were both trapped in this loveless marriage. But I intended to make her divorce me, and soon.

I started to vary the shrimp salad, refusing to slice the jumbo shrimp into a zillion tiny pieces. No, no…only giant big hunks of shrimp for my salad customers! Same goes for chicken salad. Nobody wants to eat a tiny cube. Whole great big hunks of chicken breast went into every bite. And celery? Who needs celery? Oh, and when I told Nancy that I had started using albacore packed in water—and not the cheap tuna packed in oil—I thought her head would explode.

Soon, Nancy was scheduling me for 5 am, about an hour before Bob was even supposed to arrive. Or worse, she would put me on when a big catering order had to be filled. Nancy's grin was infused with sheer evil whenever I struggled to roll the cold cuts "just right" or tie the frosted saran wrap with "the right festive touch." My deli inadequacies proved I was a total loser, even if I could beat her at *Wheel of Fortune*. And for that, at last, Nancy was grateful.

When I finally told my mother that I would have to quit, she only smiled.

"Oh, that's all right" my mother said. "I'd rather shop at C-Town anyway."

Lesson #3:
Learn to really talk with your mother.

Recipe:

Maria's Neapolitan Cream Cake (not Nancy's recipe)

This cake looks hard to make, but it's really very easy. You can make a simple layer cake or a sheet cake, depending on how many people you are serving; boxed cake mix cuts down the prep time, but hey, if you want to make the cake from scratch, go for it.

1 pound fresh ricotta

½ cup sugar

1 pound chocolate chips

½ teaspoon vanilla extract

½ cup amaretto

2 cake layers (boxed or from scratch)

¼ cup confectioner's sugar

2 cups heavy cream (for whipped cream)

8 ounces semisweet chocolate bars

1. Put the ricotta through a strainer and into a bowl. Add the sugar, chocolate chips, vanilla extract, and amaretto. Mix together.

2. Place the ricotta filling on top of the first layer and then put the second layer on top. If you're creating multiple layers, portion out the filling accordingly so you have enough for each layer.

3. To make the icing, add confectioner's sugar and cream to a chilled bowl. Whip until tiny peaks form. Add a drop of amaretto and continue to whip. Ice the cake with this mixture.

4. Shave chocolate bars into curls and add to cake for decorative purposes. Fresh strawberries or blueberries are also delicious on top.

5. Chill for at least 2 hours before serving.

Serves 6-8.

Chapter 26: My Salad Days, or Sizzle This

Now that Nancy and her deli were out of my life, I had to find a new job. Luckily, Chris was working as a busboy at the Mecca of 1980s fast food dining: Sizzler Family Steakhouse, with its all-you-can-eat combos, salad, soup, and ice cream fixings bar.

Since only boys were cooks at Sizzler, I had to settle for a job as a counter girl. That was okay with me, especially since I got a big bump in pay—I now made $3.35 an hour and I got to wear a lovely brown polyester uniform that some busboys said matched my eyes, a brown baseball cap with the word "Sizzler" emblazoned across it, and the requisite smile for the hungry, violent masses who would accost me at my new post.

Most hot summer nights, the lines would stretch out the door as hordes of hungry people waited to place their orders. Usually, the ordering went without incident, and a look of sheer delight would cross the customers' faces as they took their trays and headed down the line to the cashier.

But on nights when my barely-out-of-his-teen-years manager hadn't ordered enough (1) baked potatoes, (2) rice, (3) soda, or (4) the killer—steak, I was the first line of defense against the vicious, torch-bearing mob.

ME: May I take your order?

CUSTOMER: Yes. I'd like a sirloin steak, a baked potato, and a Coke.

ME: I'm sorry, Ma'am, but we're out of steak.

CUSTOMER: How can you be out of steak? Aren't you a steak house?

ME: Actually, I'm just a sixteen-year-old trying to save up for college. Would you like chicken?

Thirty or forty customers later, the exchange would go something like this:

ME: Can I take your order?

CUSTOMER: I heard you're out of steak, potatoes, and drinks. How can you possibly help me?

ME: You can have the chicken, rice, and water. Or you can go down the block to Burger King. Is that helpful?

It was usually at about this point in the evening that my place at the microphone was handed over to someone with a whole lot more patience, and I was banished to the salad bar.

The salad bar wasn't all that bad. I'd wheel a cart of empty canisters to the walk-in fridge, where I could spend lots more time than necessary filling up on carrot sticks, lettuce, croutons, olives, four different types of salad dressing, watermelon, cantaloupe, broccoli, and cheddar cheese.

I could also spend at least another hour heating up soups for the soup bar and gathering crackers before heading out to the dining room floor and actually restocking the salad bar.

Smelling of salad dressing and split pea soup was a small price to pay for my moments far away from the general public. That is, until my manager would come looking for me and say in his squeaky, just-about-to-change, Peter Brady of *The Brady Bunch* voice, "For the love of God, get out there and fill up that damn salad bar!"

So, eventually, I'd push that cart out there, stopping along the way to chat with my brother and the other busboys as they washed dishes and sprayed each other with the hose-like faucet. Then, I'd stick my head into the cooks' line of vision, making sure to catch up with anyone I'd missed on my way back to the freezer. Next, I'd stop at the tables where all the waitresses were on breaks, and then I'd seek out any neighbors or acquaintances that happened to be in the dining room. When I finally had no more excuses, I was forced to face my own personal Vietnam.

The salad bar usually looked like the Mekong Delta after a U.S. strafing mission had leveled it to smoke and fiery ruins. Carrots, broccoli, and kale were strewn everywhere. Gobs of sticky, swamp-smelling salad dressings oozed from all four edges of the salad bar like a festering wound.

The mixed salad bowl was almost always empty. I'd run past the gaggle of "Charlies," the customers hungry for reinforcements and willing to kill me if I didn't give them any, dropping the new bowl of mixed greens in place as I surveyed the landscape. I'd yank out the empty canisters and slap in the new ones, pulling out my Fantastic spray and paper towels from my apron to wipe away the swampy, sticky stuff that clung to the salad bar like Agent Orange.

Meanwhile, the Charlies would bleat at me. "Miss, I want chicken noodle soup. Do you have chicken noodle soup?" Never mind that there was a four-foot-high sign just over my head that said:

Our soups today are:

Split Pea with Ham

Beef Barley

I'd point to the sign and say, "Sorry. No chicken noodle soup today." This complicated explanation would leave the customers dazed and confused. "How can you not have chicken noodle soup?"

I wanted to say, look, this is a steak house and sometimes we don't even have steak, but I figured if I ran away fast enough, I would avoid the inevitable skirmishes and necessary hiding from another irate manager who would make me sit through more training videos titled "Why the Customer Is Always Right and YOU ARE ALWAYS WRONG!"

I did my best to tidy up the Saigon of Salad Hell and run back to the walk-in fridge where I could fill up more canisters and hopefully freeze to death before having to go out on the floor and face more angry customers. That is, until my "Peter Brady" manager would fling the freezer door open and say, "So that's where you're hiding! We need you back on orders."

Ever the optimist, I'd fling off my salad bar apron and burst through the doors to the front counter. Like Marcus Welby, M.D., on his way to surgery, I was glad to be getting back to what I was truly meant for. My coworkers called me the "Sizzler Sinatra" because I would take orders and make them sing, ensuring that the staff fully understood what the customer wanted, and the customers were always satisfied.

Well, sort of.

One little old lady in particular used to drive us all crazy at Sizzler Family Steakhouse. She'd toddle up to the counter, her blue hair gleaming in the dim restaurant light, and grip my arm with her bony, viselike hand. "Miss," she said, "I must have my steak rare. Do you understand?"

I looked past the counter wall at the "chef," Steven. Steven was a sixteen-year-old, acne-ridden boy wearing his cook's hat at a crazy angle. Around him, flames shot upward in every direction, engulfing every piece of meat on the grill.

"Yes, ma'am. I understand," I replied.

I gripped the microphone and began my song. "One sirloin steak, extra rare. One baked potato, sour cream on the side. Sanka. Salad bar. Make sure that steak is rare now." The old lady smiled at me.

I looked back at Steven and we both laughed.

There were few things more embarrassing—and amusing—than working at the restaurant and having people you knew come in to be served by you. It was one thing that they knew you worked at the Sizzler; it was another thing entirely to have the people you knew and loved show up and expect to be waited on.

My parents thought it was great fun to drop in with forty of their closest friends, and they would all giggle and point at me like I was a dancing bear working the counter. Well, with my lack of patience and that brown polyester uniform, maybe a brown bear and I did have certain things in common.

My brother Louie and his friend, Boots, would drop by sometimes to eat there, bother me, and plant themselves in Chris's section, making as big a mess as possible at the table he would have to clean after they left. Boots was a 600-pound bouncer who owned a nearby bar. He would sidle up to my counter and order the following:

"All-you-can-eat steak and shrimp, all-you-can-eat-soup and salad bar, all-you-can-eat dessert bar, and a Tab."

"Boots," I replied, "why not go for it and have a Coke?"

"Maria," he would laugh, "I need to cut calories somewhere."

The staff at Sizzler consisted mainly of high school students, and there was a great feeling of camaraderie as we fought off the hungry hordes. One night, as the line reached outside the air-conditioned restaurant and onto the street, I saw a familiar head bobbing up and down.

"Who's that?" my coworker and classmate, Hope, said.

I peered at the line and squinted. "I don't know," I said, as I took another order and the crazy head kept bobbing up and down. Somebody was waving at me.

"I think that's Mr. Reines," she said, and I was horrified. Hope smiled at me and poked me in the ribs. "How come *my* English teachers don't come to visit me?"

There he was, with his beautiful wife and daughter in tow. He came up to me and ordered.

"Hello, Maria darlin'," he said, and I thought I'd die of embarrassment. I wanted to crawl underneath the counter and hide. I felt absolutely ridiculous in my brown uniform and baseball cap, in all of its scratchy polyester glory and scent of salad bar.

"Hi," I replied. "What can I get you?" I took his order and giggled nervously. He smiled at me.

"Do they give you a break in this place?"

"Yes. I go on break in ten minutes."

"Perfect!" he boomed. "Meet us at our table in ten minutes. We'll spend some time together."

"I doubt you came all this way to spend my break with me."

"Of course not! We came to eat at the salad bar." He smiled and winked. "See you in ten minutes."

I laughed to myself. There was a Sizzler only half a mile away from his house, yet he'd driven all the way to Bayside.

What a character! I watched him saunter up to the salad bar as I helped other customers. He piled his food on his plate about three feet high. When I got to his table, I teased him.

"The salad bar is all-you-can-eat. You can go back more than once, you know."

He laughed. I twirled my brown cap and took a seat.

"Love your outfit," he said.

"I'm getting lots of great material for when I become a writer," I replied.

We made chitchat for a few minutes, until Chris came out on his break too.

"Join us," Mr. Reines said, and Chris pulled up a chair. We sat and laughed with Mr. and Mrs. Reines and their daughter for the next ten minutes. Instead of wishing the night would just come to an end, it suddenly felt like a party. I was sorry when my break was over.

"Thanks for coming," I said.

"We'll be back," Mr. Reines said, and smiled.

Of course, there were perks when you worked at the Sizzler. Your meals were free, so you could come in an hour before your shift started and chow down. My favorite meal was a well-done teriyaki steak (why bother asking for rare when you're only setting yourself up for disappointment?), a baked potato with sour cream and chives, and a salad. A big hunk of cheesy bread completed the meal.

Chris and I would sit with our coworkers, trading customer

horror stories, eating and laughing. During Lent, "Pete Brady" would let us have fish. So we'd get the all-you-can-eat shrimp or the baked cod. If Pete was feeling really generous, we might even get a chocolate pudding or a piece of carrot cake.

On vacation days or half days off from school, I'd pick up extra hours and work the opening shift or a midday shift. My companion on those days was a woman (note, not a girl) named Lisa.

Lisa was the oldest living counter girl in Sizzler history. At twenty-two, she had been manning the counters for six long years, getting passed over for promotions to waitress so many times that she had high heel tracks across her forehead. Lisa was not pretty, or smart, or able to make change if the register was down. She also was unfriendly and approached customers like they were the enemy. There was no way Lisa would ever be promoted. As a new counter girl, I would soon be eligible for promotion above and beyond the confines of the counter, and this made me a potential threat that Lisa felt needed to be handled.

"You're wrapping the silverware all wrong!" she'd bark, undoing the napkin I'd just wrapped around the fork, knife, and spoon and redoing it the exact same way.

"It looks the same," I'd reply.

"Of course it does, to the untrained eye," she'd say. "But the silverware will never come out now."

"Don't you want the customer to be able to get their silverware?" I asked.

Her purple-tinged complexion and huffy breathing as she walked away made me think of Nancy Martinelli. I knew I was in trouble.

A minute or two later, she would come back to me and roar something like "You're making the iced tea all wrong!" The next four hours of my shift would be filled with her helpful comments: "Do the orders like this," "Count the change out like this," "Put the whipped cream on the pudding like this," and, my personal favorite, "Stir the soup like this."

I was pretty sure after three or four days working with Lisa that I was going to blow, and they were going to find her in fifty different canisters on the salad bar. I would have, too, if I hadn't dreaded hearing "You're chopping me up all wrong!"

On days like that, I would gladly return to the land mine area known as the salad bar. Dealing with crazed, cranky customers flinging shredded cheese and croutons at me was a small price to pay to escape Lisa and her counter girl tyranny.

The salad bar truly brought out the worst in people, regardless of their age, race, or religious affiliation. I'm not sure if it was the novelty of it: "All you can eat! Even though I hate everything under the sneeze glass, I MUST EAT IT ALL!" The challenge transformed people from kind, caring, and compassionate to mean, selfish, and heartless faster than you can say "free olives!"

Men and women old enough to know better would push each other out of the way to get an extra helping of kale—

which was there only for decorative purposes. Old ladies who probably spent hours cleaning their own kitchens thought nothing of sloshing soup all over the soup bar, dripping it all the way back to their seats. Men would grab fistfuls of croutons, dropping them as they moseyed on back to their seats, perhaps fearing they'd never find the "Make Your Own Taco Salad" bar again if they didn't.

Cleaning up after scores of thoughtless, rude, and inconsiderate slobs made me really appreciate my mother. It also made me understand something so profound that it brought tears to my eyes: the food service industry was not meant for the likes of me.

As if I needed proof, one night, my old friend John H. came to eat dinner at the Sizzler with his mother. John and I had known each other since he played "The Jolly Green Giant" in a first-grade play. He was a natural for the part, considering he was about ten feet tall even then.

His mother was known by those in the "customer service industries" as something of a pest. While John towered over her, Mrs. H. could enter any store and make cashiers quiver in fear, knowing that her mere presence meant trouble: "I want this item. It was on sale two weeks ago. It's not my fault I didn't come here then. I want it. What do you mean you don't have it? I want you to search the cellar and then call every store in a 400-mile radius to find it. And when you do, I won't want it anymore. But do it anyway."

When Mrs. H. placed her order, I held my breath.

Thankfully, we were not out of steak, potatoes, or soda that night, or Mrs. H. would have spent hours telling me why the Sizzler had disappointed her in ways too unbearable to relate—even though she intended to relate them again and again.

No, her sirloin steak and baked potato were on order, and I handed her and John two big salad plates and sent them off to the salad bar. I knew we were in for some fun as Mrs. H. elbowed her way into the throng at the salad bar, jockeying for position near the mixed greens and fresh fruit bowls.

She piled her plate high with lettuce, kale, carrots, taco fixings, quesadillas, corn relish, mini egg rolls, apples, oranges, and ranch dressing. When she tried to push the food over to make room for some chocolate pudding, I waved to her.

"Mrs. H.," I said, "it's all-you-can-eat. We'll give you a clean plate. You don't have to pile everything onto that one."

But she couldn't hear me over the noise of the Muzak and the crush of the crowd.

"What?" she said, taking one hand off her plate and cupping it to her ear.

Big mistake…

In that instant, an elderly man bent under the sneeze guard to reach for some chickpeas. As he reached forward, Mrs. H. lost her grip on her plate and dumped its contents on his head.

While Mrs. H. picked kale out of his lapels and tried to wipe the ranch dressing off his face, she admonished him for being clumsy and making her drop her salad. John ran out the side door exit and I laughed so hard that tears streamed down my face. I had to crouch down under the register to hide while the manager ran out to help the dripping customer. He wasn't the first salad bar casualty, but he was by far my favorite.

As my salad days were coming to an end, my "I have to have it rare" lady showed up again. I didn't really blame her for getting mad when her sizzling, smoky, charred remains-of-the-day steak was delivered to her table with a "rare" sign sticking out of it. She ate half of it and then complained bitterly to her waitress, who tried to appease her with a new Chicken Malibu dinner. Then she complained some more until Al, the only manager actually old enough to shave, would give her a free meal.

Al was a kindhearted person who always went out of his way to make the customers happy. If someone complained that the restaurant was too hot, he'd jack up the air conditioner. If they whined that the salad bar looked like downtown Hiroshima after the bomb, Al would have five of us out there in a flash, cleaning and scraping and mopping until the salad bar shone. And if customers complained about their food, Al would usually give it to them for free. He didn't run for the back when Mrs. H. came to the Sizzler, like all the other managers did.

Al was the sort of guy who probably never kissed a girl and lived in his parents' basement. At thirty-three, he was by far the closest thing we had to the wisdom of the ages in a place run by a crew that usually wasn't old enough to pour wine. Al was short and squat, with thinning brown hair and a patchy moustache that he was always pulling on.

It took an awful lot to annoy Al, but "rare" lady somehow managed to do it. Eating for free must have been the high point of her life, because it started becoming a weekly event. Al became incensed when it dawned on him that this gray-haired, Clara Peller "Where's the Beef" look-alike was playing him. So, after several weeks of two free meals (half a steak, plus one whole Malibu Chicken platter), Al decided to try a little experiment.

When Clara came through the door on her walker, we were ready for her.

"I must have my steak rare," she told me.

I sang her order over the mike, making sure to give Steven the high sign. He pulled out a frozen sirloin and threw it on the grill. When it had the faintest hash marks, he pulled it off—uncooked, half frozen, and definitely rare.

When Clara started complaining that her steak wasn't rare enough, Al practically ran to her table.

"Listen, lady," Al said. "The only way this steak could be more rare is if I led it out here on a leash. Do us all a favor: go to Burger King from now on."

It wasn't exactly like the training videos, but it made my heart burst with pride for Al. I felt proud enough to kiss him… well, almost.

Recipe: Teriyaki Steak

Here's my take on the Teriyaki Steak I used to enjoy so much. Just remember: rare does not mean you should lead it out on a leash, and well done does not mean you should burn it.

½ cup vegetable oil

½ cup brown sugar

5 ounces soy sauce

3 cloves garlic, chopped

1 cup pineapple juice

1½ pounds flank steak

Mix first five ingredients well and pour over flank steak. Marinate steak overnight. Grill to medium rare and slice against the grain. This goes great with rice.

Serves 4-6.

The Five People I WON'T Meet In Heaven

Nancy Martinelli

Vanna White

A busload of stampeding soup and salad bar senior citizens

Lisa the counter girl

The rare beef lady

Chapter 27: Tony and Kathie Get Married

It never really occurred to me that my brothers would grow up and meet girls who would actually agree to marry them. It's not that there was anything wrong with my brothers; it's just that, as a kid, growing up was this far-away thing that never seemed like it was going to come. But it did, much to my surprise.

After years of dating, Tony and Kathie got engaged, set a wedding date, and chose their bridal party. As one of the lucky bridesmaids, I got to go shopping to pick out dresses.

At 16 years old, I was so excited to be a part of this. I imagined that we bridesmaids would go off together, sharing inside jokes, laughing at everything we said to each other, and agreeing on everything. In between shopping for gowns, we would go out for lunch and eat. I mean, eating was important when you were doing all the hard work of searching for a dress, wasn't it? Besides, I hated shopping and was really only looking forward to the meal afterwards.

This is where I learned the real truth about being a bridesmaid.

Girls, understand this: those bridal magazines lie. They show women who weigh about twelve pounds, looking happy and beautiful in taffeta, silk, satin, or chiffon. They even look good in hats! Everyone has perfect skin and the cutest haircut. Everyone is smiling and laughing, with a basket of daisies in her hands and the sun shining in the sky.

Since this was my first bridal party (the first of many), I did not understand that fighting over the color, style, fabric, and type of dress was mandatory. Apparently, choosing the right color to match the napkins at the reception hall is something the bride undertakes as a solemn vow, and getting shoes that can be properly dyed to match the dress (and by extension, the napkins) is a must.

I was too young to care which dress we chose. All I knew was, I didn't want to wear a hat. Hats were very popular in the 1980s, but I thought they looked dumb. Here you were, decked out in a gorgeous dress, and you had the equivalent of a Stetson hat perched on the side of your head. Only it wasn't as big as a Stetson; it was a dwarf Stetson, in a lovely shade of teal.

I probably wasn't true bridesmaid material.

Kathie was pretty patient with me. She appreciated that I didn't cry or scream or fight over the various dresses that the group pulled out. I only remember a few dresses that I absolutely refused to wear under any circumstances.

One of them looked like the dress Carol Burnett wore in that skit where she was supposed to be Scarlett O'Hara, walking down the big staircase, with a curtain rod across her shoulders and tassels on her head. I think that would have been a better look than most of the dresses we tried on.

I didn't realize it then, but I was too young to say things like "This dress makes my hips look fat" and "This dress makes my arms look like I'm waving a flag!" The women in the party, however, had many complaints about how enormous these bridesmaids' dresses made them look.

I tried on dress after dress after dress until finally we found a pretty dress with a handkerchief bottom. By handkerchief bottom, I mean there were shorter and longer parts to the skirt, like the hi-lo dresses that are in style today. The dress was made of organza and tulle, so it draped across your body in the most forgiving way imaginable, while feeling light and airy. This made all of the women in the party overjoyed. Although it was a spaghetti strap dress, we were able to get it with a short jacket to cover us in the church. At last, everyone was happy.

Next, we spent months trying to find shoes that we could all agree on. It felt like the shopping was going to last longer than the courtship—and that lasted for five years.

Finally, after many months of hunting for dresses, shoes, and accessories, the day of the wedding arrived. I came back from my hair appointment, put on my dress and makeup, and waited for the limousine to come. I heard scuffling downstairs and then Tony appeared in his tuxedo with Jude right behind him.

"You are not wearing that suit!" Tony said.

"Why not? I think I look great," Jude replied.

Jude was in a pinstriped suit that looked as if a clown and an umpire had given birth to it. The lapels were wide, the black and white stripes were wider, and the suit was cut in a boxy shape. It would've looked great if he was playing with The Stray Cats or any other rockabilly band, but not so much for a church wedding followed by an afternoon reception. Jude and Kathie had something of a strained relationship at the moment and they were constantly fighting. She had made the mistake of telling Jude that he should look presentable at her wedding; this was Jude's response.

My father came out of his bedroom, took one look at Jude, and laughed. "Go back downstairs and get changed. You have to wear something else."

The limo pulled up, and I ran out the door into the weak sunlight of that late March morning. I jumped into the back of the car, laughing all the while at the idea of Kathie's face if Jude showed up in that zoot suit. Jude and Kathie had been arguing since, well…forever, and I was pretty sure that she wouldn't like Jude's suit one bit. The question was, would she let it ruin her day?

It only took a few minutes to get to Kathie's house, and when I got there, the photographer was already taking pictures.

"Hi, Maria!" she said.

I expected Kathie to look like a nervous wreck, but she didn't. In the months leading up to this moment, she had fretted and worried about gowns and tuxedos, flowers and entrées. Kathie had gone over so many details so many times that I was sure she'd still be sitting there now, trying to plan ahead just in case disaster struck.

But there she was, grinning for the camera, looking like we were about to head out on the best adventure ever. She didn't look like a big puffy marshmallow; her dress was tailored beautifully and her veil framed her face perfectly. She wore a big smile and was laughing as the photographer snapped photos. She looked extraordinarily happy.

"Are you nervous?" I said.

"No! I just want to get to the church already!"

About an hour later, we headed over to the church. It was strange to see everyone I knew all cleaned up and solemn. On our side of the church, I saw Angela, Pete, and Mary Lou; Eleanor and Bob; Uncle Don; Lorraine, John, Angela, and Ray; Tony and Vicki; my Uncle Nick; Aunt Nellie and Uncle John; and dozens more, all craning their heads, watching and waiting for the bridal party to march down the aisle.

I watched my grandmother march down the aisle on my brother Joey's arm as he guided her to her place of honor beside Uncle Sal, Uncle Don, and Dad. Then, Louie, Tony's best man, escorted Mom down the aisle. She looked beautiful in her long purple dress with the sequins on top. She clutched a fur coat along her shoulders and looked as glamorous as any movie star as she kissed my brother and took her place beside my father.

The organist began the wedding march, and off we went. I was terrified that I would trip on my high heels or faint (I was a world-class fainter) or break out in a sweat when everyone was watching me. But when my turn came, I managed to walk in a straight line without making an idiot of myself. It was truly a remarkable moment in time. Everybody smiled and waved at me, and I smiled and waved back. Once I got to my spot at the front of the church, I turned to see Kathie come down the aisle.

Kathie walked down the aisle on her father's arm, with a 10,000-megawatt smile and a big laugh. She did not look like a nervous bride at all. Her dad handed her off to Tony, who looked more nervous than she did.

Everything was going along smoothly until the priest said: "Should anyone here have any reason to object to this union, let them speak now or forever hold their peace," and Kathie's deaf brother stood up and objected. No, wait a second…that was the movie, *Four Weddings and a Funeral*. No one objected at Tony and Kathie's wedding. The only glitch that did occur happened when her little nephew, the ring-bearer, skipped up to the altar to hand over the rings and he tripped. The rings went flying, everyone gasped, and we waited for the ring bearer's wails of embarrassment to ring out across the church. However, the little guy got up, dusted himself off, handed over the rings, and marched back to his seat. His face may have been a little red, but he smiled when everyone gave him a round of applause.

When the priest said, "I now pronounce you husband and wife," Tony and Kathie kissed and everyone in that little church broke into applause one last time.

I was happy for my brother and sister-in-law…and as usual, hungry. Luckily, the reception was just a few miles away, and soon enough, we were all talking, laughing, and eating at the reception hall, enjoying pigs-in-blankets, stuffed mushrooms, scallops wrapped in bacon, and baked clams.

When the cocktail hour was over, we were ushered into the main dining room, and Mr. and Mrs. Anthony Lagalante were announced for the first time. They danced their first dance to Dan Fogelberg's "Longer Than," and we all got on the dance floor with them.

For the next five hours, we danced and sang and celebrated. Uncle Don made the rounds, dancing with cousins Lorraine and Eleanor, my mother, and yes, even me. Everyone wanted to dance with Uncle Don, and he didn't disappoint anyone.

When the day was done, we rolled out of the Roslyn Country Club well-fed, tired, and very happy.

We went back home, where my parents sat misty-eyed in the living room. I disappeared into my bedroom and got changed. I had a strange inkling of what it must have been like for Cinderella right after the ball. I hung up my gown and put away my shoes, and went back to being plain old Maria, not even a bridesmaid any more.

I went downstairs and looked at Tony's empty bedroom. I would miss him very much. Nothing would ever be the same now that he had left the house. Jude had moved out a year before, but he was over so much that it wasn't even like he had left.

Now that Tony was married, I imagined there would be a lot less brother/sister time. There would be no more late-night jaunts to White Castle or late-night ice cream sandwiches while we watched *Trilogy of Terror* on the Late Show. I started to understand why my mother was upstairs looking at Tony's baby pictures and my father seemed so sad.

But then again, Kathie and Tony now lived only about two miles away. I was pretty sure we'd see them tomorrow after mass. Plus, Kathie liked coming over on Saturday nights for Chinese food, and they always took me to the movies with them. The world hadn't ended after all; sure, it was different, but couldn't different be really wonderful?

The future was rolling out in front of us all: Tony and Kathie were married. Who would be next? Jude? Louie? Paul? Joey? Chris? Would I always be a bridesmaid, never a bride— or would I find someone and get to enjoy a wedding day too?

Our newest family member, Kathie, probably had an inkling that the years ahead would be filled with some happiness, some tears, lots of yelling, and a lot of eating.

She had no idea.

Recipe: Shepherd's Pie

My very first Irish sister-in-law brought a whole new dimension to our little ethnic clan, so here's a recipe that celebrates her background and heritage. It's a great go-to dish that can be counted on in a pinch—sort of like Kathie.

1½–2 pounds russet potatoes (3–4 big ones)

1 cup milk

1 stick butter, divided

2 tablespoons oil

salt and pepper to taste

1 chopped onion

2 cloves garlic, minced

4 large carrots, chopped

2 pounds lean ground beef or lamb

1½ tablespoons Worcestershire sauce

2 tablespoons tomato paste

1 cup beef broth

½ bag (8 ounces) frozen peas

½ bag (8 ounces) frozen corn

cooking spray for casserole dish

1. Preheat oven to 400°F.

2. Peel the potatoes and cut into ½-inch pieces. Place in a medium saucepan and cover with cold water. Set over high heat, cover, and bring to a boil. Once boiling, uncover, decrease

the heat to maintain a simmer, and cook until tender and easily crushed with tongs, 10 to 15 minutes. Drain the potatoes in a colander and return to the saucepan. Mash the potatoes. Add the milk, ½ stick of butter, salt, and pepper and continue to mash until smooth.

3. Put the rest of the butter and oil into a sauté pan and add onion and minced garlic. Add carrots and cook for 5 minutes. Add ground beef or lamb and cook until no longer pink. Drain off the fat and place the dish back on the burner. Add Worcestershire sauce, tomato paste, beef broth, salt, and pepper. Cook for five more minutes. Add peas and corn toward the end of the cooking time.

4. Layer meat and vegetables into the bottom of a sprayed casserole dish. Add mashed potatoes on top. Place in preheated oven. Cook for 30 minutes, until potatoes are golden brown and dish is bubbling. You can turn on the broiler for a minute or two to get the top to brown (if necessary).

Serves 6.

Chapter 28: Prom Night

One of the best parts about growing up in a big family was the sense that there was always someone who would, to quote *The Godfather*, "go to the mattresses" for you when necessary.

If I needed help creating a family tree, my grandmother and Uncle Sal would sit down with me and help me fill in the blanks. If I needed to park near Queens College but I couldn't find a spot anywhere, my cousins Angela and Pete would let me leave the car at their house. If I needed a nice outfit, but didn't have the money, Uncle Don would take me to the store he worked at, B. Altmann's, and get me something special, along with his store discount.

If my car broke down on the way to work, one of my brothers would come and rescue me. If my brothers weren't around, there was always my cousin Tommy. Once, I was supposed to be at work in twenty minutes. I was about a mile away from home, and of course this was in the days before cell phones, when my car sputtered to a stop. The ancient gas gauge said I had half tank of gas, but it lied.

Just as I began to panic, Tommy pulled up.

"Maria, what's the matter?" he said.

"I think my car is out of gas," I explained.

"Get in," he said, as he drove me to the gas station, filled up a gas can, and got me enough gas to get back and forth to work. I wasn't even late!

My luck in having this big family to draw on was never more necessary than when I was a senior in high school. As was usually the case with me, I had no boyfriend and no prospects either, but I wanted to go to the prom. I had resigned myself to missing it altogether when my friend, Denise, approached me. "I have a date! His name is Frank," she said, and I could tell she was very excited.

"Good for you. I'm glad." I said.

"Now you have to come too. I won't go without you. Bring your brother Chris along, and ask Lisa H. to come too. My dad will give us a free limo."

Denise's father worked for a limousine company, so that was one huge expense I wouldn't have to worry about if I decided to go. I always had so much fun with Lisa too, and I knew we would laugh all night long if we decided to go. It was tempting, but still, I balked. "I don't know. Nobody asked me."

"So?" Denise said. "Ask someone yourself."

I thought about it and decided to try. I asked a couple of

my friends, but anyone that I considered a good enough friend to ask either hated the very idea of the prom, or had a girlfriend who hated the idea of him going with me to the prom.

I was just about to give up on the idea altogether when it struck me that SOMEONE, SOMEWHERE must have been willing to go to the prom with me. So, I decided to go ahead and buy four tickets. I wasn't going to embarrass myself and go with Chris; instead, I had him go with Lisa.

I quickly ran out of prom date candidates, so I told Chris that I might not be able to go.

"Let's ask Tommy," Chris said.

Most of the people in my circle didn't know that Tommy was my cousin. Sure, some of them knew him because he was a member of a band called "Pee Wee Sweet" that included him, Chris, and their friend Mike. Their gigs included covers of Jimi Hendrix songs like "Purple Haze," "In Memory of Elizabeth Reed" by the Allman Brothers, and an original song they wrote called "King of the High School Prom." They played around the neighborhood and at local high schools (including ours) and colleges at the battle of the bands, the end of school year concerts, and other events.

The next time we saw Tommy, we asked if he would be willing to go. "Sure," Tommy said. "Why not?"

"At the very least, we'll get appetizers and a fancy dinner," I said.

"Oh, maybe they'll have pigs-in-the-blanket," Tommy joked.

So that was settled; I had a date for prom night. The only

hitch was that the prom was the same night that Chris and Tommy had a recital at the Drum Center and they couldn't get there very early. However, faced with the prospect of being late or not being able to go at all, I was more than happy to wait for my brother and my cousin to show up.

In the days leading up to the prom, Lisa, Denise, and I got our hair done, got our dresses pressed, and searched for shoes. Lisa chose a dress she bought off the rack at Bloomingdale's and I used my bridesmaid's dress from Tony's and Kathie's wedding. Once I ditched the jacket, I had the perfect prom dress, and lucky me—I even had the shoes to match.

When prom night arrived, Chris looked very debonair in his tuxedo and new haircut. Tommy looked tall and handsome, with long brown hair cut in an '80s bi-level, and dressed in a white tuxedo jacket with black pants. I couldn't have had a better date for the night.

"Come outside and line up," my mother said to Chris, Tommy, and me. We stood outside in our prom finery, smiling, as Mom clicked away while we waited for the limousine to arrive.

Mom's photographic skills were always a bit shaky. Between standing about twenty feet away from us and fighting the impending dusk, the photos were a bit blurry and dark. I'm just glad she actually had film on hand, which was something of a coup for us; there is hardly any photographic evidence of Chris's and my existence since there was never film or flash cubes in our house.

We paused just long enough to take group photos when Denise, Frank, and Lisa showed up. Lisa looked beautiful with her wine-colored dress and her big '80s hair, and Denise looked very chic in an off-the-shoulder white dress. After a few more quick photos, off we went for a night of dancing, laughing, and, hopefully, eating.

As soon as we arrived, Chris, Lisa, Tommy, and I ran over to the photographer's booth and had our photos taken. Lots of the girls there recognized Tommy and asked, "Isn't he the guy in Chris's band? Is that your boyfriend?" I shook my head, while Lisa and I laughed.

It was fun to see everyone from school dressed to the hilt. The girls wore bright taffeta gowns and the boys wore spiffy tuxedos. Everybody was in a good mood and ready to celebrate the end of high school. The night's theme was "The Way We Were," which seemed kind of out of date when we were dancing to Boy George, The Stray Cats, and Cyndi Lauper.

We joined our friends on the dance floor for a bit, until Chris and Tommy went back to the table. Lisa and I danced together, and then I started to dance with some of my friends. Lisa danced with a boy who always seemed to like her, and they were having a great time.

At one point, I started to walk off the dance floor when a boy who had liked me in the tenth grade came over and asked me to dance.

"Sure," I said, and he smiled.

I was acting in a much more mature way than I'd acted

two years before, when this same boy, named Richie, had asked me out. He shocked me by sending a gorgeous bouquet of flowers to me on Valentine's Day. I responded like a five-year-old, said thank you, and did my best to avoid him after that. I wasn't ready when he liked me, and that was too bad. He was such a good person.

We danced a string of fast dances together when a slow song set started.

"You don't have to dance this with me," Richard said. I could tell he was praying I wouldn't leave him there on the dance floor.

"That's okay," I said. "I'd like to."

"Won't your boyfriend mind?" he said.

"Tommy?" I laughed. "He won't care. He's my cousin."

"Your *cousin*? Why on earth did you come with your cousin?"

"Nobody else asked me."

"I would've asked you!" Richard said.

"Well, you didn't. You came with someone else. So why don't you go ask her to dance now?"

"I like this arrangement better," Richard said, and we continued to dance. Just then, a couple that I knew slid across the dance floor to our side. They thought they could "save" me by having the boy cut in.

"May I?" he said, and I could see that he and his girlfriend were laughing. What was worse, Richard could see it too.

I started to dance with this boy until he looked at me and said, "Now isn't this better?"

I glanced over at Richie, who looked miserable. I didn't want to hurt him. I thought of how he probably had to screw up a lot of courage just to come over and ask me to dance in the first place. "Thanks, but no thanks," I said, as I walked back to Richie. "May I cut in?"

Richard smiled. "Sure," he said, and my friend just shrugged. She went back to her boyfriend and they danced off. In between dinner, dancing, and laughing with Tommy, Chris, Lisa, Denise, and her date, I danced quite a bit with Richie. He was really a sweet kid, and I was sorry I'd never given him a chance before. At the end of the night, Richie gave me a kiss. And it was pretty nice!

Once the prom was over, we went into New York City for a night of dancing at the legendary Copacabana (yes, the same one in the Barry Manilow song, and no, we didn't see Lola the Showgirl there). When we were too tired to dance anymore, we left the club and went to a local diner for eggs, pancakes, and French toast.

My brother and I got home at sunrise, and I gave Tommy a big hug. As far as I was concerned, he was the King of the High School Prom.

Recipe: Post-Prom French Toast

This dish is perfect for the morning after a big event, or any time you want something sweet and satisfying on a lazy, danced-all-night-and-now-I'm-hungry kind of morning.

6 eggs, beaten

2 cups half and half

½ teaspoon vanilla extract

1 teaspoon kosher salt

1 large loaf thick bread (preferably challah bread or brioche)

2 tablespoons cinnamon

1 tablespoon oil

Sifted confectioner's sugar (optional)

1 cup maple syrup (warmed)

4-6 pats of butter

Raspberry or blueberry preserves (optional)

Put eggs, half and half, vanilla extract, and salt into bowl and mix together. Cut the bread into thick slices (about ¾ inch) and dredge in egg mixture. Soak for about 5 minutes. Heat up a sauté pan or griddle and fry the slices in oil; transfer to a warm cookie sheet and place in oven while you fry up the rest of the slices. Sprinkle frying slices with cinnamon; you can add confectioner's sugar if you like. Top with butter, warmed maple syrup or preserves. Enjoy!

Serves 4-6.

Chapter 29: Gary at Last

Since high school was ending and I couldn't face another bleary-eyed day at the Sizzler Family Steakhouse, I decided to find a new job. So, with Lisa H. by my side, we jumped into my little blue car and went off to apply for jobs at Stern's Department Store. It seemed like the perfect place for me to work, since I would be going off to college in the fall and I needed a job that paid better and would work around my class schedule.

Stern's was the equivalent of another planet compared to Sizzler. I would no longer be required to wear a brown polyester uniform and cheesy hat; now, I was expected to come to work in a dress or skirt or a blouse and slacks. There was no food to handle and I would no longer go home smelling like bacon bits and ranch dressing.

Lisa got a job in the Juniors' department and I got sent

downstairs to China. Tucked away in the corner, surrounded by china, crystal, and silverware, I whistled songs like "Where Have All the Customers Gone?" while I swear tumbleweed bounced by. Most nights, working at Stern's was about as difficult as closing my eyes and drifting off to sleep (which I really had to fight, since my bosses seemed to frown on sleeping at the register).

Depending on my coworkers, the job could be great fun. I spent many nights telling jokes and laughing with Ginny, the middle-aged woman I worked with when I first started there.

When customers did actually come into the department, Ginny was always bright and cheery; she was so delighted to have human beings actually shopping in our department that no request was ever too much trouble for her. She didn't lose her patience or wish death on any customers, as some of my other coworkers did. She never ran away when Mrs. H. came running down the aisle toward the China department. Phone calls to all twenty-five other Stern's stores were never a problem; if you wanted that wine set, Ginny would find it for you!

By watching Ginny, I learned that customers were really just people with needs, and if I met those needs, they would be my allies forever.

Unfortunately, Ginny left to work in the post office a couple of years later, where her relentless good cheer and focus on customer attention might have led to the rash of shootings and the phrase "going postal."

Meanwhile, coworkers came and went. No one wanted to

work in China, mainly because it was a deserted wasteland and our floor manager was as humorless and unyielding as Darth Vader. If Frank ever came around the bend from Domestics and saw you standing still at the register—with no customers in sight—he would descend on you quicker than a hungry hawk grabs hold of a rabbit.

"Why are you just standing here?" Frank would say.

"There are no customers anywhere in sight and I'm supposed to stand here and ring them up if and when they show up," I'd reply.

"Why aren't you polishing the silver?" Frank asked.

I looked at the rows and rows of gleaming silver. "I polished everything last night. There's nothing left to do."

I learned quickly that this was the exact wrong thing to say to Frank. It was like a challenge, and Darth Vader could never refuse a challenge.

"Unlock the Waterford case and wash all the glasses. When you're done with that, go to Gifts and clean all the Lladros. Next, dust all the shelves."

And so it would go every night. Whether I was alone or with a coworker, we would polish, wash, dust, and clean, silently praying that someone, anyone, would need dishes or glasses so we could stop cleaning and start ringing up orders.

The only person I ever met who managed to get out of this chore was a girl named Helena. She was about as bright as a burned-out light bulb, and Frank should've known better than to ask her to clean anything. But ask her he did, night after night, until our department manager went to Frank and begged him to stop.

"Why?" Frank replied.

"When she takes the sculptures out of the case, she breaks their heads off. Then she puts them back into the case, headless. I have over $2,000 worth of broken merchandise in the display case. But they are clean."

Helena was quickly dispatched to the Domestics department, where Frank figured she could fold towels and not cost the store any more money.

The job would have been a complete bust if it hadn't been for the fact that it was a fabulous place to meet people. College and high school students came and went as staff members at Stern's; the constant turnover was just the thing I needed to meet someone.

I dated a few of the boys at Stern's but didn't really connect with anyone at first. It never occurred to me that I would be so totally mystified by boys, having grown up in a house that was full of them. Eventually, however, I learned a thing or two about how to relate to boys that I wasn't actually related to.

I learned that I could no longer punch them and run to my bedroom, using a large plank of wood shoved under my doorknob to keep them out.

I learned that saying "You're just fat/lazy/stupid/boring" made men outside of my immediate family angry and less prone to stick around.

I learned that men don't like to lose. Of course, my brothers didn't like to lose, but they weren't men, exactly. They were adversaries to be vanquished. But no one took me aside and said, "Listen, Maria, when you go to Tiffany's Wine & Cheese and start playing board games, let him win at least one or two rounds of backgammon. Don't pump your fist and yell 'Who's yo' daddy!' when you beat him at chess, and don't, for the love of God, scream 'Loser!' when you beat him at Trivial Pursuit. Even if he seems to be enjoying himself, you will almost certainly never see him again."

I learned that food wasn't like an additional family member to most men. They could go practically days without sitting down at the table and talking to anyone, let alone fifty immediate family members, over a glass of sangria and a hunk of cheese.

I made the shocking discovery that they didn't find my grandmother's eating off their plates funny. I mean, c'mon! Who doesn't find the antics of my eighty-year-old grandmother delightful and amusing? So what if that's the last piece of pie—what Nonnie wants, Nonnie gets!

Yes, it was almost destiny that dating and I would have some rough patches. It's not that I didn't like boys—on the contrary, I sure did—it's just that I never understood them. I was soon to find out that I hadn't grown any more enlightened just because I worked in a place called China.

There was Teddy, my fellow sales associate, who was

madly in love with me and asked me out a few times. Once we went out, though, Teddy became less communicative than Helen Keller before Anne Sullivan cranked the water pump. To be honest, Teddy was the antithesis of "my type." He was a skinny, nervous boy with bright blue eyes and black hair. He reminded me of one of the Lollipop Kids from *The Wizard of Oz*, only a little bit taller.

I was shocked when he asked me out on a date since it had never occurred to me that we were anything more than friends. But I recognized that Teddy was a genuinely nice person, and as Mr. Reines had said years before, just because I dated someone didn't mean I had to marry him. So I said yes.

Almost immediately, I could tell that my attachment to Teddy was tenuous. I wasn't the least bit nervous when he came to get me that night, although he looked like he'd just swallowed a goat...and it was kicking him. Teddy's face was pale and he looked frightened. I introduced him to my parents, and my father jokingly said, "Now make sure you get her back here by 12 or I'll beat you with a pumpkin!"

We went to the movies and then out for ice cream. Teddy spent the entire time checking his watch. This bright, funny boy who always had so much to say at work didn't utter a single word to me for two straight hours. When we got to Swenson's Ice Cream Parlor, I said, "Let's get a booth."

"We can't," Teddy stuttered. "I have to have you home by 12."

"It's 9:45," I replied. "We'll be done and home by 12, even if we get a booth."

But no, Teddy paid for our ice cream cones and we stood awkwardly in the parking lot, slurping away. I was home by 10:30. There was no awkward goodnight kiss. Teddy was in such a panic to get me home on time that he practically dragged me to the front steps, knocked on the front door, and delivered me safely to my parents.

"How did it go?" my mother asked me.

"I don't know," I replied. "I think he likes me, but if I go out with him again, you might have to use a defibrillator on me just to keep me awake."

I think Teddy was being polite, but his irrational fear of my father and his sudden muteness made my heart sink. There was no chemistry between us, and no way to get that spark to roar into flames. If he was a caveman and I was two sticks, we never would've discovered fire.

For months Teddy begged me to go on another date with him, but I kept saying no. Finally, after months and months of being asked by him and only him to go—well, anywhere, I relented when he asked me to go to a party given by a friend one October night.

"I'm not going on a date with you," I said.

"It won't be a date," Teddy replied. "I'll have other people in the car."

When he picked me up, the car was empty.

"Where are your other friends?" I said, still not wanting to believe that we were on a date.

"They got other rides," Mr. Smooth replied.

I shook my head. Oh well, might as well go along. I had nothing else to do now that *The Rockford Files* had been canceled.

We got in his car and started to drive. Once again, Teddy was struck mute. He said not a word to me as we drove to College Point and walked into his friend's house.

The next thing he said to me was, "Excuse me." He promptly walked over to his friend Charlie, and they disappeared into the basement. I thought he would come back up a few minutes later, but as the hours ticked by, I wondered if my date had fled the scene. What was I doing here? I walked over to the dining room table and poured myself a Coke.

"Hi," a young man said.

I looked over my shoulder and, not seeing anyone behind me, realized this boy was speaking to me. "Hi," I replied.

"My name is Joe and I see you've been standing here alone for a while. Did you come by yourself?"

I introduced myself, and we started to talk. Joe came from a huge Catholic family, had eight brothers and three sisters, was very pleasant, and best of all, he was a Yankees fan. He had sandy-brown hair and blue eyes, and he could actually string together more than two sentences at a time when he spoke to me.

By the time Teddy came back up the stairs from the basement, Joe and I had covered what we'd been up to from the late 1960s to the present. We were laughing and enjoying ourselves, so much so that when Teddy tapped my arm, I couldn't figure out why he was wearing a wounded look on his face.

"I'm back," he said.

I arched my eyebrow. "I can see that."

I turned back to Joe and we started to chat again. Teddy wandered away.

"You should go back to your boyfriend," Joe said.

"He's not my boyfriend," I replied. "We came here together tonight, that's all."

"Oh," Joe said. "Do you have a boyfriend?"

"No," I replied.

"Do you think we could go out some time?"

Before I could answer, I felt Teddy's vise-like grip on my arm. "It's time to go, Maria."

We walked out of the house and did not utter another word to each other on the drive home. I wanted to kick him for taking me away from Joe just as he was about to ask me out.

When we got to my door, I could see that Teddy was expecting a kiss on this, our supposedly second date.

"So where were you all night?" I said.

Teddy shrugged. "I went downstairs to hang out with the guys."

"Then what did you need me there for?"

"You didn't seem to mind. Made yourself a new friend."

"Teddy, this is the most you've said to me all night! You bring me to a party and then go downstairs for three hours, leaving me alone upstairs where I know no one. Am I not supposed to talk to other people?"

"He was asking you out on a date!"

"So?" I said. "What do you care? You were busy with the guys!"

Teddy tried to hug me. "Look, Maria, I really like you!"

I broke free from the bear hug. "I like you too, Teddy, but not like that. This isn't working out for us, so let's just stop before I say something I'll regret."

Teddy closed his eyes and tried to kiss me. I slapped his shoulder like he was my old football buddy.

"Good-night!" I said, as I slipped from his grasp and ran inside.

The flowers, candy, phone calls, and coincidental "bump-intos" started coming fast and furious then. Teddy would leave flowers, balloons, and chocolates on my car hood. Many nights, he'd call to ask me along on a group outing to the movies or bowling. Then, he started walking by my classes at Queens College. I would've despaired, but a funny thing happened a few weeks later. Joe, the friendly boy from the party, came to Stern's to buy his mother some china.

In the end, Joe finally asked me out while Teddy stood across the sales floor and glowered. I didn't let regret or guilt hold me back; I said yes. I thought for a week or two that I had found someone worth keeping.

Joe was a nice-looking young man, funny and polite, and always a perfect gentleman. But I soon realized that he didn't mean all that much to me. If I saw him on Friday or Saturday, that was fine. If I didn't, that was fine too. He looked a lot like my Psychology 101 teacher, and I confided in Chris that when

I saw the psych teacher, I'd forget what Joe looked like.

"True love, huh?" Chris snorted.

By the end of December, Joe and I had fizzled out. Our last conversation wasn't exactly the stuff of high drama.

"I don't think I can be tied down," Joe said to me.

"Is that why you came an hour late tonight?" I said. "You think I'm tying you down?"

"It's not that I don't like you," Joe replied. "I'd like to be your friend."

I shrugged. "Nah," I said, without a moment's hesitation.

"What do you mean, nah?" Joe said in disbelief.

"I've already got enough friends," I replied. "See you."

I walked to my friend Hope's house and told her the story. Hope laughed.

"Do you feel bad?" she asked.

"No," I said, and I meant it. In fact, I was pretty sure that not having Joe in my life wouldn't be a big deal. Especially now that Psych 101 was over.

I got used to the idea that I wasn't going to have a boyfriend. I was eighteen and already convinced that I'd end up one of those pathetic old ladies who lived with twenty-five cats until the day the city workers came to uncover the bad smell emanating from my house, where I lay dead and all twenty-five of my cats were eating me.

So the years passed. I dated one or two other people who

were really good people, just not right for me. Sometimes my head would ache. Would I ever find the right one?

One night about two and a half years later, I stood in the China department chatting with my coworker, John. John and I loved shopping and going to the beach; we were good friends from the start. We were having a great time standing around, sharing funny stories and laughing, when the training manager turned the corner from the escalator and headed toward us.

"Oh, good God, no," John said, fear creeping into his voice. "Here comes Gia, and she's got some newbies with her!"

I watched Gia as she barged into the different departments, introducing the new sales associates. Each of them had the same look of having been beaten into submission that you wore after three endless nights of training stuck in a small room with Gia.

Most people meant well. Not Gia. She lived to teach newcomers the minutiae of life at Stern's Department Store, and she reveled in the fact that most people couldn't remember any of it. Meanwhile, Gia could—at any moment—make you feel small and worthless by asking you what it was about that skirt you were wearing that put you over the dress code line, in violation of store policy #3754321.

So it was with considerable glee that Gia harrumphed her way over to our department with a new sales associate. She was obviously pleased to be breaking up John's and my little tea party; here was a newcomer, her feline smile said. Now you two will have to be nice, and it will probably kill you.

"Look at him," John said as the two walked our way. "I hope he knows how to polish silver."

The new guy walked behind Gia with a bit of a smile on his face. He was tall and broad-shouldered, with lots of short-cropped, light brown hair, a beard to match, and glasses. He wore a white blazer and a thin white tie over his impeccably pressed dress shirt and slacks. Gia would never get him on a dress code violation.

"This is Gary," Gia said, as Gary shook hands with John and me. "Now you should all play nicely. Gary will be working on the Monday-Wednesday-Friday-Saturday shift." Since John and I worked on the Tuesday-Thursday-Saturday-Sunday shift, we would only work together a few hours a week on Saturdays.

"Nice to meet you," I said.

As Gia walked away, John turned back to me and immediately launched into the conversation we were having before Gary got there. Gary smiled and turned to look around the department.

When John left to help a customer, I turned to Gary. "Three days in a room with Gia—and you lived to tell the tale!"

"They wanted me to do a fourth day," Gary said, "but I told them I had to have my eye put out with a hot poker."

I laughed. Hey, the new guy was funny and cute! Of course, he also looked about ten years older than me, so I figured he was married and maybe had kids. Probably took this job to supplement his income, to help pay for the new baby or a new house. I figured he was out of my league.

But wouldn't it be nice if he liked me too?

A few days later, I was in a car accident. With the summer just starting and no car, I had to take on lots of extra hours at Stern's so I could save up the money for tuition in the fall term.

I became night selling manager at this point, and I looked very official with my blue badge and neck brace. Whenever customers had a problem, they would seek me out and whine to me. It was my job to make them happy, or at least satisfy them enough so they would go away.

I started working the additional Monday-Wednesday shift, so I suddenly was in contact with Gary and his coworker, Juanita. I had to help them very often because they were new and didn't know how to write up special orders.

"Miss," one lady said to me, "I would like to special order some china."

Since I was in the Draperies department that night, I wasn't sure why she was telling this to me. "Okay," I said. "Just go over to the China desk and one of those two will help you."

"No," the lady said. "The lady told me I'd have to get you."

Juanita spent most nights looking pale and anxious; she was a single mother with a teenage son who spent his life spending more money than Juanita would ever make in this lifetime.

Each night, I'd have to go back to the employee lounge and wake Juanita, who was sprawled out on the couch, snoring.

"Juanita," I said, as I pushed her arm. "You have to get

up and go back onto the floor. If Frank finds you here asleep, we'll both get into trouble."

"I'm sorry, Maria," Juanita replied. "My son, Yeffrey, wants a Euro Pass, and I worked all day at one of my other yobs to raise money so I could buy him one. I'm tired now."

It never ceased to amaze me that Juanita:

1) Named her son Jeffrey, when all she could say was "Yeffrey."

2) Hadn't turned to selling blood to raise money for Yeffrey's exploits.

3) Was not yet selling organs to raise needed cash.

4) Arrived at work fully clothed; hadn't she discovered the market for vintage clothing? Would she come in naked one day because Yeffrey wanted a Ferrari while touring through Italy?

5) Saw nothing wrong with sleeping at this, her third job/ "yob," while her son was sightseeing his way through Europe.

After I begged Juanita to get back out on the selling floor, I went back out onto the selling floor and spent time with Gary.

I spent the extra hours polishing, cleaning, and helping customers. The upside to all this was, once Frank found Juanita asleep in the employee lounge and she was fired, Gary and I spent more time together.

I discovered something quite amazing. This cute, funny, and smart person was not ten years older than me, married and with kids. In fact, he was a year younger than me, unmarried, and not much more than a kid himself. He loved baseball (he was a Mets fan, but I was forgiving), endured Catholic school, and most of all...he loved to eat.

We started going out with the others on our breaks and at night, after quitting time. Together, we sampled Italian, Chinese, and Greek foods. I took him to the Sizzler, where my old boss, the Pete Brady look-alike, gave us a free lunch. We also devoured seafood nachos and margaritas at Chi Chi's in Great Neck and ate boatloads of buffalo wings at Bennigan's. White Castle welcomed us like we were the palace owners, and we were on a first-name basis with Wendy, Mickey D., and, of course, The King himself...Burger King.

At this point, I knew I liked Gary. So I broke it off with the person I was dating at the time and hoped that maybe, just maybe, Gary liked me too.

A few nights later, as we stood in the China department, I decided to let Gary know it. Unfortunately, Helena walked in at that precise moment with another headless statue. "I think Frank is going to get mad," she said, as she showed me the price tag. "This one's worth $450!"

I tried to console her, but what I really wanted to do was throw her and that headless sculpture as far away as possible. "Just go back to Gifts and I'll come over and do the expense report," I said, as I pushed her out of the department.

I came back to find Gary smiling at the register. "So," he said. "You were saying that you like someone?"

"Yes," I said.

"What does he look like?"

"He's got glasses and he wears a thin white tie."

"Like this one?"

"It is that one."

Gary smiled. "Want to go out to dinner with me tonight?"

I smiled and nodded yes. This guy got me!

We went out to dinner after Stern's closed. We drove to Katie Cassidy's, an Irish pub and restaurant on Woodhaven Boulevard in Queens. Gary ordered pot roast and I ordered a turkey dinner with all the fixings. As Gary plowed through his food, I chatted away, too nervous to eat. This was a first for me. I had never been too nervous to eat before in my life.

"Aren't you hungry?" Gary said, as he pointed at my plate.

"No," I replied. "You can have it if you want it."

Gary ate his dinner and mine as I sat shivering underneath the air-conditioning vent.

"Are you cold? Because I'll go back to the car and get you my coat."

I felt a wave of panic wash over me. "No!" I said. "I'm fine."

Gary frowned. "Your lips are blue. Don't worry. I'll be right back."

He jumped up and ran outside. For some reason, I was in the grip of an inexplicable fear. What if he was about to dine and dash? I didn't have enough money on me to pay for both meals. What if I had to wash dishes to pay? I didn't have my car either. Would I have to call home and get a ride? I would die of embarrassment!

Gary walked back into the restaurant and held his coat up for me as I slipped it on. "Is that better?"

"Yes," I replied. "I was afraid you were going to dine and dash."

Gary almost spit his dinner across the table. "Why would I do that?" he said, choking back laughter.

"I don't know," I said. "I thought that maybe you were bored or decided you should leave. I got panicky."

"We work together," Gary reminded me. "What would I have said to you on Friday night when you got to work? 'Sorry I left you at that restaurant. Now can you help me write up that special order?'"

I shrugged. "So maybe I wasn't thinking all that rationally."

"No," Gary said. "But that's okay. You're cute and I forgive you." He finished eating and called for the check. "Do you want to come with me to Zum Stammtisch on Friday night? It's a fantastic German restaurant in Glendale. You'll love it, and I promise not to dine and dash. Besides," he said, "I don't think you want to cross any of those German waitresses."

Maybe I wouldn't end up living with those twenty-five cats after all.

We drove to Zum Stammtisch and Gary translated the menu to me. "Sauerbraten is like pot roast, only a thousand times better," he said. "And the dumplings and red cabbage are great too! You've got to try it!"

I looked around. The walls were decorated with paintings of the Fatherland, beer steins, and bric-a-brac. The waitresses

328

were all wearing dirndls and had their hair tied up in pigtails. The waiters wore lederhosen. The only thing missing was Captain von Trapp singing "Edelweiss" while Julie Andrews strummed on her guitar.

"Did you ever see *The Sound of Music*?" I asked Gary. "My college English professor used to sing 'How Do You Solve a Problem Like Maria' to me all the time. This place reminds me of that movie."

"Of course I know *The Sound of Music*! That was the play we did in the seventh-grade," Gary chimed in.

I laughed. Maybe he would know how to solve a problem like me after all.

Recipe: Sauerbraten

This recipe comes from my mother-in-law, and it is delicious! It takes a little work but it's worth it. Go ahead and try it, and don't be afraid if it makes you want to sing "Edelweiss" too.

1 (3-pound) rump roast, trimmed and cut in half crosswise

1 cup sliced onion

1 cup water

2 tablespoons salt

2 tablespoons sugar

1 lemon, sliced

10 whole cloves

6 peppercorns

3 bay leaves

5 gingersnaps, crumbled

1. Place roast halves in a deep glass bowl. Combine the next 8 ingredients (through bay leaves). Pour mixture over meat; cover and marinate in refrigerator for 24-36 hours, turning meat occasionally.

2. Remove roast from marinade, reserving 1½ cups of the liquid. Discard the rest. Place roast in a 6-quart slow cooker and pour reserved marinade over meat. Cover with lid; cook on high for 1 hour. Reduce to low-heat setting and cook for 7-8 hours more, or until roast is tender.

3. Remove roast from slow cooker and set aside; keep warm. Increase to high-heat setting. Strain cooking liquid through a sieve into a bowl; discard solids. Return liquid to slow cooker. Add gingersnaps, cover, and cook 12 minutes. Serve gravy with roast.

Yield: 6 servings (serving size: 3 ounces meat and ½ cup gravy)

Chapter 30:
Nonnie's Stroke and the Midnight Buffet

After a whirlwind of holiday shopping, celebrating, eating, and a multitude of other happy stresses, December 31, 1991, came along.

On that night, my grandmother, Uncle Don, parents, brothers, sisters-in-law, nieces, nephews, Gary, and I gathered in a local restaurant to celebrate the coming New Year. It was almost two years since Uncle Sal died, and we all missed his dry, scorched-earth wit. My grandmother missed her baby brother most of all.

We gathered with family and friends, sang songs, and ate our fair share of great food. We also raised a glass to Uncle Sal, who we knew was there even if we couldn't see him. By midnight, we were back at my parents' house, sipping champagne and kissing everyone at the stroke of midnight.

Then, we celebrated some more with my mother's Quiche Lorraine, sandwiches, and cakes.

Kathie may have been the first sister-in-law, but I was blessed with many more over the years. Joey was the next to get married, to a woman named Christine. Then Louie would marry his long-time girl-friend, also named Christine, causing endless confusion at parties and in email chains. I would get to be a bridesmaid in lots more wedding parties, wearing forest green or deep dark blue dresses with shoes dyed to match. Eventually, Jude also got married to a wonderful woman named Barbara and Chris married his beautiful girl-friend, Anne.

Our family was growing every year; Tony and Kathie had a little girl while Joey and Christine had three children already, and I was sure Louie and Christine would be having children soon. Gary and I were getting married in October, and the days ahead spoke of excitement, milestones, and big changes.

What I didn't know was that the next day would bring a huge change that none of us saw coming.

On New Year's morning, I got up early and found my grandmother sitting at the kitchen table. She was having a bowl of shredded wheat and a cup of her favorite decaf coffee.

My grandmother had been staying with us for the past few weeks. She hadn't been feeling well since before Thanksgiving. I knew this, because she had asked me to take her shopping on Black Friday. She wanted to get toys for all of her great-grandchildren.

"I don't have the energy to go by myself," she said. "But I want to hit the mall while the big sales are on."

"Nonnie, are you sure? The mall is going to be packed!"

"Yes, I can do it if you take me," she replied.

So I drove to her house in Port Washington and picked her up. She tottered down the stairs and was already out of breath.

"Are you all right?" I said.

"I'll be fine. Let's stop for breakfast first," she said.

We swung by "her" Burger King on Shore Road and got some eggs and juice. I was itching to get going since I knew the mall was going to be a madhouse, but my grandmother wanted to linger over her coffee. She was in a good mood, full of stories and enjoying having my undivided attention.

When we finally got on the road, my grandmother launched into some stories about her life.

"Your grandfather was so handsome," she said.

"I know," I said. "Where did you two meet?"

"On the subway," she replied. "We used to see each other every morning on the way to work."

I smiled. Since my grandfather died when I was little, I didn't remember him well. Nonnie knew that and always liked to tell me about him. "What was he like?"

"He was tall and thin, with dark hair and big brown eyes. His teeth were straight and clean too. I really liked his teeth."

I laughed. "Wow, his teeth? Nonnie, that's not very romantic. You sound like you were buying a horse!"

Nonnie shrugged. "In those days, it wasn't easy finding someone who was clean and had all of his teeth," she said, and I laughed again.

While I snaked through the packed roads, my grandmother told me about her dating days, early marriage, life as a young mother, and, now, life as an old lady. It was fun hearing about her as a person who lived a long and full life. I always knew she was a character, but I tended to view her as "my grandmother" and not someone who filled many roles before and even after I joined the planet.

The only time I wanted to jump out of the car was when she started to tell me about how she and my grandfather would fight...and how much fun it was making up.

"Your grandfather wouldn't talk to me for days, and that got me crazy! But then, finally, when we were in bed, he'd reach for me and kiss me—"

I nearly crashed the car. "Please, please, please—stop there. Don't tell me anymore!" I begged, and she laughed.

When we got to the mall, I offered to drop her off at the door, but she refused. So my normally brisk-walking grandmother hung on my arm and I helped her walk about half a mile from the farthest parking lot back to the door. It took us about half an hour to get there.

We headed straight for the store she was dying to get to and she finished her shopping quickly. "Go shop for a bit while I sit down," she said. She settled herself in a chair in the middle of the mall. "Go on. I won't run away," she said, and smiled.

I didn't want to leave her, but she was insistent, so I ran into a toy store and bought a few things for my nieces and nephew. I found my grandmother right where I left her, looking a little bit revived and smiling.

She hung onto my arm and we walked back to the car. For the first time in modern history, my grandmother was quiet.

I drove her home and helped her climb the stairs to her apartment. At this point, my grandmother would usually beg me to stay for tea and cake, because she was lonely and never wanted any of us to leave her. We would linger there for as long as we could, and then go back outside to our cars. When we looked up, my grandmother would be in her living room, waving from the picture window. My father would always say, "I hate seeing her there, all alone."

So of course, when you were visiting my grandmother, you built in as much time to spend with her as you could, telling stories, laughing, and eating with her at the table in her big, pink kitchen.

But not today.

"Let yourself out," she said, as she went right into her bedroom and lay down.

"Are you okay?" I asked.

"I'm just tired," she replied, as she blew me a kiss. "See you soon."

And she did see me soon. The following week, Nonnie came to stay for the weekend and my parents decided to ask her to stay with us for the rest of December.

Nonnie's exhaustion was very unlike her. Any time of the day now, we'd find her napping. Exertion of any kind just leveled her.

"Mom, you should go to the doctor," my dad said.

"No, I'll wait until the New Year," she replied.

Unlike when I was little, I now enjoyed having my grandmother around. We planned excursions out for lunch and went shopping for my bridal gown. We hit two boutiques, but by the tenth dress, my grandmother was tired of giving me the thumbs up or down.

"Go back to the first store," she said, as we walked back to the car. "The beading on the fourth dress you saw was beautiful. I should know, since I was a crochet beader back in my time. If you buy that one, I'll pay for the matching veil."

"Do you want to come back with me?" I said. "We can go after lunch."

"No," Nonnie replied. "I'm exhausted. Sarita, can we go home and eat? Do you have anything there?"

"Sure, Mom," my mother replied.

We got back to our house and Nonnie pushed the front door open. Suddenly, she tripped. Since I was helping her in,

I tripped on her and fell on top of her, and my mother tripped and fell on top of both of us.

We lay there like the Three Stooges, laughing hysterically.

"What happened?" I said, gasping for air, stuck in between my grandmother and mother. We were a three-generational sandwich.

"I think I tripped on my heels," Nonie said, in between fits of laughter.

"What the hell are you three idiots doing?" my father said. We'd woken him up, and now he was standing over us as we lay on top of each other, still laughing. Dad looked very annoyed.

First, he pulled my mother up, and then me, and then we all helped my grandmother stand. Of course, the three of us couldn't stop laughing.

We dusted Nonnie off and checked her from head to foot.

"Ma, why don't you go to the doctor? And stop wearing heels," he said, as he helped his mother out of her coat and my mother, grandmother, and I kept laughing.

Here we were, a few weeks later on New Year's morning. My grandmother looked perkier than she had in quite some time.

"Did you take your medicine?" I asked.

"Nah," she said. "I'm not going to take it anymore. It makes me feel sick."

The product she was talking about was the same one I had just spent the last year writing about at the pharmaceutical advertising agency where I worked. "Nonnie, you can't just stop your medication like that. You could get really sick!"

"Ahhh," she said, waving me off because obviously I was still a small child and knew nothing. "I'll be fine."

The thing is, she was fine for most of the day. She had more energy than usual and was in great spirits.

"I'm going home today!" she said to everyone who crossed her path.

Uncle Don was coming by later to take Nonnie, Chris, and me out for lunch at the Sizzler Family Steakhouse. Then, afterward, he would drop Chris and me off and take Nonnie home with him.

As lunch time neared, Gary called and asked me to join him at his law school for an unexpected break.

"I have to miss lunch, Nonnie," I said.

"That's okay," she replied. "Next time."

Later that afternoon, as I was sitting in the living room with my dad and my brother Joe, we heard Uncle Don's car door slam outside. My father went to open the front door.

"What's wrong with them? Do they serve liquor at the Sizzler?" my father said.

Joe went to the door and peered out. "What are they doing? Why are they dragging Nonnie down the street?"

I joined them at the front door and laughed for a second, but as Nonnie got closer, I could see the panic on Uncle Don's and Chris's faces. I thought about the side effects of cutting off your medication like Nonnie had.

"She's having a stroke!" I said, as I ran for the phone.

The next few hours were a blur of activity. An ambulance whisked Nonnie away to the hospital, my parents and uncle rushed off to be by her side, family members dropped by to wait for more news, and the phone never stopped ringing for hours and hours.

My parents and uncle finally got home about ten hours later, worn out and starving. They hadn't eaten anything since breakfast, so we decided to have our own midnight buffet.

We pulled out some Quiche Lorraine, cold cuts, Italian bread, cheese, salads, and cakes left over from our New Year's celebration, and they told us about Nonnie's medical condition.

"She's had a massive stroke," my father said. "She's paralyzed and unable to walk, talk, or even eat."

My grandmother was unable to walk...talk...or eat? This was the same person who loved to jump up and dance the chicken dance, tell long stories about her life, and eat off everyone's plate. It all seemed very cruel.

"The next few days are going to be tough," Uncle Don said.

"The doctors said she may not make it through the night," Mom said.

"That doctor doesn't know my mother," Dad said.

We didn't know it then, but we would be hearing those predictions from the doctors for the next fourteen and a half years. As my grandmother fought off the Grim Reaper, there was always another disaster looming around the corner. We were so focused on her illness and her care that we didn't notice how someone so crucial to our little world was also starting to slow down, forget important things, and be gripped by something truly devastating.

That someone was my mother.

Recipe: Italian Hero

My grandmother would have eaten this off your plate, minus the cheese. I think this recipe is apropos because she was my Italian hero (heroine). This is a very satisfying, hearty, last-minute, thrown-together kind of sandwich.

1 loaf Italian bread

¼ pound mortadella sausage

¼ pound Genoa salami

¼ pound prosciutto

¼ pound capicola (this is an Italian cold cut made from
    dry-cured pork)

¼ pound mozzarella or provolone cheese

4 tomatoes, sliced

4 cups shredded lettuce

1 cup sliced, roasted red peppers

1 cup Italian dressing

Salt and pepper to taste

Sliced red onion (optional)

Sliced black olives (optional)

Slice Italian bread lengthwise. On the bottom, arrange cold cuts, cheese, tomatoes, lettuce, and red peppers. Drizzle Italian dressing on top. Add salt and pepper to taste, red onions, and black olives. Place a layer of bread on top and press down. Slice into 4 or 5 sandwiches. Enjoy.

Chapter 31: Cooking Momma

And so, the years passed. My grandmother would get sicker and sicker, and then rebound, telling everyone: "I'm never going to die." In fact, when my grandmother told me "I'm not going anywhere," I believed her over the doctors.

My mother devoted herself to my grandmother's care, until a heart attack sidelined her and my father and Uncle Don stepped in. They cared for my grandmother at home for seven more years, until she went into a nursing home at the age of 90.

My mother, meanwhile, survived the heart attack only to begin her own long struggle with Alzheimer's disease. This is something that I wouldn't wish on anyone, let alone my beloved mother.

Mom would come to my house and we would spend the day together sometimes, whenever my father took a much-needed breather from care giving.

Life went on, somewhat sadder, but now that my brothers and their wives were having children, there was also great joy. By this time, I had four beautiful nieces and four handsome nephews, and eventually, a great-nephew too.

Then, ten years to the day after Gary and I met in Stern's Department Store, a miracle happened: our daughter, Maddie, was born. Three years later, we welcomed a second miracle: Paige. In no time at all, I morphed into the Cooking Momma.

Unfortunately, I am not one of those mothers who can whip up a four-course meal by running out to the garden, picking fresh herbs and vegetables, hunting down a free-range chicken from a local farm, and skinning it myself.

No…I am the kind of mother who needs to plan out a week's worth of meals to the last ingredient or there's a good chance you'll be eating cereal for dinner. I tried to plant an herb garden once but the squirrels ate it, and a neighbor had a chicken running loose once but I don't think I was supposed to kill it (since it was a pet, and I remembered poor Mrs. Murray and her heartbreak over eating the family pet, all those years ago).

Most nights, while I walk my dog through the streets of our hometown, I enjoy the smell of wonderful food coming from other people's kitchens and I wish I were eating there. Instead, I have to go home and cook something, and, yes, there's the smell of food…but it's not always wonderful.

There are my tacos, which often leave the house smelling like I've smuggled in an illegal immigrant with a body odor problem who's hiding in my stove. Then there's the fish that either smells burned because I leave it in the oven too long or just stinks up the house because, well, it's fish. My experimentation with curry has also been known to leave my house smelling like Mumbai during the monsoon season.

Some nights, however, I get lucky, and my triumphs are greeted with great joy from the masses that are my husband, daughters, and dog. There was the night I made an herb-rubbed flank steak with sweet potato mash and green beans, and that great smell wafting through the streets actually came from my house! Lasagna with meatballs and sausage in homemade tomato sauce also left many people smiling—so much so that I took the dish into work for our Thanksgiving Pot Luck, and no one died.

Like my mother before me, I am capable of creating amazing things that defy the imagination…or a trail of carnage that lacks description.

Take, for example, the year my daughter Maddie needed to bring in some food for Heritage Day at school.

"I want to make something German," she said.

"But I'm not German," I replied. "Can't I make lasagna?"

"No," Maddie said. "Someone else took Italy. I have to do Germany."

"Why don't you bring in pfeffernüsse?" Gary said.

"I made that last year, and the kids hated it. What kid wants to eat spice cookies?"

"What about Black Forest cake?" Maddie said. We had

just taken her to Zum Stammtisch, the German restaurant that Gary took me to on our second date.

"I don't know," I said.

"You bake all the time," Gary replied. "How hard could it be?"

That's right, I thought to myself. I can make a Cassata à la Napolitano (Neapolitan Cream Cake) without even looking at a recipe. My chocolate layer cake and chocolate chip cookies are always met with great applause. What's so hard about making Black Forest cake?

So like anyone who is too stupid to know better, I got a recipe and started assembling the ingredients. I wanted it to be authentic for Maddie's class—as if those third-graders were about to say, "Um, Mrs. Schulz, this is not authentic cherry liqueur you used on this cake." After several trips to different liquor stores, I found the perfect kirschwasser—cherry brandy—to use on my cake.

The night before the party, Maddie and I baked the cake and let it cool. We put stainless steel bowls and mixing beaters in the refrigerator to chill so the whipped cream would form perfect peaks. Then, we went off to bed, and I set my alarm clock to 5 am so that I could create a Black Forest cake that no one would soon forget.

The next morning, in complete darkness, I pulled out the bowls and created perfect homemade whipped cream. Next, I took a brush and glazed the layers with kirschwasser, just as the recipe told me to. I put whipped cream and maraschino cherries on the layers and then put everything together, adding whipped cream on top. I shaved chocolate bars to nubs in order to create perfect curlicues to decorate the cake and placed cherries strategically around the top. When Maddie woke up at 7:30, she rushed out to see my progress and let out a delighted whistle.

"It's great! My class is going to love it!"

Maddie and I finished the cake and I even taught her how to make rosettes on top, just like in the bakery.

"It's beautiful!" Maddie said, as she ran off to get dressed.

I placed the cake on a platter and got out the aluminum foil to cover it. That's when I noticed the cake leaning over to one side. Within seconds, the Leaning Tower of Black Forest Cake began to cave in the middle, until the entire cake imploded under its own weight.

Gary came out to the kitchen when he heard me scream. "What's wrong?"

I fought back tears. "My cake collapsed!" I said.

Maddie and Paige ran out to see what was going on. "Oh no!" they both said in unison.

My once spectacular, three-layer Black Forest cake was now falling to pieces, like it was being sucked in from the middle and fanning out to the sides. I immediately thought of Steve McQueen and The Blob. In the space of just a few hours, I had gone from Martha Stewart, creator of a culinary masterpiece, to just plain Maria, creator of a black hole cake.

"Maybe you put too much kirschwasser on it," Gary said, trying to decipher the physics of my collapsing cake.

"I followed the recipe exactly," I said, wiping whipped cream and tears off my face. "Maybe I can put it back together?"

Gary laughed as we tried to smash the blob-like cake back together. "I'd say your cake is the equivalent of Humpty Dumpty: you can't put it back together again."

Heritage Day was just a few hours away and I was supposed to go to work. "What am I going to do?" I wailed.

Maddie shrugged and then smiled. "You could just buy something at the store."

I turned to face her. "You mean to tell me I didn't have to bake something from scratch? Why didn't you tell me that in the first place?"

"I thought it would be more fun this way," Maddie replied. "And it was, for a while."

Gary and I got the kids off to school, and then I called a local German bakery.

"Yah, you can come over here now," the baker said. "I got two Black Forest cakes. And fresh strudel!"

In the end, I showed up at Heritage Day armed with the bought Black Forest cake and fresh strudel. No one cared that I didn't make it myself; in fact, most people were delighted that I'd gone to the local bakery instead.

"Why on earth did you try to make it?" one mother said to me. "The kirschwasser probably cost more money than both cakes combined!"

Okay, so perhaps that was true. Maybe, just maybe, I should stick with making things I know how to do well: Italian cream cakes, chocolate layer cakes, cookies, brownies, and the occasional ginger snap. Maybe next time I'll even read the instructions that were in my daughter's homework folder...the ones that said, "The world won't end if you get a store-bought cake."

That teacher was very wise.

Recipe: Black Forest Cake

Are you feeling adventurous? Go ahead and try this recipe for Black Forest cake. The remnants of mine were delicious!

1 cup milk

1 tablespoon vinegar

1¾ cups all-purpose flour

2 cups white sugar

¾ cup unsweetened cocoa powder

1 teaspoon baking powder

2 teaspoons baking soda

½ teaspoon salt

2 eggs

½ cup vegetable oil

1 cup strong brewed coffee, cold

1 teaspoon vanilla extract

1 (21-ounce) can cherry pie filling

½ cup cherry liqueur

3 cups whipped cream

3 chocolate bars (for chocolate ribbons)

1 jar maraschino cherries

1. Preheat oven to 350°F. Grease and flour two 8-inch cake pans. Make sour milk by combining milk and vinegar. Set aside.

2. Sift together the flour, sugar, cocoa powder, baking powder, baking soda, and salt. Set aside. In a large bowl, whisk together the eggs, oil, coffee, and vanilla. Stir in the sour milk. Gradually beat in the flour mixture, mixing just until incorporated.

3. Pour batter into prepared pans. Bake in the preheated oven for 30 minutes, or until a toothpick inserted into the center of the cake comes out clean. Allow cake layers to cool completely before filling.

4. To make the cherry filling: Combine the cherry pie filling and cherry liqueur. Refrigerate cherry mixture until chilled, then place between layers, along with 1 cup whipped cream.

5. Decorate the entire cake with the rest of the whipped cream and shave chocolate bars to create chocolate ribbons. Add maraschino cherries in a ring around the top of the cake. Dust with cocoa powder.

Serves 6-8. Enjoy!

Chapter 32: The Final Course

"'Cause life is just a party, and a party isn't meant to last."
—Prince, from his song "1999"

In my family, there are only two things that are certain in life: eating and dying. So it stands to reason that we would find some way to combine the two. When someone we love dies, we immediately plan the funeral. And as soon as that's done, we call a restaurant we really, really like and book a room so that our mourning can be followed by an unforgettable meal.

When my grandmother died exactly one week after my father's house got hit by lightning, we skipped the wake entirely. After a fourteen-year-long illness, we decided she'd done enough lying around. So we had a simple funeral followed by a burial at a local cemetery on the hottest day of the year. The funeral of a loved one on a blazing hot day might not make some people hungry, but that never stopped us. We immediately drove to Giordano's, an amazing Italian restaurant in Queens, and ordered everything off the menu.

Four months later, when Uncle Don lost his fight with lung cancer, we did it all over again. No wake, just a funeral at the nursing home and burial at the same cemetery, on a much colder day.

When we finished the final prayer at the grave, my father made an announcement.

"Meet us for lunch at Monahan & Fitzgerald's—and Donny, you can't come!"

A sudden gust of wind blew one of the grave wreaths straight at my father.

"Donny never could stand to be left out of a party," Dad said, as we headed off to the restaurant.

In 2008, it was my mother's turn to go off to that big restaurant in the sky.

My beautiful mother died after her long, brutal battle with Alzheimer's disease. In the end, the woman who always used to say "Mangia tutti cosi"—"Eat everything"—would finally depart this life as the result of being unable to swallow or eat anything anymore.

But we couldn't bear to say goodbye to my mother quite so fast. One day of visitation and a funeral at our favorite hot spot, the nursing home, would make the Trifecta complete.

On the day of her wake, I walked through the doors of the

funeral home where Gary stood waiting for me. He gave me a hug. I turned to see all my brothers, sisters-in-law, nieces, and nephews gathered quietly toward the front of the room, near my mother's casket. My father promptly came to the back of the room to retrieve me.

"Come up and see your mother," my father said, as he took me by the hand.

My father, brother Louie, and I went up to the casket. There lay my mother wearing the peach suit we had picked out together so many years before. Just last summer, Kathie and I had talked about my mother wearing this suit at her funeral.

"It will never fit her! It will be too small!" Kathie said.

"We'll see," I said. "She loved that suit. That's the one we're going to use. It will be fine."

Now, of course, after four months of eating absolutely nothing, the suit swam on her.

"She looks good, right?" Dad said, as we stood next to the casket.

My mother did look pretty good, for a dead person. Her hair was finally styled like she used to wear it when she was well, long before she went into the nursing home and the in-house salon started styling her hair like the ninety-year-olds who lived there. Her makeup was perfect and it occurred to me that she didn't have a single line on her face. There was only one thing wrong.

"They put a frown on her face," I said. "Mom looks like

she's on the wrong end of a practical joke."

"She is," Louie replied.

Sometimes, in those made-for-TV movies, everyone starts off really young and by the end of the show they've been aged thirty or forty years. That's what my mother's wake was like.

People I hadn't seen since I was a small child came parading through, telling me so many things about my mother that my head began to swim. By the time the first visitation was over, I half expected my mother to sit up in that box and tell everyone to just go home.

"Let's go back to our place for dinner," Kathie said. And so my family and I headed back to the house in the hills… Bayside Hills.

Yes, despite the lightning strike, the endless marches from the nursing home to the grave, and the endless negotiations and pitfalls with the insurance companies and adjustors, the house had risen once more.

Now, Tony and Kathie lived there with their two girls, Sara and Kate, and my dad lived in his own rooms upstairs.

My friend, Lisa, came back to the house with Gary and me. I gave her the nickel tour so she could see how everything had changed.

"Wow! Look at this place! Who ever knew it could be so nice!" Lisa said.

The upstairs was completely redone; my father had a big,

spacious room and a private bath. In the basement, the big room where the band used to play was now a family room, and Jude's old bedroom was now Sara's. My parents' room was now Tony and Kathie's.

I stopped in Kate's bedroom and looked around. This had been my refuge for more than twenty years. This is where Chris and I laughed and played and talked late into the night until our mother told us to go to sleep. It was where I told my grandmother not to leave, that I really did love her and wanted her to stay after Chris told her I wanted her to pack up and leave. It was where I was sleeping the morning Joey came in and told us that Tony had been rushed to the hospital with a burst appendix.

"Do you like my room, Aunt Maria?" Kate said.

"Yes," I said. "I always have."

We ate cold cuts and salads on crusty Italian bread and downed Coke and 7-Up to fortify ourselves for the night ahead. Too bad my mother wasn't around anymore; we could've really used a Quiche Lorraine or some sausage bread to make the meal complete.

One more exhausting night followed by one last exhausting morning ritual, and we were at the end of the wake. As my family filed quietly past the casket, my father stopped and gazed inside.

"I'll be seeing you real soon," he said, as he kissed my mother good-bye.

I walked up to the casket and touched my mother's now cold face. I leaned in and said, just loud enough for my father to hear, "I won't be seeing you for a long, long time."

Once the funeral and chapel service at the cemetery were over, we headed off to the only logical destination: Giordano's, the Italian restaurant where we'd gathered after my grandmother's funeral just one and a half short years ago.

The waiters brought out trays of bruschetta, crusty Italian bread with tomatoes and olive oil, as well as tomatoes and mozzarella, calamari, and antipasto trays. We raised our glasses and made a toast to Mom as the next course, Ziti Bolognese, was served.

My stomach chafed against the food. Could I ever feel hungry again in a world that didn't include my mother?

"Eat something," Gary said. "You'll get sick."

Maddie and Paige handed the menus to me. "What should we have?"

We pored over the menus and chose fish, and chicken, and beef. The girls laughed with their cousins as I traded funny stories about my mother with my husband, brothers, and extended family around the table.

My mother, grandmother, and uncles were all gone, but somehow I knew they were all here, enjoying the family get-together beside us.

The food came out to the table and the girls picked at it.

"Mangia tutti cosi," I said to them.

Maddie and Paige laughed. "What does that mean?" they said in unison.

"It means 'eat everything,'" I replied. "And enjoy every last bit of it."

Recipe: Sausage Bread

No party was ever complete without Mom's cooking. Her Sausage Bread always made those Sunday meals extra special.

1 pound Italian sausage links,

    removed from casings and chopped

½ cup chopped green onion

¼ cup chopped green pepper

2 tablespoons olive oil

1 egg

¼ cup Parmesan cheese

1 can Pillsbury French Bread

Brown the sausage, onion, and green pepper in olive oil. Drain well. In small bowl, beat egg and Parmesan cheese. Add to sausage mixture and mix. Unroll bread and cover with sausage mixture. Roll up and seal ends and edges tightly. Bake according to bread instructions.

Serves 4-6.

Epilogue

For those of you who came to this book looking to learn the secrets of the universe or to gain deep insights into the meaning of life, I'm sorry. You probably know by now that you've come to the wrong place.

I started writing this book in the fall of 2004 because my mother had early-onset Alzheimer's. She couldn't remember how to shower or feed herself, and she would sometimes even forget to eat. Despite her adamant belief that she could never possibly forget us, she did. Alzheimer's is a cruel thief.

I was losing my mother and, with her, all the stories and happy times that made our life together so unique and so much fun. After all, what makes us who we are, if not our memories? Since my mother couldn't remember the stories, I decided to remember them for her. In the process, I remembered lots of things about myself, too.

My book is a combination of stories about our big, and raucous, and just a little bit crazy family and the friends who let me into their little worlds. Some of the names and places have been changed to protect the innocent (me), but the stories are as real and accurate as my memories will allow.

In the end, none of us were malicious or scary; most of our crimes were the kind that will make you laugh, not run and hide. We were the Sopranos without the money, murder, or blood on our hands—and with a Puerto Rican twist.

Dad was loud and hot-headed; Mom was quiet and thoughtful. But sometimes my parents would switch roles. Dad dabbled in poetry and music; Mom chased us around the house in a rage. Every day was an adventure with my parents, who were just two normal people trying to make their way through life.

My six brothers were all gifted with an incredible sense of humor and a penchant for getting into trouble. As their sister, I watched it all, enjoyed their antics, and got into my fair share of hilarious situations with them by my side.

My grandparents, uncles, aunts, cousins, sisters-in-law, nieces and nephews (and of course, my own husband and children) all added spice to our lives and are represented here as faithfully and lovingly as possible.

If you ask three people what happened at the exact same family function, you will probably get three very different versions of the same story. Sorry if you were there and you want to say, "It didn't happen like that." I feel your pain. Now go write your own book.

Of course, no book about my family and friends would be complete without recipes! We loved to cook, and bake, and sit around our dining room table for hours. Some of the most hilarious stories I ever heard were told in the fifth hour of sitting at that table. What I remember most were the smells of lasagna, baked bread, or turkey; the expectant look of delight on my relatives' faces as someone told a funny story; and the ringing of laughter from my mother, father, uncles, grandparents, and brothers. I'm still laughing about it right now.

This book is a celebration of all the memories that made us who we are, and the people that made life such a joy. Thanks for coming along for the ride.

MARIA SCHULZ is an author, copywriter, and the blogger behind Tales From A Hungry Life. She has been writing stories since she was eight years old and decided to turn an English class assignment about Alaska into the story of Lola the Eskimo, her Siberian husky sled dog, and their quest for food. Maria grew up in a family of six boys, one girl (yes, she's the girl), two dogs, one cat, one rat, some hamsters, a Mynah bird with an Italian accent, a raft of extended relatives, and two very tired parents. This book is a celebration of all the good times, good company, and good food (check out the recipes!) these wonderful people shared.

Acknowledgments

To my husband, Gary, and daughters, Maddie and Paige, my best supporters and biggest fans.

To my parents, brothers, relatives, and friends, who gave me all the love, support, and material I ever needed.

To Lisa, for listening, reading, making suggestions, and encouraging me through the entire process.

To Grace, for designing an amazing book cover and for helping me to finally make this book happen.

To Suzanne, who has been a wonderful cheerleader, and who can't wait for the book tour.

To Laurie, whose thoughtful questions and copyeditor's eye for detail made this book so much better.

To Mr. Reines, my English teacher and friend, who taught me how to tell a story, love the written word, and believe in myself.

To anyone who ever listened to my tales over the years and said, "You should write a book!" Well, here you go.

Thank you.

21932515R00208

Made in the USA
Middletown, DE
15 July 2015